The Ultimate Player's Guide to

MINECRAFT

Third Edition

Stephen O'Brien

que®

800 East 96th Street,
Indianapolis, Indiana 46240 USA

The Ultimate Player's Guide to Minecraft, Third Edition

ISBN-13: 978-0-7897-5572-8
ISBN-10: 0-7897-5572-6

Library of Congress Control Number: 2015943749

Printed in the United States of America

First Printing: August 2015

Trademarks

All terms mentioned in this book that are known to be trademarks or service marks have been appropriately capitalized. Que Publishing cannot attest to the accuracy of this information. Use of a term in this book should not be regarded as affecting the validity of any trademark or service mark.

Minecraft ®/TM & © 2009-2013 Mojang / Notch

Minecraft is a trademark of Mojang Synergies/Notch Development AB. This book is not affiliated with or sponsored by Mojang Synergies/Notch Development AB.

Warning and Disclaimer

Every effort has been made to make this book as complete and as accurate as possible, but no warranty or fitness is implied. The information provided is on an "as is" basis. The author and the publisher shall have neither liability nor responsibility to any person or entity with respect to any loss or damages arising from the information contained in this book.

Special Sales

For information about buying this title in bulk quantities, or for special sales opportunities (which may include electronic versions; custom cover designs; and content particular to your business, training goals, marketing focus, or branding interests), please contact our corporate sales department at corpsales@pearsoned.com or (800) 382-3419.

For government sales inquiries, please contact governmentsales@pearsoned.com.

For questions about sales outside the U.S., please contact international@pearsoned.com.

Editor-in-Chief
Greg Wiegand

Executive Editor
Rick Kughen

Development Editor
Rick Kughen

Technical Editor & Contributor
Timothy L. Warner

Managing Editor
Sandra Schroeder

Project Editor
Seth Kerney

Copy Editor
Keith Cline

Indexer
Tim Wright

Proofreader
The Wordsmithery LLC

Publishing Coordinator
Kristen Watterson

Book Designer
Mark Shirar

Compositor
Bronkella Publishing LLC

Contents at a Glance

Table of Contents

About the Author

Stephen O'Brien is an Australian-born writer and entrepreneur currently residing in Sydney after too many years in Silicon Valley. He has previously written 28 books across multiple editions with publishers such as Prentice Hall and Que, including several best-selling titles. He also founded Typefi, the world's leading automated publishing system, and invented a new type of espresso machine called mypressi. He has been using Minecraft since its alpha release and remains astounded at the unparalleled creativity it engenders. The first edition of this book was an international bestseller. Stephen is also the author of *The Advanced Minecraft Strategy Guide*, published by Que.

Dedication

To Mika, for the singular joy that is the blessing of every parent

Acknowledgments

Having spent many years wordsmithing, I have to say that my experience writing the first two editions of this book was one of the most enjoyable projects with which I've ever been engaged.

I can point to several reasons.

First, Minecraft truly is an astonishing work of technical art. Its endless limits create a canvas that can only bring joy to a writer's soul.

Second, the amazing team at Que created a fabulous support network. I must thank Rick Kughen for spearheading the effort; Keith Cline for superb copyediting (any typos, etcetera that remain are entirely my own fault); Tim Warner for the technical edit and many other contributions; Mark Shirar for the cover design; and Seth Kerney for keeping production running just the way it should.

I am also ever grateful to Preeti Davidson for not only everything that makes life as one might always have dreamed, but also for her huge help in proofing the final galleys of this title.

Finally, to you, the readers, I owe an enormous debt of gratitude. The first two editions of this book brought delight to many a young (and not so young) Minecrafter's gameplay, just as I hope this one also does for you.

Thank you all.

We Want to Hear from You!

As the reader of this book, *you* are our most important critic and commentator. We value your opinion and want to know what we're doing right, what we could do better, what areas you'd like to see us publish in, and any other words of wisdom you're willing to pass our way.

We welcome your comments. You can email or write to let us know what you did or didn't like about this book—as well as what we can do to make our books better.

Please note that we cannot help you with technical problems related to the topic of this book.

When you write, please be sure to include this book's title and author as well as your name and email address. We will carefully review your comments and share them with the author and editors who worked on the book.

Email: feedback@quepublishing.com

Mail: Que Publishing
ATTN: Reader Feedback
800 East 96th Street
Indianapolis, IN 46240 USA

Reader Services

Visit our website and register this book at quepublishing.com/register for convenient access to any updates, downloads, or errata that might be available for this book.

Introduction to the Third Edition

Imagine a world where the possibilities are the limits of your own imagination!

Welcome to Minecraft, one of the most interesting open-ended games ever produced.

From the first moment I started playing this game, back in the beta, to today's extraordinary experience, Minecraft has developed into a tour de force of absolutely splendid gameplay—one that, with a little help from this book, anyone can enjoy countless hours exploring, creating, and digging.

Before I even thought about writing the first edition of this book, I found it popping up more and more often in random conversations among all age levels—everyone from my 9-year-old's best friends going on up... way up. Minecraft's unique open-endedness offers an equally open-ended fascination to people of all ages.

The first edition of this book came at a time where there were few reliable online resources. One could spend hours watching YouTube videos without really going in depth or truly capturing the nuances of the game. And, among all that, there are literally thousands of junk sites trying to trick you into clicking on ads or installing malware.

This third edition continues to fill the gap, bringing together all the key information you need in a single place. Written from the player's perspective, it takes you through the essentials and then far beyond, with all the background information, crafting recipes, strategies, and ideas you need to make your Minecraft world truly your own. It covers everything from first-night survival to hosting your own multiplayer server.

If you have ever wondered how to sculpt completely customized worlds, explore underwater dungeons, play Minecraft multiplayer in Spectator mode (and more), this edition has you covered.

If you are a parent wondering whether Minecraft is suitable for your own kids, consider that as of 2013, students at Viktor Rydberg school in Stockholm, Sweden, have been taking a mandatory course on Minecraft, teaching them various skills such as

- Environmental issues
- City planning
- Getting things done

- Planning for the future
- Interactivity
- Safe online habits
- Building and making objects using your creativity
- Computer skills

To this list, *The Atlantic*, in a recent article about the benefits to children of playing Minecraft, adds:

> The most clearly visible are visuospatial reasoning skills—learning how to manipulate objects in space in a way that helps them create dynamic structures. Visuospatial reasoning is the basis for more abstract forms of knowledge like the ability to evaluate whether a conclusion logically follows from its premises.

Minecraft also helps youth learn how to collaborate to solve problems, and collaborative learning improves critical thinking skills that support motivation for learning.

No matter who you are or how you play, you'll find Minecraft to be an endlessly fascinating, wonderful, enjoyable world.

What's In This Book

Survive and thrive in Minecraft with 13 chapters of detailed step-by-step guides, tips, tricks, and strategies. Each chapter in this book focuses on a key aspect of the game, from initial survival to building an empire. Make the most of your Minecraft world today:

- Chapter 1, "Getting Started," walks you through the steps needed to download and install Minecraft and start a new game, optionally using seeds to control the world generation.
- Chapter 2, "First-Night Survival," is an essential strategy guide to one of the most challenging times in Minecraft. In this chapter, you learn to craft essential tools and build your first mob-proof shelter, all in less than 10 minutes of gameplay.
- Chapter 3, "Gathering Resources," teaches you the skills you need to build a permanent base of operations, build better tools, store resources, and find food to stave off hunger. You also learn how to use the built-in GPS so that you can always find your way home, even after extended forays into the wilds.
- Chapter 4, "Mining," unlocks some of Minecraft's deepest secrets. This chapter shows you the best tunneling plan to uncover the most resources in the shortest possible time, the essential tools required, and the layers you should dig to uncover everything from basic iron ore to diamonds.

- Chapter 5, "Combat School," will get you ready to tackle any mob, including the creeper. From sword-fighting techniques to armor, this chapter has you covered. You'll also learn the essential perimeter protection techniques for your home.
- Chapter 6, "Crop Farming," will help you become completely self-sufficient, ensuring that the hunger bar stays full, constantly boosting your health. Learn to hydrate 80 blocks of farm land with a single water block and how to automate your harvests at the touch of a button.
- Chapter 7, "Farming and Taming Mobs," is all about Minecraft's passive animals, the chickens, pigs, cows, horses, and more that populate its world and provide you with valuable resources. Learn to breed animals, tame ocelots to scare off creepers, and gallop across the world on horseback.
- Chapter 8, "Creative Construction," will help you unleash your inner architect. From grand constructions to inventive interiors, learn about the decorative ways you can use Minecraft's blocks and items to build the perfect abode.
- Chapter 9, "Redstone, Rails, and More," empowers your world with a host of automated devices. Control redstone power and automated doors, send minecarts on missions, and build stations, stopovers, and more.
- Chapter 10, "Enchanting, Anvils, and Brewing," will have you brewing up a storm. Cast spells, improve your weapons and armor, and fall from great heights with grace.
- Chapter 11, "Villages and Other Structures," is your key to interacting with the other nonplaying characters. Trade your way to better goods, and learn the secrets of the game's temples and monuments.
- Chapter 12, "Playing Through: The Nether and The End," is the strategy guide you need to get through these tricky sections of the game. Find a fortress fast, get what you need, and then prepare for the Ender Dragon. It's easy when you know how.
- Chapter 13, "Mods and Multiplayer," shows you how to customize the game, from new character skins to mods that add a host of functionality. And along the way, you also learn how to access multiplayer games and set up a permanent world on your own server for family and friends.

How to Use This Book

Throughout this book, you'll see that I have called out some items as Notes, Tips, and Cautions—all of which are explained here.

NOTE

Notes point out ancillary bits of information that are helpful but not crucial. They often make for an interesting meander.

TIP

Tips point out a useful bit of information to help you solve a problem. They're useful in a tight spot.

CAUTION

Cautions alert you to potential disasters and pitfalls. Don't ignore these!

Crafting Recipes

You'll also see that I've included crafting recipes throughout this book. I've included the actual ingredients in the text, so just match the pattern you see to create the item, as shown here for a wooden pickaxe. It's easy, and you'll be surprised how quickly you can whip them up after just a few uses.

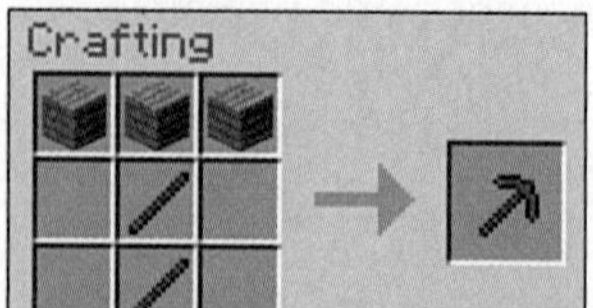

There's More Online...

In addition to the information packed between the covers of this book, I've put together a complete guide to all the crafting recipes online. Feel free to download. Visit http://www.quepublishing.com/register to register your book and download your free PDF copy.

Getting Started

In This Chapter

- Register, purchase, and install Minecraft on your platform of choice.
- Choose a gameplay mode that suits your gaming style.
- Want to change the world? Here's how!
- Confused by the controls? See the complete list.

Minecraft is an amazing place. More than just a game, it's a world of pixelated possibilities: an incredible 3D grid of blocks, resources, creatures, monsters, and pitfalls. It features multiple gameplay styles, from the safe, free-soaring Creative mode to the challenging Survival mode and the multiplayer Adventure mode.

In this chapter, you will learn how to register, download, and install Minecraft. You'll also get a full rundown on the different gameplay modes and options, determine the way the world generates, and learn how to control your Minecraft character.

Registering and Downloading

Before you can immerse yourself in the world of Minecraft and start exploring, you'll need to do a few things. You'll need to set up an account with its creators, Mojang, purchase a license (you only need to do this once), and, of course, install the software. Although you can do a lot offline, Minecraft works best when you have a steady connection to the Internet. If you have already completed these steps, turn to the next section in this chapter.

Minecraft is available in several different versions, including a free demo that runs on your PC or Mac for 100 minutes, which is the equivalent of 5 Minecraft day/night cycles. There are some limitations for this demo version, such as only being able to play a single world without any of the extensive customization options.

Although the PC and OS X versions of the game are (in general) the most prevalent and popular, Minecraft has been ported to many other operating systems and platforms:

- Minecraft: Pocket Edition for Android, iOS (iPhone, iPad, and iPod touch), Kindle Fire, and Windows Phone
- Minecraft: Xbox 360 Edition
- Minecraft: Xbox One Edition
- Minecraft: PlayStation 3 Edition
- Minecraft: PlayStation 4 Edition
- Minecraft: PS Vita Edition
- Minecraft: Pi Edition (seriously scaled-down version for the $35 pocket-sized Raspberry Pi computer; intended for educational purposes and not, strictly speaking, for fun)

In general, the versions released on platforms other than the PC and OS X lack some features, but they also undergo regular updates. If you play on the Xbox 360 or Xbox One, you might want to consider reading *The Ultimate Player's Guide to Minecraft: Xbox Edition*. *The Ultimate Player's Guide to Minecraft: PlayStation Edition* focuses on the version produced for the PS3 and PS4. This title does not cover the Windows 10 Edition, as the recently released beta lacks numerous features.

NOTE

A Few Technical Specs

I use the term *PC* throughout this book to refer to any personal computer running Microsoft Windows, OS X, or any flavor of Linux. The one primary hardware requirement for Minecraft on a PC is that the video card support OpenGL hardware acceleration. Because almost every video card in existence does that these days, you should find that Minecraft installs and runs pretty much perfectly even on a laptop with integrated graphics. If you have any problems getting the game to run, make sure you have the latest Java release installed (visit http://java.com if you are unsure) and update your video card driver.

CAUTION

Try the Demo First

If you're concerned that Minecraft won't run on your computer, register an account with Mojang (see the following section) and then download and play the demo version of Minecraft to ensure that your computer has the necessary specs. The demo will run long enough for you to test many of the concepts covered in this book, and if you decide to buy, it will unlock so that you can continue further.

Registering a Mojang Account

Before you can play the demo version or even purchase the full game, you need to register an account with Mojang. (The Xbox, PlayStation, and handheld versions are exceptions.) It's a quick process, similar to registering a free account for any other site. If you just want to check out the demo to see whether you like it (and you will), you do not need a credit card. The process differs a little from a lot of other software purchases, so I'll take you through it step by step.

Start by visiting http://minecraft.net in your browser and click the blue **Register** link in the top-right corner of the screen, shown in Figure 1.1.

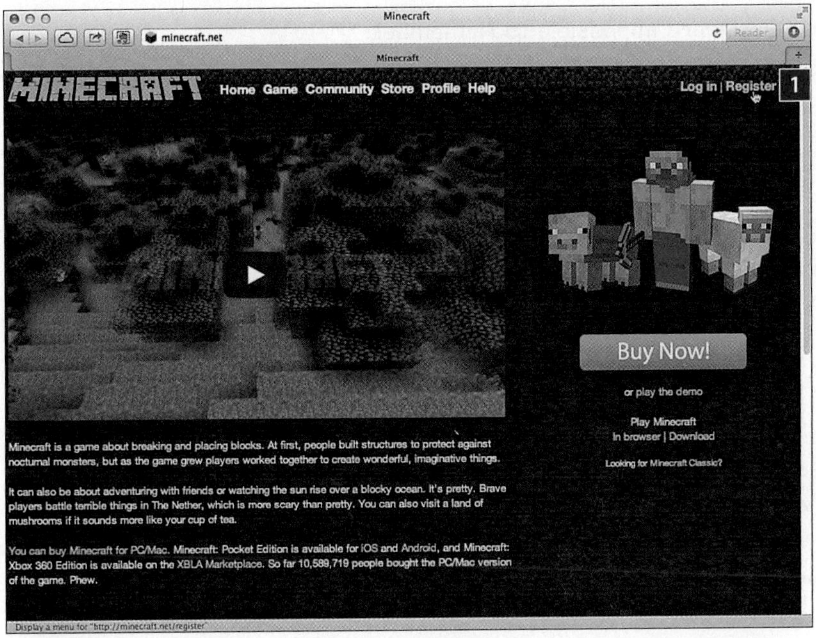

FIGURE 1.1 The first step in using the demo or download versions of Minecraft is to register with Mojang.

1. Register here

Provide your email address and create a secure password. You'll also need to give your first and last name and date of birth. Then select and provide the answers to three security questions.

NOTE

Choose Your Security Questions Wisely

Choose your answers to the security questions carefully. You'll be asked one of the three questions at random the first time you log in to Minecraft.net from a new PC.

TIP

Don't Make Your Password Impossible to Remember!

Passwords don't need to be a confusing, impossible-to-recall mishmash of letters and numbers in order to be secure. A simple strategy that defeats all but the most sophisticated attack is to choose two random words, an adjective and a noun, a separator, and then add a number. For example, redLight#29 is strong. Hackers will check your date of birth and variations of your name and initials, so avoid any combinations of these. Just to be safe, also use something different from those you use for your regular email, bank access, and so on. There's no need to make it too easy for the *real* creepers out there to hijack your accounts.

Check your inbox for an email from Mojang. Click the link contained in the email to confirm your email address, and you're ready to go.

In the next two sections, I'll take you through the process of purchasing and downloading Minecraft. If you've already done that, you can skip to Chapter 2, "First-Night Survival." You can also bypass this section if you just want to play the demo version in your browser.

Purchasing Minecraft

After you've purchased Minecraft, it is permanently linked to your Mojang account. There's no need to worry about losing the install software, misplacing serial numbers, or changing PCs and being unable to reinstall. Just log in and download again.

There is a way to download Minecraft after you've registered. But don't get too excited about seeing the download link there unless you just want to try it in demo mode. You still need to have the actual purchase of Minecraft linked to your account before you can play a complete game. The good news is that you need only log in once from within the Minecraft Launcher to verify the purchase. After that, you can still play, even offline. And if you are online, the site conveniently checks to ensure that you have all the latest files installed, updating as it goes.

To purchase and download Minecraft, follow these steps:

1 Log in to http://minecraft.net with the account you set up earlier and click the big **Get Minecraft** button on the right of the web page. This takes you to the Mojang store.

2 Complete all the fields on the Buy or Redeem Code screen. From there, the rest is standard online purchasing. Provide your credit card details and billing address, and you can complete your order. Note that you can also use PayPal to pay for your purchase. After you've completed your purchase, you can return to http://minecraft.net at any time.

3 Log in if you haven't already, and you'll see that the **Get Minecraft** button has changed to **Download**. Click it to move to the actual download screen, shown in Figure 1.2.

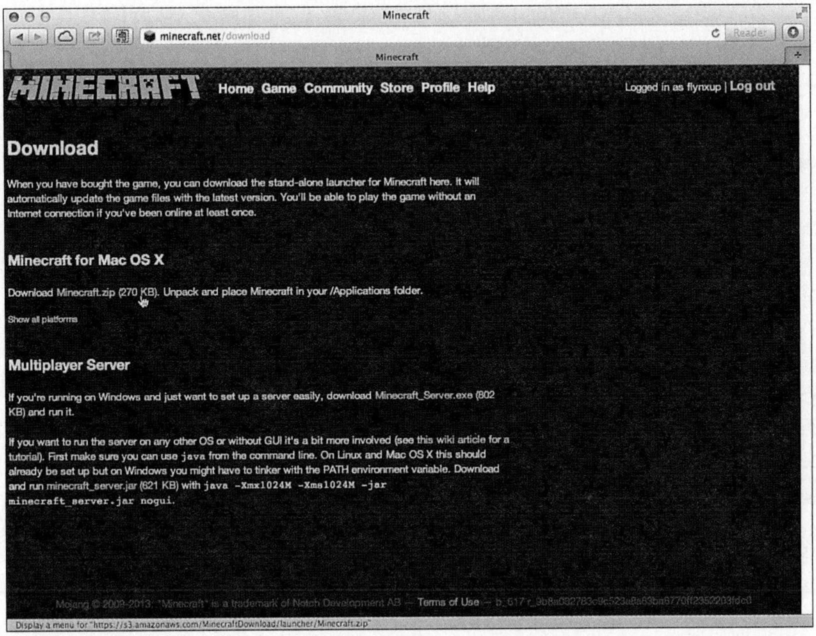

FIGURE 1.2 The download page provides links to the Minecraft download for your current platform. Click ***Show all platforms*** if you don't see the correct version.

These days, application and game files tend to run to hundreds of megabytes, if not gigabytes, in size. So you may be surprised at the relatively small size of the Minecraft download. It's actually just a few hundred kilobytes for OS X and Windows, and even less for Linux. That's because you aren't really downloading the game, just a utility called Minecraft Launcher. The launcher takes care of checking for updates, downloading the main Minecraft application files (around 190MB in all), and checking your account credentials. You always use the launcher to access the actual game.

TIP

Other Custom Launchers Available

Some enterprising developers have created their own compatible versions of the Minecraft Launcher with additional features that let you easily manage mods, resource packs, and other third-party add-ons to the software. One of my favorites is *MultiMC*. You can learn more about this handy utility by visiting http://multimc.org. See Chapter 13, "Mods and Multiplayer," for more on mods, and my other book, *The Advanced Strategy Guide to Minecraft,* for even more. Be careful using a "cracked" Minecraft launcher that supposedly allows you to play the game for free. These launchers are likely to also install malware that will unleash a plague of problems on your system.

NOTE

Giving the Gift of Minecraft

Want to give the gift that keeps on giving? When you reach the Minecraft purchase screen, you can also choose to email a gift code to someone else or receive the gift code yourself and then pass it on personally. You can then participate in cooperative online sessions on your local network and join sessions that are hosted on the many independent multiplayer servers available online, or subscribe to Minecraft Realms to use Mojang's own server system. For more information on multiplayer servers, see Chapter 13.

Different browsers treat downloaded files in different ways. I'll assume you are already familiar with the process of opening downloaded files for your particular computer platform. Following are a few notes to keep in mind:

- **Windows**—On Windows, you can save the file anywhere you prefer, perhaps in a special Minecraft folder within the Documents folder or to your desktop.
- **OS X**—On Mac OS X, you should copy Minecraft Launcher to your Applications folder, just to keep things tidy, although I've had no problems running it from elsewhere. After you launch the game, you can attach it to the dock with a right-click.
- **Linux**—The Linux version can also run from just about anywhere, but you'll probably want to move it to its own subfolder in your home folder as well.

Launching Minecraft

You've set up your account, and you've purchased and downloaded Minecraft. It's time to get the show on the road!

1 The first time you launch Minecraft, ensure that you are online, and then go to your install location and double-click the Minecraft icon to open the Minecraft Launcher.

2 Fill in these two fields:

- **Username**—Enter the email you used when creating your Mojang account.
- **Password**—Enter your account password.

TIP

It's Just Java

If you see a message that Java is either not installed or an older version, visit http://java.com to do a quick update, and you'll be good to go.

3 Now click **Log In**. The screen shown in Figure 1.3 will become the default screen you see the next time you launch Minecraft. If you are not currently connected to the Internet, **Play** changes to **Play Offline** after a short delay, although you must have at least logged in once online from the Minecraft Launcher before this option becomes available.

4 If this is the first time you've run Minecraft, wait while the game components download; on a broadband connection, this takes only a few minutes. The Minecraft title screen, shown in Figure 1.4, is pleasantly spare. Although it's tempting to party up and hit Multiplayer mode, let's head into the Singleplayer mode first because that is the best place to learn Minecraft.

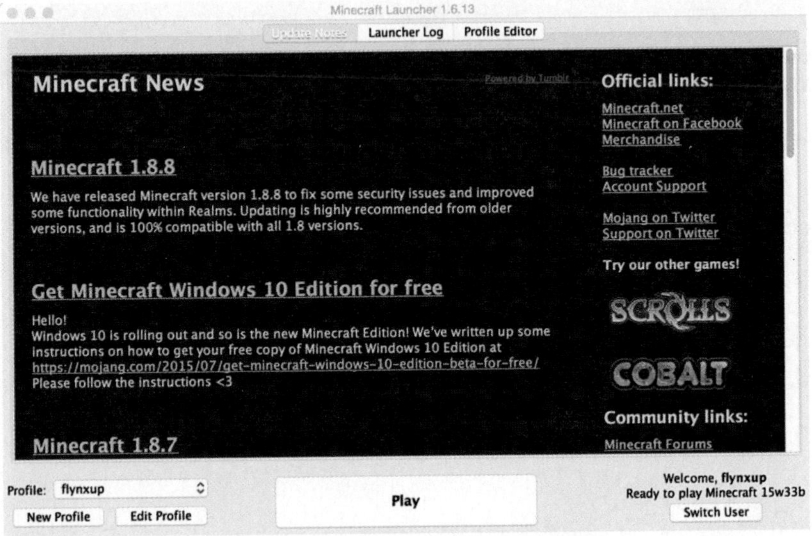

FIGURE 1.3 The Minecraft Launcher provides the latest news, links to Minecraft-related sites, and the Twitter handles of the Mojang team.

FIGURE 1.4 The Minecraft title screen provides your launch point for single-player and multiplayer games, as well as global and language options.

1. Singleplayer offers access to the Creative and Survival modes, new games, and previously saved games.
2. Use Multiplayer to explore worlds with other players, often in highly customized environments.
3. Minecraft Realms provides you with an easy way to create small Minecraft multiplayer servers without having to know much about the Internet or web development.
4. Click the World icon to change the default interface language.
5. Change the global options such as video settings; you can also change these in-game.
6. Quit to your operating system.

5 Click **Singleplayer** and let's get started!

NOTE

Single-Player and Multiplayer Terminology

Minecraft calls single-player games *singleplayer*, so I also use that spelling here. Multiplayer games are also often referred to as PvP (or Player versus Player), although those games can be cooperative, creative, or a faction-based mix of both.

Starting a New Game

The Create New World screen shown in Figure 1.5 allows you to set a few essential parameters. Just follow these steps:

1 Type a name for your world in the **World Name** text box. You can use the default New World multiple times because Minecraft keeps the saved game files separate, but doing so can become a little confusing over time.

2 Click the **Game Mode** selector to choose between Survival, Hardcore, and Creative modes. (See "Singleplayer Game Modes," later in the chapter, for more information.) For now, leave it on Survival.

FIGURE 1.5 Rename each of your Minecraft worlds as you go so that you can return to them (and keep track of them) easily.

3 Click **More World Options**.

4 For the options that appear, ignore the **Seed for the World Generator** field at the top of the window for now. (You'll read about it later in the chapter, in the section "Seeding Your World.") Ensure that **Generate Structures** is On so that Minecraft can populate the world with villages, temples, pyramids, dungeons, and ocean monuments. This is an essential gameplay element. Leave the **World Type** as Default (see the next section). Set **Allow Cheats** to On. (We walk through a few of the basic cheat commands in this and the next chapter.) Finally, leave **Bonus Chest** set to Off. When turned On, this option places a chest with a few random but typically useful items near your spawn point, but here you're going to start from scratch.

5 When you've finished, click **Create New World**. Welcome to Minecraft!

TIP

Game Lingo

Minecraft, like most other games, has its own vocabulary, and it helps to learn the terms quickly.

Spawn refers to the appearance of any new entity in the world.

Your *spawn point* is your starting location in the world. Until it's updated by sleeping in a bed, this becomes the place you reappear should you be slain by monstrous mobs or other misfortune.

NOTE

Cheats, Really?

Minecraft's *cheats* are a series of commands accessed by tapping the forward slash (/) key (or the **T** key). You'll also see them referred to in community forums as *slash commands*, to get away from the negative connotation of the word *cheat*, but given that Minecraft refers to them as cheats, I'll stick to that here.

Cheats reset the time, change game modes and difficulty on-the-fly, and allow you to set a spawn point, teleport to another location, and more. They mostly provide a host of commands that help with managing players on shared servers, but they can also save your bacon in Survival mode. I've suggested setting cheats here so that you can explore some of the different options, but after you know the ropes, it's not a bad idea to turn them off for a survival experience that's true to form.

Now that you're up and running, you can turn to Chapter 2 to start the survival tutorial, or you can keep reading for a little more background information.

Choosing a World-Generation Style

Minecraft provides three basic world-generation styles. The default World Type provides a traditional Minecraft world, even if each of those worlds features different topology above and below ground. The three others are **Large Biomes**, **Superflat**, and **Amplified**. Usually biomes (think of them as individual ecosystems) are quite small and can be traversed easily, providing diversity of terrains and ecosystems in each world. Selecting Large Biomes increases their size 16x. A superflat world is actually completely flat except for any generated structures. If you select Superflat, you also gain access to new customization options and a range of presets for different types of superflat worlds.

The Amplified world type is intended just for fun and, according to Mojang, requires that you have a fairly powerful computer to run it (due to the abundance of complex geometry). For instance, the Amplified world features out-of-proportion landforms, huge oceans, and mountains that reach the top of the Minecraft address space. Figure 1.6 shows a screenshot from the Amplified world type.

FIGURE 1.6 Each Minecraft world brings you its own personality, which is to say, its own collection of biomes and geostructures. Here we see the curious (and dangerous) Amplified world type in action.

There is one final option: **Customized**. Use this to create worlds where almost every aspect of the terrain generation has undergone a tweak or even a major change. This is an astonishingly flexible system, but if it becomes a little boggling, you can also load a range of presets that, like an Amplified world, may place excessive demands on any but the fastest PCs. See Chapter 8, "Creative Construction," for more on fully customized worlds.

So, which biome world type is for you? The default setting is great for starting out. Each biome contains different resources, and their smaller size in this setting makes them easy to traverse, which means you can move quickly from open land to a jungle, through a forest, and so on, gathering all the bits and pieces you need as you go.

Large biomes open up the terrain, making it more like the real world. These worlds present a greater challenge for the intrepid explorer, with Columbus-confounding oceans that disappear over the horizon, large flat grasslands perfect for galloping across at high speed on horseback, dense endless forests, and majestic mountains. They force you to get out and see more of the world, and you'll need to be prepared for a lot of impromptu camping on the way.

The term *biome*, you may be interested to know, is distinct from a world type. Specifically, a biome refers to the regions or terrains that are contained within a Minecraft world. In Minecraft worlds, we see one or more of the following types of biomes:

- **Snowy**—Includes Frozen River, Ice Plains, Ice Spike Plains, Cold Beach, Cold Taiga, and Cold Taiga M(ountainous).
- **Cold**—Includes Extreme Hills, Extreme Hills M, Taiga, Taiga M, The End, Mega Taiga, Mega Spruce Taiga, Extreme Hills+, Extreme Hills+ M, and Stone Beach.
- **Medium/Lush**—Includes Plains, Sunflower Plains, Forest, Flower Forest, Swampland, Swampland M, River, Mushroom Island, Mushroom Island Shore, Beach, Jungle, Jungle M, Jungle Edge, Jungle Edge M, Birch Forest, Birch Forest M, Birch Forest Hills M, Roofed Forest, and Roofed Forest M.
- **Dry/Warm**—Includes Desert, Desert M, Hell, Savanna, Savanna M, Mesa, Mesa (Bryce), Plateau, and Plateau M.
- **Neutral**—Includes Ocean, Deep Ocean, and Hills.

The superflat world is less interesting in that sense, with nary a bump to disturb the ground, but you might prefer its blank canvas to explore different techniques in Creative mode, such as creating redstone circuits.

By the way, each block in Minecraft measures 1m per side, or 1 cubic meter. Each world in the PC edition has a maximum size of 60,000,000 blocks squared, or 60,000 kilometers per side. Curiously, the Pocket Edition, playable on portable devices, has an infinite size.

TIP

Track Their Trek

If you need inspiration, see Far Lands or Bust at http://farlandsorbust.com, where you can track Kurt and Wolfie's daily journey to the fabled Far Lands. Kurt is journeying to raise money for *Child's Play*, a charity for sick children, and has been trekking since March 2011. He and his canine companion probably have quite a few more years to go, but as I write this, they have already raised over $270,000—quite an achievement! Kurt is using an earlier version of Minecraft with a large, but still finite, world.

The current Xbox 360 and PS3 editions create a world of 1024×1024 blocks, whereas the Xbox One and PS4 editions are approximately 36 times larger, although all other features are in parity between all four console versions. Surprisingly, the Pocket Edition worlds are truly infinite in size.

Happy exploring.

Singleplayer Game Modes

In each of your Minecraft worlds, you have a variety of gameplay modes:

- **Survival**—This is the default mode for all new games and is the one I mostly focus on throughout the book. Survival mode is made up of two phases: day and night. During the day, you have a 10-minute window to gather resources, mine, build, farm—do whatever you need to do. During the first few days, this is usually made up of a few key activities, but after you've established your base, be it underground, in a walled fortress, in a building, or even in a tree, you can rest a little easier. If you spawn near sheep, you can also kill a few to quickly build a bed, even out in the open, and blissfully slumber the night away, as long as no hostile mobs are present. I show you how in Chapter 2.

  Daylight is followed by 1.5 minutes of dusk—time to get back to your base. The night-time phase lasts 7 minutes and is a time you definitely don't want to be outside, protected by nothing more than your stumpy fists. They might be able to beat chunks out of trees, but they won't help you in a deadly scrap. Sunrise and dawn last another 1.5 minutes and cause some hostiles, although not all, to burn up. Then it's a brand-new day. Death in this mode is only temporary. You'll respawn within 20 blocks of your original spawn point and live to fight another day.
- **Hardcore**—After you've cut your teeth in the regular Survival mode and presumably made it all the way through, you may want to revisit the game in this mode. The difficulty level is set to **Hard** (described in the next list), and you get only one life—no respawning. It's quite a challenge, if you're up for it. In case you're curious, you can see the end game screen in Figure 1.7.
- **Creative**—This is where Minecraft really shines. If you're looking for an artistic outlet, this is the mode you want. It's a great way to build enormous structures, intricate redstone circuits, and fantastic rail systems; anything is possible. Build a model of the human heart or a gigantic floating castle, or, as UK user Squadhob did, create a simplified version of a functioning iPad in virtual space.
- **Adventure**—Although surviving Survival is an adventure in itself, Minecraft's Adventure mode adds some specific challenges by limiting the destruction of blocks to specific tools. For example, you can use an axe to harvest only wood-based items and a pickaxe to extract only ores. Adventure mode is used most often on multiplayer servers but can be accessed from a singleplayer game by using the cheat command **/gamemode adventure**. It's also often turned on for you in downloadable Adventure maps that provide their own plot lines and challenges.

NOTE

Set Difficulty for Each World

In Minecraft 1.8, the global difficulty setting has been disabled; difficulty it is now set per world. This prevents accidentally changing the difficulty when joining a world. It can be locked for each world, taking away the temptation to change to an easier difficulty in challenging situations. Locking, however, cannot be undone without the use of external editors.

FIGURE 1.7 The Hardcore game mode in Minecraft is pretty harsh. If your avatar dies, you lose everything, including your world.

Survival mode offers four levels of difficulty, and you can switch between them at any time through the in-game Options window:

- **Peaceful**—All hostile mobs disappear instantly and permanently until the difficulty setting is switched to any of the other three mentioned here. Your hunger bar also remains at maximum, or the level it was when you switched to peaceful. You can still die, and therefore respawn, so you need to be wary of long falls, lava pits, trapped temples, and other threats; but it is, as the name suggests, a peaceful existence.
- **Easy**—You see hostiles, but they deliver less damage than normal. Your hunger bar does deplete, but it still leaves you with 10 health points at a minimum, or 5 hearts in the Heads Up Display (HUD). Some other mob effects, such as poison, are minimized.
- **Normal**—As the name suggests, this is the default mode. Hostile mobs deliver normal damage (which without armor can quickly kill you), and running out of food reduces

your health to just half a point, making you particularly vulnerable and unable to sprint away from the mobs to a safer location.

- **Hard**—Hostile mobs cause more damage, and running out of food kills you...eventually.

NOTE

Mobs, Spawning, and Respawning

In Minecraft, any other creature besides your player and villagers (known as NPCs, or nonplayer characters) is called a *mob*. The term originates from *mobile entity*. You'll meet three kinds of mobs in future chapters: peaceful, neutral, and hostile. The sudden appearance of any entity in the game world is called a *spawn*. Your own character will probably also die at some point. It's practically unavoidable. In any difficulty level except hardcore, you'll respawn shortly after death. There is no limit to the number of times you can do so.

Seeding Your World

Minecraft worlds are randomly generated using an algorithm that takes a number, or seed, as its starting point. This seed comes from the clock that keeps track of the date and time in your PC. As time marches on, the clock provides the seed for trillions of worlds, each one unique. However, you can also override this and provide your own seed. Each world created with that seed will be identical in terrain, including the location of mining resources and also generally the same in mob spawn locations. You can use just about anything for the seed, including a random set of numbers or letters such as a phrase (Minecraft rocks!) or even your birth date. Actually, something quite fun to do is to create a Minecraft world seeded with your own real name, your unique Minecraft username, or your email address. Essentially, it is a world created just for you. Try it and explore your new domain.

TIP

Sharing Seeds

Share the seed you used with a friend, and your friend can play in Singleplayer mode in a world similar to your own. Some worlds happen to be more interesting than others, so this makes for an easy way to share the better ones. If you don't know it already, you can discover the seed in-game by using the cheat command **/seed**. Some websites also provide lists of seeds that create unusual worlds. Keep in mind that Mojang, the makers of Minecraft, change the world-generation algorithm now and then, which in turn changes the world that results from any particular seed. Match your Minecraft version with the seed for best results; otherwise, you might end up with something completely different.

About Snapshots

The good developers at Mojang AB are an enthusiastic bunch! To that end, you'll discover that the Mojang team publishes prerelease Minecraft versions, called snapshots. The easiest way to learn what's new in each snapshot is to visit the blog at http://mojang.com.

The naming format used for the development snapshots is YYwWWx, where YY represents the two-digit year, w stands for week, WW is the two-digit week, and x is a sequential identifier for releases within that week.

Many Minecraft players, myself included, are eager to play-test these prerelease snapshots so that we can get a feel for new or changed game features. For instance, as of this writing, the big hubbub in the Minecraft world is what v1.9 will look like when (not *if*, contrary to some people's belief) the final version is released.

Here's how you can play-test development snapshots if you're so inclined:

1. Fire up the Minecraft Launcher as usual. If you want to use your current player profile, click **Edit Profile**. Alternatively, if you want to be safe, you can create a new profile for use with experimental game versions.
2. In the Profile Editor dialog box, shown in Figure 1.8, tick the **Enable experimental development versions ("snapshots")** option and then click **Save Profile**. You'll be prompted to confirm your choice.
3. You now can open the Use Version drop-down menu, and you'll see snapshot IDs in addition to released Minecraft versions. Pretty cool, eh? Select Use Latest Version to ensure that your game is running the most recent snapshot, but keep in mind that you may need to create a new world to see the latest changes.

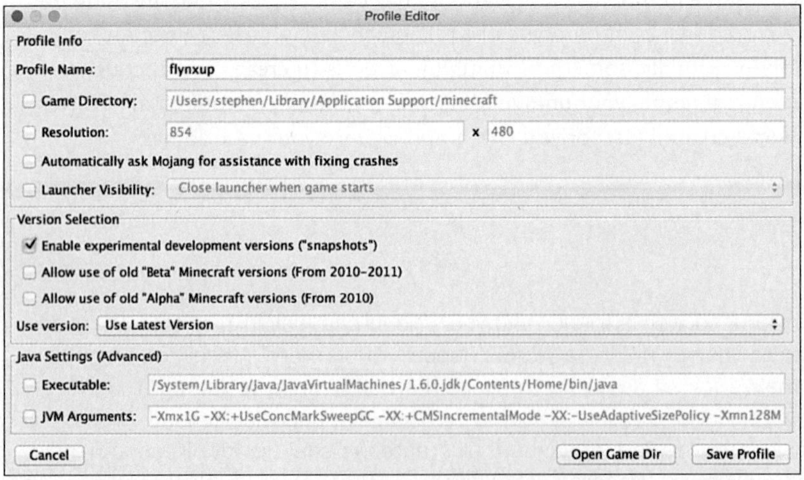

FIGURE 1.8 The Minecraft Launcher enables you to play-test prerelease versions of the game to get a feel for new or changed features.

It's important to recognize that these prerelease snapshots are volatile and do not necessarily represent the state of a final game release. To that end, I suggest that you concentrate the majority of your Minecraft gaming efforts on stable public releases and leave the prerelease experimentation to just that—experimentation.

Controls

You'll find it helpful to memorize a few control keys for when you begin playing Minecraft. Fortunately, there aren't too many. Table 1.1 lists the full set available. You can reassign all the controls through the Options menu (accessed by pressing **Esc** while in-game). While you're still learning, it's probably best to leave the controls as they are; once you start developing your skills, you'll be able to customize to suit your playing style.

> **TIP**
>
> **Controls for Lefties**
>
> If you've played any other first-person game on a computer in the past 20 years, your fingers will probably fall naturally to the WASD keys with your left hand and to the mouse with your right. If you are left-handed and prefer to have the controls reversed, consider remapping each key under the Options menu so that you use IJKL with your right hand and the mouse with your left. Change your dominant hand in the game (the main hand that uses items and attacks) through the Options screen under Skin Customization.

TABLE 1.1 Minecraft Controls

Control	Action
Left mouse button	Attack, destroy blocks, open or close doors.
Right mouse button	Place blocks, use items.
Mouse scroll wheel	Change hotbar slot.
Middle mouse button	Pick block or item, adding to your current toolbar slot (Creative mode only). If your mouse doesn't have a middle button, you can reassign this control.
Keys 1 to 9	Select hotbar slot.
Mouse movement	Look around (change the direction you are facing).
Esc	Pause game (not available in Multiplayer mode).
W	Move forward (double-tap to sprint).
S	Move back.
A	Move left.

Control	Action
D	Move right.
Left-Shift	Sneak forward slowly and avoid falling off ledges.
Space	Jump, fly up (Creative mode only).
Double space (press the spacebar twice, quickly)	Change to Flying mode (Creative mode only).
Shift	Fly down (Creative mode only).
E	Open your inventory.
F	Swap dual-wielded items between hands.
Q	Drop item.
T	Open the Chat menu in Multiplayer mode.
L	List all players in a multiplayer world.
/	Enter a cheat command.
F1	Hide the GUI.
F2	Take a screenshot.
F3	Show current data, such as your avatar's coordinates, the biome, and more.
Shift+F3	Show current performance statistics, along with the standard F3 data.
F5	Switch the view from first person (the standard view) to third person, following your avatar, and to an avatar-facing view.
None (recommend changing to F8)	Smooth your mouse movements, which is handy if you want to capture a video but not much use otherwise.

In addition, Minecraft supports streaming directly to Twitch, an online service that allows you to broadcast your gameplay to the world, and optionally earn revenue from advertising. You'll need to set up a Twitch account at http://www.twitch.tv and then bind that to your Mojang account via the account settings page on the Mojang website. Once you're ready to roll, use the keys shown in Table 1.2 to control your broadcasting.

TABLE 1.2 Minecraft Controls

Control	Action
F6	Start and stop your broadcast stream.
F7	Pause and unpause the stream.
None (change to F8)	Push to talk or mute your mic.
None (change to F9)	Add commercials to and remove them from your stream.

TIP

Mac Users Press the fn key

Use a Mac? You may need to hold the function key (marked as fn in the bottom-left corner of your keyboard) while you press any of the function keys (F1, F2, and so on) listed in the preceding table to access these additional commands. You can change this in your keyboard preferences so that the function keys work as assumed by default. Another option is to buy a third-party USB PC-style keyboard, available at most electronics stores, to use while playing Minecraft.

If you're playing Minecraft on a touch-capable monitor, be sure to consider toggling on **Touchscreen Mode** on the Minecraft Options screen.

The Bottom Line

It's difficult to decide whether to call Minecraft a game or virtual Lego blocks. It straddles both in a way that has hardly been achieved before.

Although the registration and launch systems are a little different from those in many other games, they have advantages. You'll never need to worry about updating the game because that happens automatically, and from time to time there'll be some surprises in store with continuous, steady improvements.

Once registered, you can even change the skin of your character. Search online for "Minecraft skins." When you find one you like, you can install it through your account profile on Minecraft.net. There are plenty to choose from, even copies of popular superheroes or *Doctor Who*. The next time you launch the game, you'll see the new you. Use **F5** to switch views so that you can see the result.

Minecraft world seeds also provide some useful opportunities. Not happy with how your gaming is working out? Select your old one and click **Re-Create** in the Select World window to automatically generate the same terrain and spawn at or close to the same point.

Finally, don't feel daunted by the control list. It's actually quite short compared to the lists in many other games. The main controls are your mouse, the WASD key set, the spacebar, and the inventory key.

The Bottom Line

First-Night Survival

In This Chapter

- Welcome to your new world.
- Harvest your first resources and start crafting essential tools.
- Head for the hills and build a fast shelter in style.
- Cut your clicks with inventory shortcuts.
- Bring some light into the night.
- Skip the night in seconds.

When you start a Minecraft world, your in-game character arrives with nothing but the shirt on his or her back, some dodgy-looking pants, and fists of fury. You have work to do! There are many ways to meet your demise in Minecraft, and you're bound to discover quite a few of them in time, but it's actually quite easy to survive your first night and get enough done to set you up for a great next day. There's no need to become spider bait, zombie fodder, or a handy target for skeleton archery practice when darkness falls and the mobs come out to play.

This chapter shows you how to make it through that first night and come out in better shape than ever.

Surviving and Thriving

Your first day in Minecraft is an important one because you need to accomplish a few things quickly to prepare for the dangerous night ahead. As soon as you spawn into a new Minecraft world, take a quick look around. Just move your mouse. Your first target is trees for their wood because they provide the starting point you need for crafting tools and, frankly, it's difficult to get anywhere without them.

NOTE

Welcome to The Overworld

The Minecraft world is composed of three dimensions. You arrive in The Overworld, the largest dimension. Over time, you'll make your way through a portal into The Nether, Minecraft's very Dante-esque "hellish" dimension, and then finally into The End, a small dimension where you'll fight the Ender Dragon. That being said, most of your time is spent in The Overworld. Chapter 12, "Playing Through: The Nether and The End," will help you move back and forth between the three, but don't worry too much about that for now as there are many interesting challenges ahead before the final boss fight.

Your second task is to scout for a handy cliff or mound into which you can dig your first shelter or, failing that, a little bit of level ground so that you can build the Minecraft equivalent of a shepherd's hut, even if it's just made from some dirt blocks.

Here, then, is a brief list of your first-day tasks:

- Find a few trees and punch their trunks to obtain wood.
- Turn the wood into planks and build a crafting bench.
- Turn some of those planks into sticks.
- Craft a wooden axe out of planks and sticks to speed up the collection of more wood.
- Craft a wooden pick to dig up stone so you can turn it into the cobblestone required to build a furnace.
- Craft a wooden sword, just in case.
- Dig out a basic shelter.
- Build a wooden door for your shelter, although if time is pressing, you can just block off the entrance with some of the materials you've gathered as you go.
- Build a furnace and smelt some wood to make charcoal.
- Use the charcoal and sticks to create torches.
- Optionally, find three sheep so you can use their wool to build a bed.

This is quite a list, but it won't take you long. Think of it as survival of the quickest.

TIP

Make Good Use of Pause

Minecraft days are short, so feel free to press your keyboard's **Esc** key any time you need to pause the game. Just keep in mind that time does not pause in multiplayer games, or even those you're playing on your own and have opened up for sharing on your local network. Given that the sharing setting isn't turned on by default, you more than likely don't need to worry about that just yet.

Heading for the Trees

Start by heading toward the trees. You need a few, so look for a group of them. Use your mouse to set your direction and the **W** key to move forward, **A** and **D** to move left and right, and **S** to back up. Most biomes contain trees, so they shouldn't be too far away, and if you spawned into a jungle, forest, or taiga biome, trees are all around. Figure 2.1 shows a spawn point by a river biome. (I'll use the world shown in Figure 2.1, henceforth dubbed *Elysia*, for the remainder of the book.)

There is a chance you won't be lucky enough to have so many trees. Some biomes, such as the desert, simply don't have trees. If that's the case, head straight for the nearest hill and jump to the top to get a good view. Press the spacebar to jump up each block while you hold down **W** to climb. If you spot any trees in the distance, make haste—the countdown to nighttime has already begun!

FIGURE 2.1 My verdant valley: trees, hills, a pleasant river, and a game of spot-the-sheep.

TIP

You Can Always Punt

If you don't spawn anywhere near a decent chunk of wood—it is possible, although rare, to spawn on a small island in the middle of a large ocean—you might want to consider abandoning the current world and creating a new one. With an infinite variety of worlds available, it's fair enough to reset your situation if you find yourself starting out in a tough position.

When you reach those woody perennials, start swinging. That fleshy appendage you can see to the right of the Heads-Up Display (HUD) is your arm. Hold down the left mouse button while pointing the crosshairs at the trunk to chip away at the tree, as shown in Figure 2.2. The tree develops a spidering of cracks as you wear it down, and it takes only a few seconds to punch out the first block of wood. You see a smaller representation of the block fall toward the ground and float, bobbing gently up and down. Congratulations on your first harvested resource. Well done!

FIGURE 2.2 Punching out wood takes a little patience, but you will build some tools shortly to speed that up quite significantly.

If you are close enough, the block is scooped up into your inventory automatically. If not, just move closer until the block jumps in. Now take out the rest of the blocks, or as many as you can reach, and do the same to another two or three trees. You'll need about 15 blocks to get off to a good start. Don't worry about that mass of foliage remaining behind. It fades away, although if you do hack away at some of it, you have a good chance of getting a few saplings that you can replant in the interests of sustainability. If you thwack oak, you might also score an apple or two that you can collect and save for snacking on later.

TIP

Lumberjacking Tips

There's an easy way to get most of the blocks from the trunk. Start by taking out the two blocks just above the one that is on the ground. Then jump onto that block and look straight up. Finish punching blocks out of the rest of the trunk above you. They fall on you and go straight into your inventory. When you've gone as high as you can go, look straight down and take out the block on which you are standing. You can take out most tree trunks this way. If for some reason you can't jump onto the block after you remove the two above it, you might need to clear out some foliage directly above you.

Now that you've harvested your first resources, it's time to get familiar with your inventory and crafting.

Using Your Inventory

The inventory screen is central to your management of resources as you start collecting and crafting various materials and items.

You've already seen part of it: Those nine slots at the bottom of the screen represent items you've already collected, such as the wood blocks from the trees and perhaps a sapling or two. However, this is only one-quarter of your total inventory.

Press **E** to open the inventory screen. You see the window shown in Figure 2.3, with at least the blocks of wood showing.

Let's take a closer look:

- **Armor slots**—These four slots allow you to don armor. From the top down, they represent: your helmet, chestplate, leggings, and boots, and each can be made from five different materials. Initially, you'll probably start with armor made from leather or iron, because these materials are relatively easy to obtain. I'll show you how to craft them as well as handy armor stands on which you can store them in Chapter 5, "Combat School." Shift+click a piece of armor to automatically place it into the correct slot.
- **Crafting grid**—Use this grid to create basic items on the run—torches, planks, sticks, and so on. In the next section, you'll use this to build a crafting table with a larger grid so that you can make more complex items. Figure 2.3 shows the wood blocks being crafted into wooden planks.

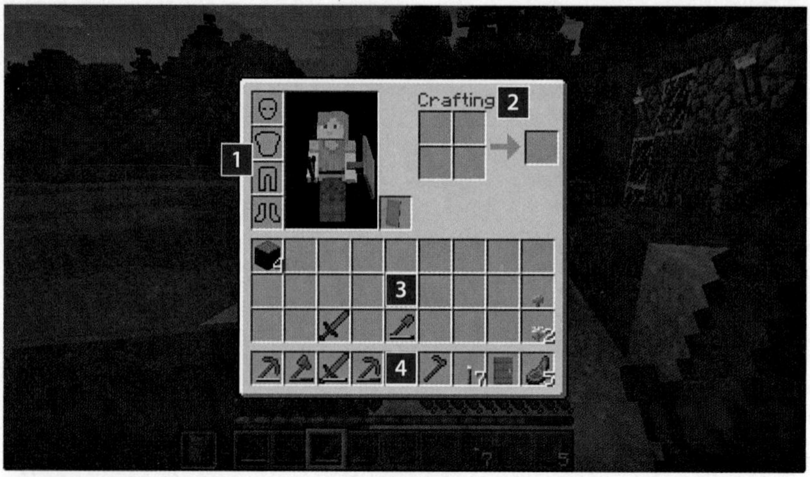

FIGURE 2.3 The inventory screen has four sections.

1. Armor
2. Crafting
3. Storage area
4. Hotbar

- **Inventory slots**—These slots represent your full inventory:
  - **Hotbar**—The bottom row provides quick access to items either with your mouse scroll wheel or by using the 1–9 keys on your keyboard. You can use any selected item in this row with the left mouse button as the action key, or you can discard it with a quick press of **Q**.
  - **Storage area**—The top three rows of the inventory slots provide storage space for items you don't immediately need but want to carry with you. This may include items you've collected on your travels and intend to carry back to your shelter for longer-term storage or to use for construction and further crafting.

Typically, you should store weapons and tools in the hotbar slots, along with some food to quickly rebuild your health and other vital items you think you'll need. Keep the rest of these vital items upstairs in the storage area.

NOTE

Stacking Items

The inventory shows 36 empty slots but can store many more items than this through *stacking*. Typically, items of a similar type can stack up to 64 units high in each slot, although some items are limited to stacks just 16 units high. Tools, weapons, armor, and some other specialized items can stack only 1 unit high.

Minecraft has some neat tricks up its blocky sleeve that make it easier to move items between the slots in your inventory. Here's what you really need to know:

- **Pick up items**—Left-click on a slot to pick up its full stack of items. Right-click to pick up just half the items in that slot.
- **Place items**—Left-click to place all the items you are holding into a slot. If that slot is occupied, the items are swapped so that you end up holding the item or stack of items that was there initially. Right-click to place just a single item from the stack you are holding into a slot or hold down the button and sweep through the different positions to place a stack of held items in multiple slots.
- **Move items between the storage area and the hotbar slots**—Shift+click a slot to transfer its items to the first available position in the other grid. Items of the same type are automatically stacked in the target grid until they reach their stack limit.
- **Distribute items evenly**—While holding a stack of items, press and hold the left mouse button and drag it across a group of slots to automatically split the stack into equal amounts across those slots. (This is particularly handy when you're crafting a stack of similar items simultaneously.) If there is any remainder from the split, it stays selected, and you can place it elsewhere.
- **Discard an item**—Drag and drop items from any inventory slot to the outside of the inventory window to discard them. This way you can discard an entire stack of items simultaneously. You can also quickly discard any single item in a hotbar slot at any time by selecting it with your scroll wheel or the 1–9 keys and pressing **Q**.

Now that you are familiar with the inventory, let's take a look at crafting.

Building a Crafting Table

Why, you may be wondering, do you need a crafting table when the inventory already provides a crafting grid? It's simple, really. The inventory provides a 2×2 grid, which is big enough for building only a limited set of items. The crafting table provides a 3×3 grid, which you need for more complex items, such as tools and just about everything else. However, you can't build a crafting table without first using the inventory crafting grid. Follow these steps to knock together your own:

1. Open your inventory screen by pressing **E**.
2. Remember those wood blocks you punched out of the tree? You need to turn them into planks. Left-click on the stack of wood blocks to pick them up and drop them into any

of the four squares in the crafting section. Bingo! A stack of four wood planks shows up in the output square to the right.

3. Click the stack of planks in the output square three times more to create a total of 16 planks.
4. Click to pick up any unused blocks left in the crafting grid and click on an empty storage slot to move them back out of the crafting grid.
5. Click on the planks in the output square to pick up the entire stack and right-click once on each of the four squares in the crafting area. Well done! You've just created your first crafting table.
6. Click on an empty storage slot to move your unused planks back there.
7. Finally, click to pick up the crafting table and move it to one of the empty hotbar slots that run along the lower edge of the inventory window.

CAUTION

Mobs Can Strike Even with Your Inventory Open

Don't walk away with your inventory screen open, thinking you've paused the game. Time still passes, night still falls, and you're still vulnerable to hostile mobs. You can easily come back to find that your character has keeled over after an attack right there in the inventory window. Remember to use the **Esc** key to really pause the game if you need to duck away for a while.

Okay, now the fun really begins. Let's place the crafting table and build some tools.

Use your mouse wheel to scroll until you have the crafting table selected or press the number key that corresponds to the crafting table's hotbar slot. For example, if the table is in the third slot from the left, press **3** to select it directly.

Now look for a clear space to put the table, point your crosshairs down, and right-click. You can see an example of the result in Figure 2.4.

Building Some Tools

Your initial crafting list includes an axe, a pickaxe, and a sword. Building tools takes no time at all, and once you have tools, your fists will get a bit of a break from punching.

Right-click on the table to open the crafting window. You'll notice that the 3×3 grid provides more room to place crafting ingredients. You're going to use all of that space.

FIGURE 2.4 You don't have to find a nice scenic spot for your first crafting table, but a view doesn't hurt.

1. Crafting table

First, craft some sticks to form the handles for your tools. Stack two plank blocks vertically, using any two of the squares in the crafting grid to create four sticks. Drop these into your inventory.

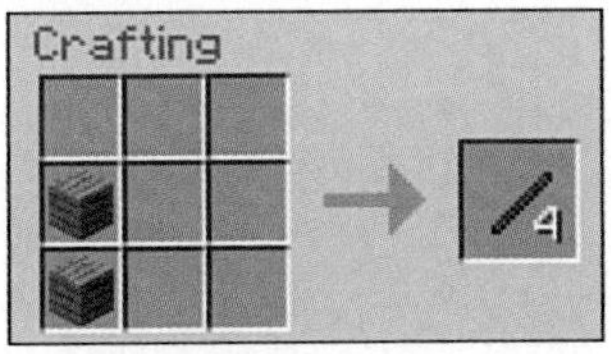

NOTE

Crafting on the Other Editions

The Xbox, PlayStation, and Pocket Editions use a simpler crafting interface that lists all the available crafting recipes and makes recipes selectable when all the required ingredients are included in your inventory. You'll still need to craft the base components, such as turning wood blocks into planks and then those into sticks, to open up the derivative recipes, but you won't need to worry about remembering the components of each recipe or where they should be placed on the crafting grid. It's all in view. On the Xbox, press the **X** button to open the initial 2×2 inventory crafting area so you can build a crafting table and then use the left trigger to access the table's grid. On PlayStation, use the ▢ button and then the left trigger. Access the Pocket Edition's crafting menu with the ellipsis (...) block on the hotbar. Figure 2.5 shows the Pocket Edition crafting interface.

FIGURE 2.5 Crafting in the Minecraft Pocket and Console editions is easier as it saves having to remember the crafting recipes, but in my opinion, that's not quite as satisfying as memorizing them in the full version of Minecraft.

Now craft an axe by placing two sticks in the middle and lower-middle slots in the crafting table. Then arrange three wooden plank blocks in the upper-middle, upper-right, and middle-right slots to build an axe.

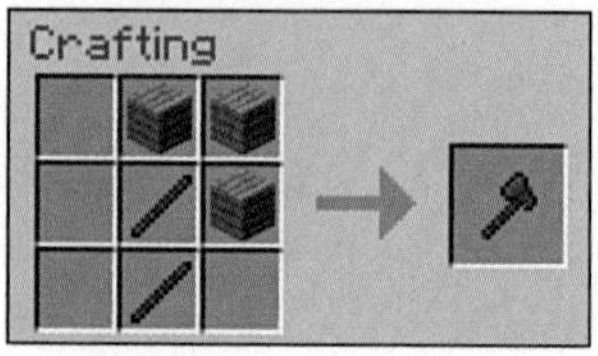

That's all there is to it. Easy, right? There are hundreds of crafting recipes in Minecraft, all with different arrangements of items in the grid, using many different materials, but the actual arrangement of items usually shares some similarity with the physical object. You can see this especially with the pickaxe and sword, and it won't take long for you to memorize the most useful recipes. See "There's More Online..." on page 4 in the Introduction to download a complete list of all the crafting recipes.

To create your first pickaxe, set another two sticks in the middle and lower-middle slots. Then arrange three wooden planks across the top row.

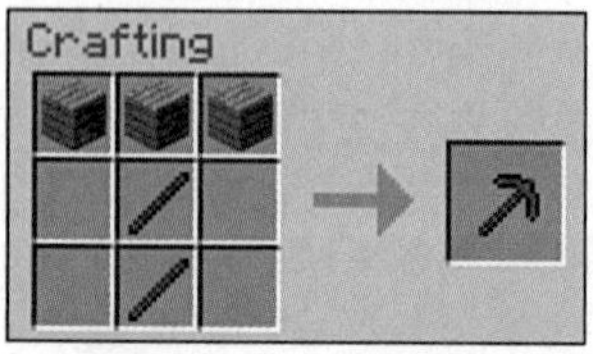

Create more sticks and planks if you need to, but don't go overboard. Just make what you need. The inventory looks like it has plenty of space right now, but it quickly fills, and although you can stack most items in piles of 64 in each inventory slot, it's more efficient to store wood in particular in its most efficient form. You see, if one wooden block can create 4 planks of wood, then converting 64 wooden blocks to planks creates 256 planks, and they completely fill another 4 slots. Converting all those blocks to sticks fills 8 slots. So just craft what you need when you need it.

Now create a sword using one stick block and two plank blocks, using any column of three slots in the crafting grid.

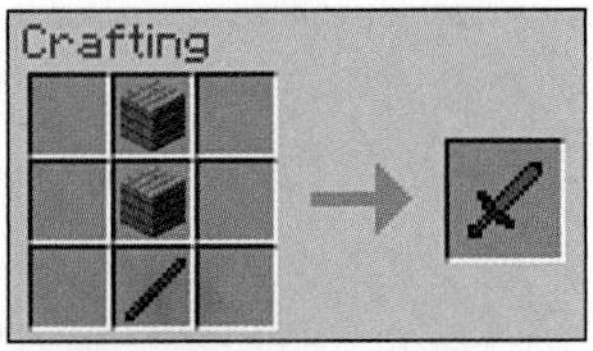

If you're enjoying crafting, also create a shovel. It's a faster choice when digging through dirt, sand, and gravel.

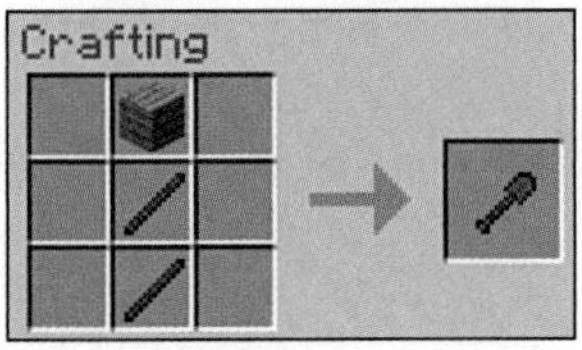

When you've finished, your inventory should look something like the one shown in Figure 2.6.

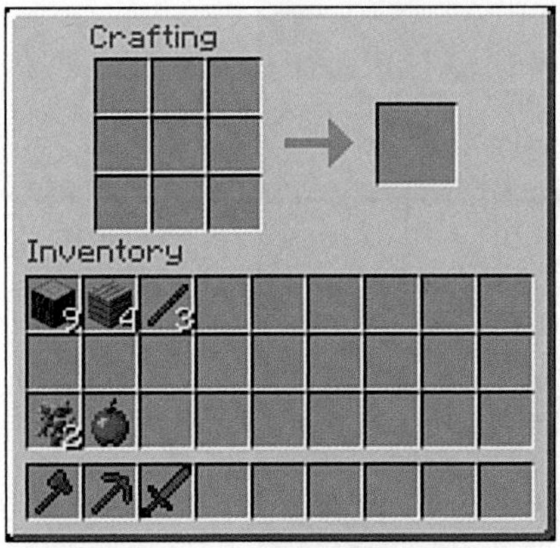

FIGURE 2.6 Your first set of tools, but they definitely won't be your last.

You're done for now, so switch to an empty slot in the hotbar and break down the crafting table with your fists. Walk over to it and scoop it up into your inventory so you can use it again.

Creating a Shelter

Now that you have some basic tools, it's time to prepare for the night. By far the quickest way to do this is to dig a little hideout into the side of a hill. Don't just duck into a cave because you might get a nasty surprise.

NOTE

Building an Above-Ground Shelter

If you have spawned into a flat area, you can build an aboveground shelter (see "Finding a Building Site" on page 68) or dig into the ground to create a small cave.

Head toward any convenient hill, cliff, or mound and select your pickaxe. You'll be digging a space that's two blocks high, but because you also need a roof over your head, the target area should be at least three blocks high. Left-click to swing the pickaxe and quickly break up the block in front of you at ground level, and the next one above it that's at eye level. If you are facing a terraced hill (Minecraft doesn't have any hills that aren't terraced), just dig out a couple of blocks at ground level until you've created a path to a three-block-high space, like the one shown in Figure 2.7.

FIGURE 2.7 Tunneling into a hill is as effective as using a cliff face for a shelter.

Move forward and keep swinging that pickaxe, because you need to carve out a little bit of room to fit your crafting table, a furnace, and possibly a bed. A space 4×4 should do for now, although you can certainly expand it later. As you move forward, you automatically collect the blocks you're breaking. If you break out into a cave or through the hill and outside again (see Figure 2.8), open your inventory and pull some of the blocks you've collected back down into your hotbar, select them as your active tool, and point your crosshairs at the top of the block beneath the gap. Then right-click to drop a new block in place.

FIGURE 2.8 Whoops! Better fill the gap.

Unfortunately, your shelter still lacks a door. In a pinch, you can just place a block in the gap and huddle in for the night. (You just need to make sure to stay out of the line of sight of the gap just in case a skeleton wanders by and starts firing arrows at you.) But you can do a better job than that.

Place your crafting table in a corner of the room, right-click it, and then arrange two columns of wooden planks to create three doors.

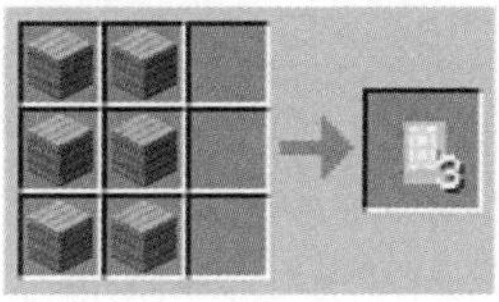

Crafting Shortcut

Crafting can seem like a lot of clicking, but one handy shortcut to remember is that you can left-click to pick up a stack of items such as wooden planks and then hold down the left mouse button as you paint them into the desired pattern in the crafting grid. Minecraft does its best to balance the number of items in each grid position as you go. When you've crafted enough of the final object, don't worry about dragging all the unused crafting elements back; just press **Esc** to exit the inventory, and any unused items float to the ground, ready to be scooped back into your inventory.

TIP

Multicrafting

Crafting a bunch of the same item at once is easy. Hold down **Shift** while clicking the output slot, and you pick up as many of the same item as can be produced with the raw materials in the crafting slots.

Now head outside your shelter, select the doors in the hotbar, and point your crosshairs at the ground block that is under the first section of your shelter where you have a true two-space-high tunnel with a roof. Right-click to place the door. Figure 2.9 shows mine. You can then right-click to open the door, step through, and right-click once more to close it. Now the cave is getting more homelike, but it's still missing something vital—light! There are no energy-saving bulbs in Minecraft. For light, you need a torch fashioned from a stick and a lump of coal or charcoal.

CAUTION

Close the Door While You're Gone

Always remember to close the door when you leave your shelter. Leaving it open is like leaving out the welcome mat for mobs, and you don't want to find anyone lurking inside when you return.

TIP

Airlocks, Iron Doors, and More

In the Hard difficulty level, zombies can break through wooden doors. Give yourself a better chance of survival by building airlock structures, using two doors instead of just one. If a zombie breaks through the first door, it will take him some time to break through the second. Hopefully, creepers aren't lined up behind. Iron doors are impervious to a zombie's attack but can be opened only with buttons or other redstone devices. Perimeter structures such as fences, moats, and lava pits also keep mobs away. See "Protecting Your Perimeter" on page 176 for a few examples.

FIGURE 2.9 Shelter secured. In Easy and Normal difficulty levels, zombies still try to break down your door, and you even see some worrying cracks appear. Don't panic! Zombies give up before they break through.

You can find coal in the ground here and there. The blocks are patterned with flecks of black and are often visible on the sides of cave walls. But you can't dig too far or venture too deep into a tunnel complex without the lack of light becoming a problem. Fortunately, there's an easier way to make torches, and that's by using charcoal instead of coal. To make charcoal, you need a furnace, and for that you need cobblestone.

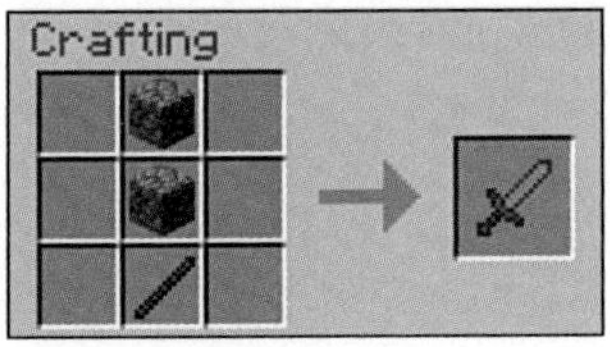

NOTE

Emergency Shelters and Pillar Jumping

Caught out exploring as night falls? You can easily survive a night in the open if you can't get back to base. Here are a few techniques. First, find the most precarious ledge you can on a cliff. Hold down the **Shift** key as you approach the cliff edge to avoid a potentially fatal fall. The "cliff edge" location doesn't guarantee survival, but mobs are less likely to find you there. You can improve the situation by digging into the cliff a little way to create a corridor two blocks high. Go sideways at the end to create an L- shape where you can hide out of sight. Block the lower half of the doorway with sand, dirt, or gravel—whatever you have that's handy really—and wait out the night in your nook.

Another way to protect yourself quickly is to dig down three blocks in anything other than sand or gravel. Just take out the first two blocks, jump in the hole, and dig out the last one, hoping it doesn't drop you straight into a lava pit or through the top of a deep cave. Place one block of the material you removed above your head, making sure that it isn't sand or gravel, which would cause you to suffocate and somewhat defeat the purpose. Wait about 8 minutes of real time for the sun to rise. If you are impatient, knock out the block and replace it now and then to check for daylight. When dawn hits, take out the block in front of you to create a step and make your escape into a brand new day.

A final trick that can prove quite handy if you spawn in the midst of a giant desert is to dig up some 10 blocks of sand or other ground covering and then place the first block down, climb on top, and with some careful timing, jump while looking straight down to place another block directly beneath you. This is known as *pillar jumping*. Repeat until you are perched on top of a pillar 10 blocks high. This keeps you well out of reach of hostile mobs. When sunrise hits, look down and left-click your mouse to dig out the blocks beneath you and ease yourself back down to the ground.

The Furnace Is Your Friend

You craft a furnace from eight blocks of cobblestone, and to get that, you need to mine stone. Fortunately, stone is ubiquitous. It's the second-most-common element in Minecraft besides air and is usually found just one or two blocks under a layer of dirt, if not just lying around in the open, waiting for you to stub an inadvertent toe. One trick to stone, though, is that you can't render it into cobblestone with your fists. You'll just pulverize it to dust instead. You need a pickaxe to do it properly.

Check your inventory, and if you haven't yet found eight blocks of cobblestone, start expanding your shelter using the pickaxe to render any stone you find into cobblestone. Although there are many other types of ore, only stone will do in this case. Don't dig more than one block down at a time because you won't be able to jump back up. Use a shallow staircase effect if needed but try to just stick to the horizontal plane for now, expanding the perimeter of each interior wall rather than plowing into a long tunnel. Figure 2.10 shows a handy layer of stone that came to light just one block from the entrance.

FIGURE 2.10 Stone is plentiful in Minecraft, but remember to bring your pickaxe.

As soon as you have the blocks, head back to your crafting table and run eight blocks around the edge of the crafting grid, leaving the middle block empty.

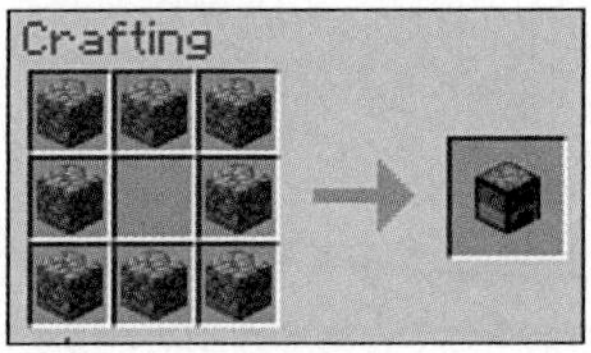

Drag the completed furnace to one of your hotbar slots and then place it with a right-click next to your crafting table. It's torch time!

Let There Be Light

Light is a great tool for dispelling fear of the dark—in any setting. In Minecraft, light keeps hostile mobs at bay. More specifically, it prevents them from spawning. Certain rules built into the software prevent mobs from springing into existence close to you, no matter the light level, but they also can't spawn anywhere near bright light. As you expand your shelter, mine, and explore, place torches to keep the coast somewhat clear. In any case, torches add much-needed ambiance to any home.

Right-click on your furnace. You see your inventory screen again, as shown in Figure 2.11, but this time with an upper grid containing just two slots. The lower slot holds the combustible to power the furnace, while the upper one holds the object you are smelting. Place a couple of blocks of wood in each of the lower and upper slots to start making charcoal, as shown. You'll soon see the charcoal pop into the output grid. Each chunk of charcoal when combined with a stick makes four torches.

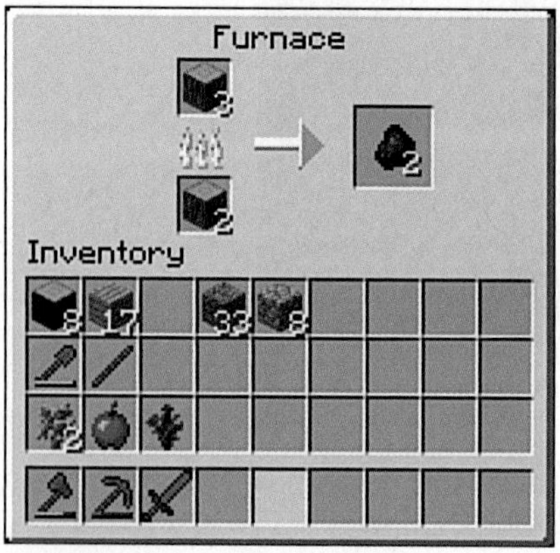

FIGURE 2.11 Burn, baby, burn. A furnace smelts objects into items more useful for crafting, building, decorating, and cooking. Keep a furnace handy at all times.

TIP

Buckets of Lava Are the Best Fuel

You can use both coal and charcoal as sources of fuel in a furnace, and they are much more effective than most other materials—able to process eight blocks apiece. But what's the best possible fuel? A bucket of lava. You'll be able to find these easily enough later on. For now, just keep it in mind. One bucket of lava equals 100 smelted blocks. It's like your own personal nuclear reactor!

The furnace can take a little time to do its thing, but you can set it and forget it. Walk away, and the furnace keeps on burning while it has fuel and something to work on. When either fuel or raw material runs out, the furnace shuts down, and you can collect the results whenever you're ready.There's no need to worry about leaving the gas on or the pot boiling over.

Now that you have some charcoal, press **E** to open your inventory window (or right-click your crafting table if you prefer). Place one stick in any lower position of the crafting grid and one piece of charcoal above it. Great work! You've just created four torches, and in Minecraft, they're going to be some of your best friends.

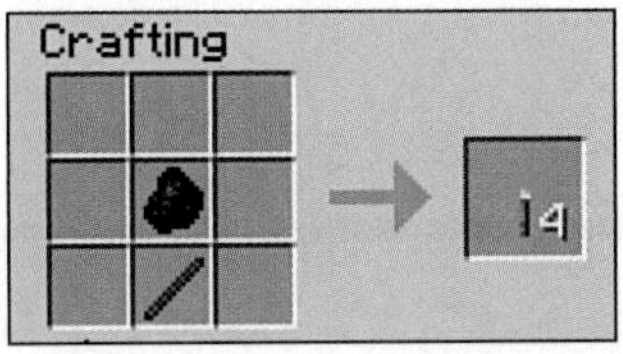

Place the torches in a hotbar slot and step back a moment. Find a nice position on a wall, select the torch, and right-click the wall to attach it. You can also place torches directly on the floor or on top of many other items, such as a crafting table or a furnace, by using Shift+right-click. Torches never burn out, so you never need to replace them, although you can knock them down with a left-click, scoop them up, and place them elsewhere if your interior decorating instinct kicks in. Torches can also provide a useful beacon function, so you might want to place a few outside your shelter. They create a nice beacon of light you can spot from a distance, which is especially helpful if you're making a last-minute dash for home at sunset.

Figure 2.12 shows the much-needed result of adding torches in the first Elysian hidey-hole.

FIGURE 2.12 Cave, sweet cave. Safe for the night and cozy enough to keep on crafting.

Slumbering with Lumber

Beds are great because they make a house a home. They lend a comforting aesthetic that a crafting table and furnace can't really provide. But more than that, they serve a purpose that gets right down to the underlying game mechanic: A bed protects you. It shelters you from harm through the night so that you can skip to sunrise and get on with your day.

Most importantly, sleeping in a bed resets your spawn point to the location of the bed so that you can venture further and further out into the world, covering vast distances, without having to restart at your point of origin should you die. Note that if the last bed you slept in is destroyed for any reason, your spawn point reverts to your original point of origin, so it pays to keep your bed safe.

NOTE

Time Is on Your Side

While you are sleeping, time doesn't really tick by. Sleeping is really just like typing the **/time set 0** cheat code, causing an instant adjustment in the game's clock to dawn but leaving everything else in the same state it was in before you actually went to sleep.

If you have cheats enabled in the game options (see Chapter 1, "Getting Started"), issue them by typing a forward slash (/) and then your cheat text. You'll see your input and Minecraft's response to that input in the lower-left portion of the screen. Check out Figure 2.13 to see what it looks like.

TIP

Spawn Point Cheat

With cheats enabled, type **/spawnpoint** to reset the world's original spawn point to your current position. If you die, you'll pop up again nearby.

Building a bed is easy, but you first need to find and kill three sheep to get their wool. Later you can build shears for a more sheep-friendly experience, but for now, lamb skewers are the only option.

If you've seen sheep nearby, take your sword in hand and have at them with a few left-clicks. Keep track of your bearings, though. The sheep make a dash for it on the first attack, and you don't want to become lost as you give chase.

tim has just earned the achievement [Taking Inventory]
Set the time to 13000
/time set day
27
64
32
2

FIGURE 2.13 You can interact with Minecraft behind the scenes by issuing cheat commands.

NOTE

Sleep Without Sheep

Getting sheep is the easiest way to harvest wool for a bed. If you can't find any, skip the bed-building and start on Chapter 3 spending the night improving your tools at the crafting table. You can quietly dig up more cobblestone by expanding your shelter. Just remember to place torches every nine or so spaces to ensure that you leave no dark places where a hostile mob can spawn. If there are simply no sheep anywhere nearby, look for spiders. Each one drops between 0 and 2 pieces of string. Collect 4 of those, and you can make a block of wool, so collect 12, and you'll have enough for a bed. Fair warning, though: This might take a while.

Each sheep drops one block of wool. When you've collected three, head back to your crafting table, lay three blocks of wood planks on the bottom layer and the three blocks of wool across the middle layer. Voilà! A bed is born.

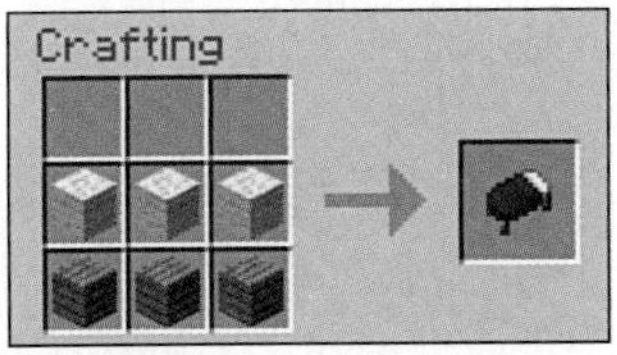
Crafting

You can place the bed anywhere there is space for two blocks. Stand facing the direction you want the bed to face, where the foot of the bed would be closest to you. Then right-click on the block where the foot should go (not the head). Figure 2.14 shows the placement, and Figure 2.15 shows the result in a now very comfortable, if simple, shelter.

FIGURE 2.14 Bed placement can be a little tricky because a bed takes two blocks. Always aim for the space you plan to place the foot of the bed.

FIGURE 2.15 The bed is now tucked against the wall in the back of the shelter.

> **TIP**
>
> **Take a Bed with You**
>
> Keep a bed in your inventory if you're trekking through the wilderness. You can place it down anywhere there's enough space and, as long as no monsters are nearby, sleep cozily through the dark. The bed is Minecraft's equivalent of a Get Out of Jail Free card. However, this technique does have its hazards should you wake and find mobs looming over you, and it really takes little effort to build a quick shelter. In other words, use this trick at your own risk.

Tools and Their (Over)Use

Take a close look at my tools in Figure 2.16. Do you see the little bar that appears beneath them? This is a property of some items, including tools, weapons, and armor, called the *durability bar*, and you should pay attention to it as you play. In Minecraft, when an item's durability expires, the item is unusable, and you have to invoke a replacement.

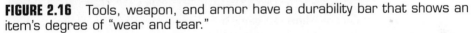

FIGURE 2.16 Tools, weapon, and armor have a durability bar that shows an item's degree of "wear and tear."

You can press **F3+H** to display the numeric durability of your items. As an item's durability decreases with use, the durability bar shortens from the right to the left, turning from green to red.

You'll learn more about tool and item durability (as well as the cool ability to repair durable items) in subsequent chapters. At this point, I just wanted to make you aware of the behavior so that you weren't surprised when, all of a sudden, that axe you've been wielding like a madman suddenly drops out of your inventory.

A Bit About Achievements

In Minecraft, achievements are intended to give you a well-deserved "pat on the back" for performing certain actions in the game. Most players find that these onscreen achievement notifications (one of which you can see in Figure 2.17) provide inspiration to continue playing the game.

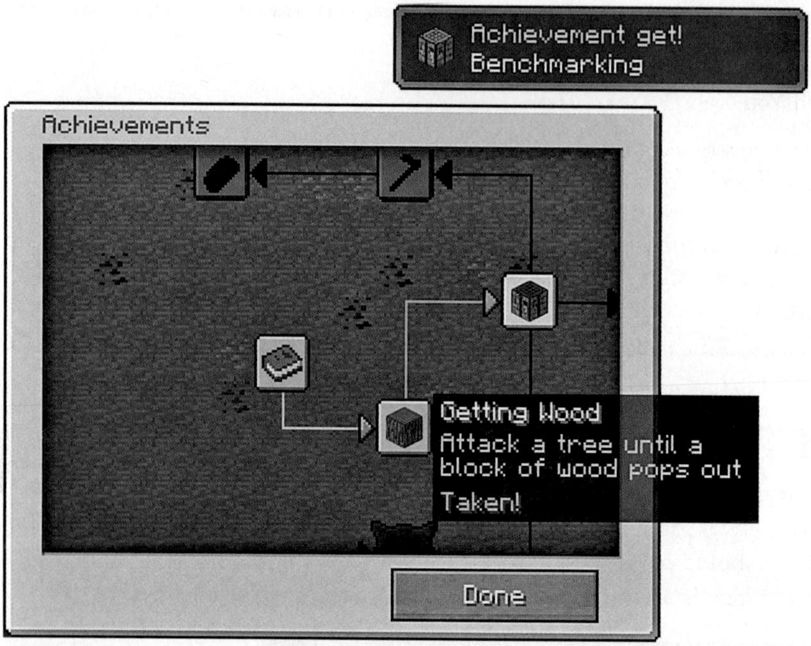

FIGURE 2.17 You can track your overall achievement progress by visiting the Achievements screen. I've superimposed an achievement notification so that you can see what those look like onscreen as well.

Press **Esc** to pause the game and click **Achievements** to see your overall achievement progress in Minecraft.

You can earn achievements in any Minecraft game mode, including Creative. However, the console editions support achievements only in Survival game mode.

To see a comprehensive list of achievements, along with their descriptions, point your web browser toward the official Minecraft wiki: http://minecraft.gamepedia.com/Achievements#List_of_achievements. You can also use this shorter version of that link: http://goo.gl/AbeKYZ.

What Is This "Bonus Chest" You Speak Of?

In Chapter 1 I suggested that you turn off the Bonus Chest option when you create a new world in Minecraft. My justification for this tip is that the bonus chest reduces your first-night incentive to punch some trees and gather your core survival resources.

For the sake of completeness, I want to briefly discuss the bonus chest with you now. In essence, the bonus chest is a sort of "starter kit" that helps new Minecraft players (or experienced players who are tired of the repetition of initially punching trees) get a leg up on surviving their first night in the world.

The bonus chest spawns just once, at world creation, and its contents are unique to the world seed. You'll find up to four torches surrounding the bonus chest. It should appear within sight distance of your avatar at game start or should at least be nearby. By the way, you can and should retrieve those torches! Figure 2.18 shows an example of a bonus chest.

FIGURE 2.18 Everything in or around the bonus chest—even the torches—can be harvested for your first-night survival benefit.

The contents of the bonus chest are variable. The chest contains up to 10 item stacks, chosen at random from the following list:

- Acacia wood
- Apple
- Bread
- Oak wood
- Oak wood planks
- Stick
- Stone axe
- Stone pickaxe
- Wooden axe
- Wooden pickaxe

Bonus chests on the console edition can also include additional content.

The Bottom Line

Surviving your first night can seem daunting at first. It's a bit of a learning curve, but get through it just once, and you'll find it much easier next time. First-night survival entails just a few simple steps: Harvest wood, create a crafting table, build tools, and hollow out a shelter.

But remember, Minecraft days pass really quickly. Keep an eye out for the sun setting in the west, and make sure you can at least create a small cave in a cliff or hillside so that you are out of harm's way when night falls. When you head out again in the morning, check for hostile mobs. Their sound gives them away. Some lurk all day, whereas others burn up in the sunlight or take cover in shade. Be especially careful if it's an overcast day or raining, though, because the lower light level makes it easier for them to survive.

Now that you've had an initial taste of Minecraft, I bet you're hungry for more. At this point, we've only scratched the surface of the crafting table, and while the shelter serves its purpose, Minecraft provides unlimited real estate and resources—enough to create any architectural dream. In the next chapter, you'll learn some essential survival tricks, including how to stave off hunger, deal with mobs, and build additional tools.

Gathering Resources

In This Chapter

- Never get lost. Learn the secrets of the HUD and its hidden GPS.
- Improve your tools with more durable materials.
- Safely store your hard-earned resources.
- Learn the easy way to manage hunger.
- Build your first outdoor shelter and enjoy the view.
- Access the full Creative mode inventory.

It might not look like it on the surface, but each Minecraft world is rich with resources. Making the most of them is the next step in getting the most out of the game. In Chapter 2, "First-Night Survival," you put together a pack of essentials sufficient to last the first night, but this is really just the smallest prequel to the real game, and describing how to find, create, and use other types of resources forms much of this book. This chapter is about building a foundation you can use to launch into the rest of the game. The focus is on a few key points: building an outdoor shelter, finding food to stave off hunger, improving your collection of tools, and building a chest to safely store items. Mastering these processes solidifies your position, makes your base more defensible, allows you to do all sorts of Minecrafty things more efficiently, and helps you set yourself up for longer excursions above and below ground.

The good news is that you already have a base, so you can explore during the day (trying not to lose your way) and head back at night. However, you still need to avoid at least some of the hostile mobs that persist during the day.

Introducing the HUD

Let's start by taking a look at the Heads-Up Display (HUD)—that collection of icons and status bars at the bottom of the screen. Figure 3.1 shows the HUD as it appears in Survival mode, with all possible indicators displayed. (The Creative mode HUD only shows the hotbar.)

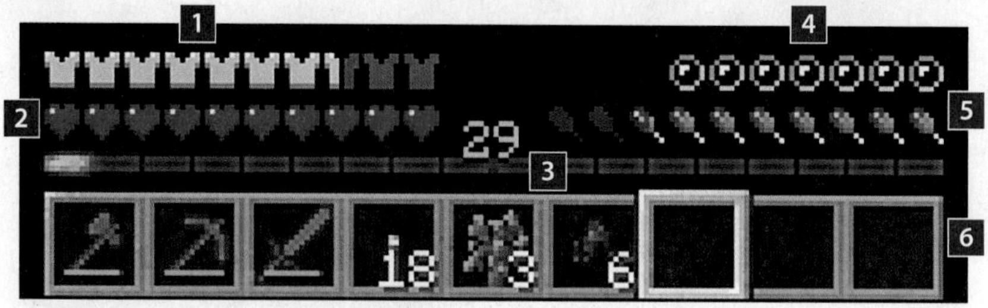

FIGURE 3.1 The HUD provides key status indications. Health is all-important, but low hunger also leads to low health, so keep a close eye on both.

1. Armor bar
2. Health bar
3. Experience bar
4. Oxygen bar
5. Hunger bar
6. Hotbar

Each section of the HUD provides a key nugget of information about the health or status of your avatar:

- **Armor bar**—The armor bar appears when you've equipped your avatar with any type of armor and shows the current damage absorption level. Each armor icon represents an 8% reduction in the damage you'll take, so a 10/10 suit of armor reduces the damage you take by 80%, whereas a 1/10 suit absorbs only 8%. Armor becomes less effective the more damage it absorbs, although the rate at which it deteriorates also depends on its material—leather being the weakest and diamond the strongest. While the HUD shows only 10 armor icons, each represents 2 points, making 20 points in all.
- **Health bar**—You also have up to 20 points of health available, represented by the 10 hearts shown. Each time you endure damage—such as from hunger, spider bites, zombie slaps, a fall, being under water too long, and so on—half a heart or more disappears, accompanied by a distinctive click noise. Health and hunger have a complicated relationship. You can read more about this later in this chapter, in the section, "Hunger Management."
- **Experience bar**—The experience bar increases the more you mine, smelt, cook, kill hostile mobs, trade with villagers, and fish. Your current level is shown in the middle of the bar. You move to the next experience level when it's full. Experience isn't generally important until you start enchanting and giving additional powers to items such as swords (see Chapter 10, "Enchanting, Anvils, and Brewing"). Unlike in other role-playing games, experience in Minecraft is more like a currency that you spend on enchantments, so it waxes and wanes. But all experience gained since your last death, even experience you spend on enchantments, counts toward the final score shown on the screen when you die. Killing a mob drops experience orbs that either fly directly toward you or float to the ground, waiting for you to collect them. You can also gain

experience by smelting certain items in a furnace and carrying out other activities such as finding rare ores, breeding animals, fishing, and more. Dying, however, drops your experience level to zero, although you can rebuild it a little by picking up your own experience orbs (seven for each level you've attained) after you respawn if you can make it back within five minutes.

- **Oxygen bar**—The oxygen bar appears when you are underwater and quickly starts to drop. You can probably hold your own breath for longer! (The world record, at an impressive 22 minutes, is held by Stig Severinsen.) As soon as your oxygen level hits zero, your health starts taking a two-point hit every second, but it resurfaces for just an instant if you hold down the jump key until you've reached air once more. There's no danger with deep dives, either. You can use this ability to do interesting things like building an underwater base. Figure 3.2 shows an example, and you'll learn how to build your own in Chapter 8, "Creative Construction," along with some tricks for staying under longer than Stig.

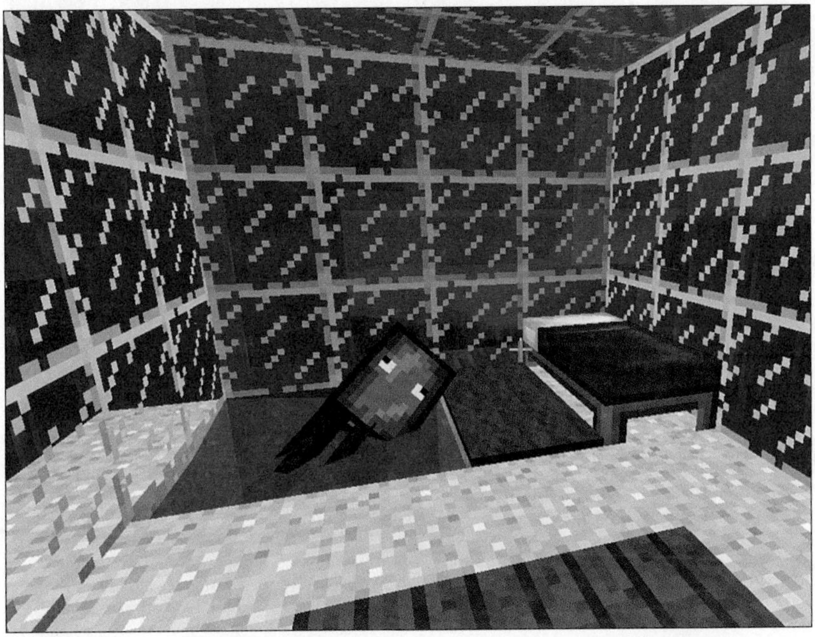

FIGURE 3.2 Underwater bases are impervious to mob attacks (but watch your oxygen while building one). In fact, the only mobs that spawn underwater outside of the huge ocean monument structures are squids, which pose no danger to you.

- **Hunger bar**—You also have 20 points of hunger available, as well as a hidden value called Saturation. Like armor and health, each hunger bar icon holds 2 points and can reduce by half an icon (that icon is, incidentally, a shank, or the lower part of a leg of meat) at a time. You'll learn more about hunger later in this chapter, in the section "Hunger Management."

- **Hotbar**—These nine slots represent items you can select with the mouse scroll wheel or by pressing the 1–9 keys. Press **E** to access your full inventory and to change the items in these slots. The white number next to a slot shows that slot's count of stacked identical items. A durability bar also appears, in green, under each tool's icon, and it gradually reduces as you use the tool until that tool actually breaks and disappears from your inventory. You'll have some warning of this because the bar turns red when it's close to zero. See "Improving Your Tools," later in the chapter, to learn more about the durability of different materials. Finally, any item you are dual-wielding shows up as an icon to the left of the hotbar.

TIP

Showing Durability Stats in the HUD

Press **F3+H** (or **fn+F3+H** on OS X) to display the current and maximum durability values of all the tools in your inventory. A durability value appears in a ToolTip when you hover your mouse over an item.

NOTE

The HUD Changes When You're Mounted on a Horse

The HUD changes when you ride a horse so that it shows the horse's health in place of your hunger bar. The experience bar also changes to the jump bar. You can learn more about horses and other mountable mobs on page 148 in the section "Taming and Riding Horses, Donkeys, and More."

In Multiplayer mode, your HUD also displays a chat window in the bottom-left corner. Press **T** to expand the chat window.

Toggle the entire HUD display off and on by pressing **F1**. Press **F3** with the HUD turned on to view a much more detailed HUD debug screen (see Figure 3.3.)

NOTE

Hiding the HUD in the Xbox/PS3 Editions

You cannot hide the HUD in Minecraft Pocket Edition, but there is an option for doing so on the console editions. Press the **Start** key and open the Help & Options menu. Scroll down to **Settings→User Interface** and deselect **Display HUD**. There isn't a quicker way to do this at present.

FIGURE 3.3 The Debug HUD provides a lot of cryptic information but can also help you navigate home. It also provides information about your system, available memory, and more.

1. Your location in blocks east of your original spawn point. Blocks west are shown as a negative value.
2. Your current vertical height in layers above bedrock.
3. Your location in blocks south of your original spawn point. Blocks north are shown as a negative value.
4. The direction you are facing and how moving forward will change the current coordinates.
5. The current biome type.

The coordinates shown in the debug screen are based on the world's origin, where x=0 and z=0. (y shows your current level above bedrock.) Take note of the current values. If you become lost before you have a chance to build a bed and reset your spawn point, you can always find your way back to your original spawn and, presumably, your first shelter, by facing in a direction that brings both x and y back to those noted values. If you sleep in a bed and reset your spawn, turn on the debug screen and write down the coordinates shown before you head out. This is particularly useful if you plan to use the teleport cheat (**/tp xxx yyy zzz**).

Incidentally, just so we're clear: *Cheating* in Minecraft doesn't carry with it the negative connotations of cheating in most other contexts. If you have enabled cheats in the game menu, type a forward slash (/) followed by the cheat text to customize the running state of the game. Make sure to press **Enter** or **Return** after you type your cheat to submit the command to Minecraft.

When you need to return to those earlier coordinates—and I should warn you that this *can* take some experimentation and a little practice—turn and take a few steps and note the change in values of your current coordinates. Shift those x and z values back toward the coordinates you originally recorded. You'll probably wander around a bit, but eventually you'll get there.

Improving Your Tools

Wooden tools wear out fast, so it's best to upgrade your kit as quickly as possible.

Each type of material has a different level of durability. Think of durability as the number of useful actions the tool can perform before wearing out completely and disappearing from the inventory. I've included the durability in parentheses after each material's description, listed from least to most durable:

- **Gold (33)**—Although it is the least durable material, gold happens to be the most enchantable material, so you can imbue it with superpowers (see Chapter 10). But given that gold is about five times as rare as iron, and it can be used to craft many other useful items, I wouldn't recommend using gold for tools.
- **Wood (60)**—Wood is easy to obtain, especially in an emergency above ground, but wooden tools can't mine the more valuable ores, such as iron, gold, diamond, and redstone. You will need a pickaxe of any kind to mine stone because digging with bare hands will just break the stone down into unusable dust.
- **Stone (132)**—With over twice the longevity of wood, stone makes a great starting point for more serious mining and other activities. Stone tools are built from cobblestone blocks, which in turn come from stone. That may seem a little circuitous, but it will feel natural enough after a while.
- **Iron (251)**—Iron is your *go-to* material. It is found between bedrock, the lowest possible level in The Overworld, and up to about 20 levels below sea level. Iron is used for building all kinds of tools, implements, and devices, including armor, buckets (for carrying water, lava, and milk), compasses, minecarts, and minecart tracks. All these require at least iron ingots, which you obtain by smelting iron ore in a furnace; each block of ore produces one ingot. Ingots and many other items are found scattered throughout the world in village chests, mineshafts, dungeons, and strongholds. You might also find them dropped from killed zombies and iron golems, if you dare tackle them.

- **Diamond (1562)**—Diamond is the strongest material of all but also the most expensive, given that it is relatively rare (about 25 times as scarce as iron). A diamond pickaxe is the only kind that can successfully mine obsidian, a material required for creating the portal to reach The Nether dimension. Use iron pickaxes as much as possible and switch to diamond only when you need to mine obsidian. You're better off saving any diamonds you find for weapons, armor, and enchantment tables.

NOTE

Different Materials for Different Items

Durability applies to all tools, weapons, and armor, although there are differences in the materials you use to make different items. For example, you can craft leather armor from leather, and you can make stone tools from cobblestone, but you can't make armor from stone or tools from leather.

CAUTION

Don't Let Tools Wear Out

Try not to let a tool become so worn that it actually breaks down completely and disappears. Instead, place two of the same type of worn tools in the crafting grid to combine their remaining strength into another and give it a second shot at busting blocks. Consider it recycling, Minecraft style. You can also repair tools and weapons at an anvil found in the smithy in villages, or at one you've crafted yourself.

The recipes for crafting tools from all materials are identical, except that you can replace the head of an implement with the material of your choice:

- To make a stone pickaxe, you need two wooden sticks for the handle and three cobblestone blocks.

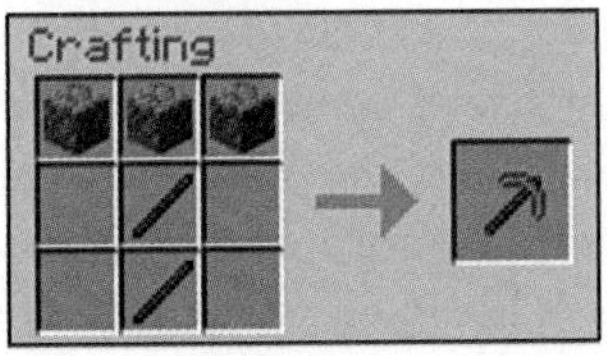

- Replace the planks with stone in the crafting recipes for the axe and the sword to create stone versions of those.

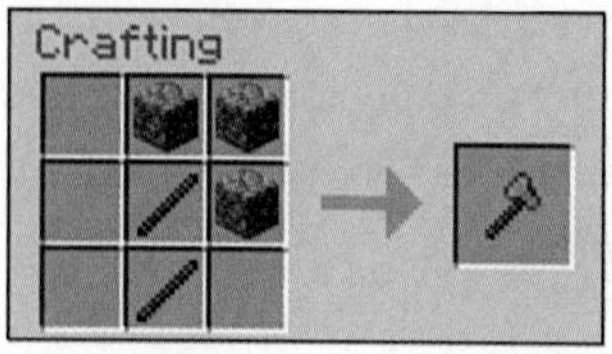

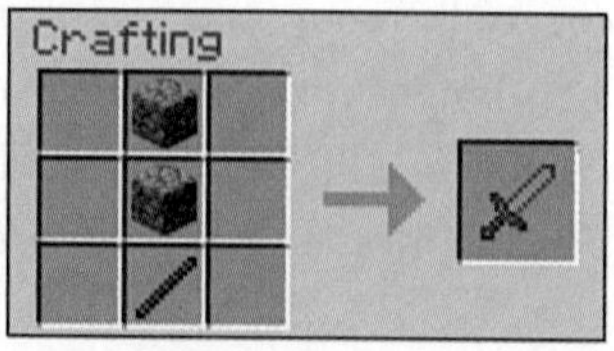

- You might also want to add a shovel to your collection, because using one is about four times faster than using hands to harvest softer materials such as dirt, gravel, sand, clay, and snow, and using a shovel helps some of those blocks deliver resources rather than just dig them out.

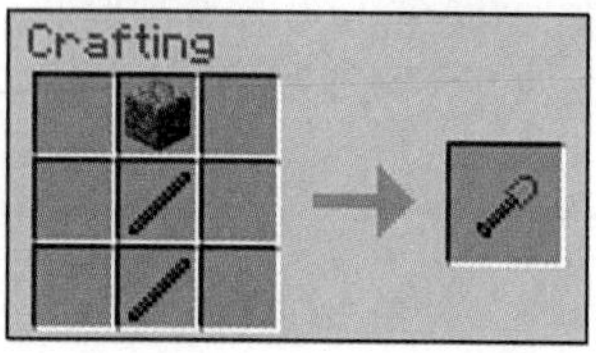

As you craft more items, you need to find a place to store the ones that you don't need to use right away. You should also store other resources and food you come across on your travels. That comes next.

Chests: Safely Stashing Your Stuff

Whenever you head away from your secure shelter, there is always a reasonably high risk of death. Creepers, lava pits, long falls—they can all do you in. While your new life when you respawn is only a moment away, the real danger is that any items you've collected will drop from your character's inventory at the place of death. You'll have about five minutes of real time before they vanish forever. If the site of your death proves impossible to return to, your hard-earned tools and supplies will be lost.

You can think of a chest as an insurance policy. Put everything you don't need in a chest before you embark on a mission, and those things will be there when you get back or after you respawn.

The natural place to leave chests is in your shelter, but you can also leave them elsewhere, perhaps at a staging point as you work deep in a mine, or far afield outside. Mobs will leave them alone, and the only real risk you face is leaving them out in the open on a multiplayer server where they can be ransacked by other players, or that you could get blown up by a creeper while you're rummaging around inside.

Chests come in two sizes: single and double. A single chest can store 27 stacks of items. A double chest, which you create by placing two single chests side by side, stores up to 54 stacks of items. Given that a stack can be up to 64 items high, that's an astonishing potential total of 3,510 blocks in a crate that takes just 2×1 blocks of floor space. If you've ever followed the *Doctor Who* TV series, consider chests the TARDIS of storage! Or in Dungeons & Dragons terms, it's a Bag of Holding. Figure 3.4 shows a chest in one of my personal hidey holes.

FIGURE 3.4 A furnace at left and a storage chest at right.

Create a chest at your crafting table with eight blocks of wooden planks arranged around the outside, leaving a space in the middle.

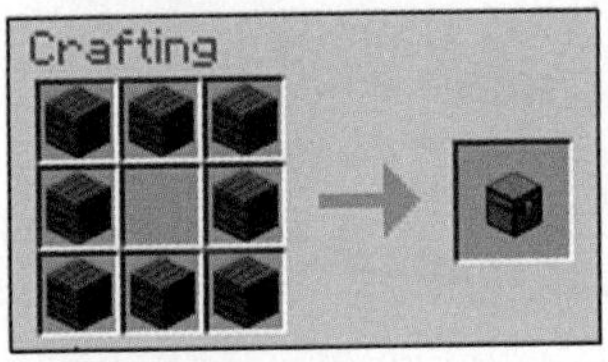

Place the chest and then right-click it to open it. You can then move items back and forth between your inventory and the chest. In Figure 3.5, I've transferred to the chest all the items I don't need for the next expedition.

FIGURE 3.5 Chests act as an insurance policy for your items so that they aren't lost if you die. Use the inventory shortcuts you learned earlier to quickly move items between your active inventory and the chest's storage slots.

THE CONNECTED CHEST

Chests are undoubtedly useful; it's difficult to survive without them. But you can't transport a chest's contents with you.

Enter the Ender Chest, which is like storage *in the cloud*. An Ender Chest isn't cheap to make. You'll need eight obsidian blocks, obtained by combining lava with water, or via regular mining and caving, and one Eye of Ender, collected by combining Ender Pearls from downed Endermen with Blaze Powder in the crafting table—and you can't get Blaze Powder without first heading to The Nether dimension. So what's so good about Ender Chests? All of them access the same virtual chest, sharing all contents between them. Say that you've built multiple dwellings across your vast world, and you have some items—a few favorites—that you'd like to be able to access anywhere you go. Place an Ender Chest in each of your dwellings, and any items that you place in any of the chests become available in all others. It's like quantum travel without all that entanglement business.

Before you head out, you should know two other things: how to avoid monsters and how to deal with hunger. Read on.

Avoiding Monsters

There's a key difference between the Minecraft world on the first day and the second day. In a word, mobs (hostile ones, to be specific). Mobs spawn only in dark areas, and some only during the night, so if you are outside during your first day and stay in well-lit areas, you'll be reasonably safe. By the second day, however, mobs have had a chance to build their numbers and wander about. It's not very likely you'll encounter them on day 2, but it's best to be prepared.

There are over two dozen types of hostile mobs: Enderman, Iron Golem, The Wither, Creeper, Ender Dragon, Zombie, Baby Zombie, Zombie Villager, Endermite, Giant, Blaze, Slime, Wither Skeleton, Ghast, Silverfish, Witch, Human, Skeleton, Spider, Cave Spider, Wither Skeleton Jockey, Magma Cube, Spider Jockey, Zombie Chicken Jockey, Guardian, and Elder Guardian. Of those, here are the ones you might meet on your second day outside:

- **Zombies**—Zombies burn up in sunlight but can still survive in shadows or rain or when wearing helmets, and, of course, they're fine in caves all hours of the day or night. They are relatively easy to defeat, and if any come after you from out of the shadows, just head to a well-lit area and keep your distance while they burn up in the sun.
- **Skeletons**—Skeletons also burn up in sunlight unless they're wearing helmets, and they can survive at any time in lower light conditions. They're quite deadly with a bow and arrow and best avoided for now.
- **Spiders**—Spiders come in two varieties: *large* and *cave*. You'll probably only see the large spiders at this stage. They are passive during the day but become hostile in shadows and can attack at any time if provoked. They'll climb, they'll jump, and they are pretty darn fast. Fortunately, they're also easy to kill with some swift sword attacks. The blue spiders are the smaller, poisonous cave spiders. They live only in abandoned mineshafts underground, but they do so in substantial numbers. If you suffer from arachnophobia, I don't have much good news for you, except that with a little time, you'll get used to them, and they won't seem quite so nasty. If you see a skeleton riding a spider, you've just encountered the rather rare spider jockey.
- **Creepers**—Creepers have a well-earned reputation as the Minecraft bad guys. They are packed to their green gills with gunpowder, and they'll start their very short 1.5-second fuse as soon as they are within three blocks of you. Their explosion can cause a lot of real damage to you, nearby structures, and the environment in general. If you hear a creeper's fuse—a soft hissing noise—but can't see it, run like heck in the direction you're facing. Remember to sprint by double-tapping and holding your **W** key. With a little luck, you'll get three blocks away, and the creeper's fuse will reset. Creepers are usually

best dealt with using a ranged attack from a bow and arrow. However, if you sprint at them with an iron or diamond sword and take a swipe at just the right moment, you can send them flying back out of their suicidal detonation range, causing the fuse to reset. Most creepers despawn around noon, leaving the afternoon generally free of their particular brand of terror.

- **Slimes**—Slimes spawn in the swamp biome and in some places underground. They initially spawn as small, medium-sized, or quite large gelatinous green blocks and are more than capable of causing damage. Attacking eventually breaks them up into two to four new medium-sized slimes. These slimes can still attack but are relatively easily killed, at which point they spawn a further two to four tiny slimes each. These last slimes don't cause any attack damage but may still push you into peril if you're unlucky.

If you come across a lone spider, a zombie, or even a slime, that's as good a time as any to get in some sword practice. Just point your crosshairs at the creature and strike with the left mouse button. Keep clicking as fast as you can, and you've got a very good chance of killing the mob and picking up any items it drops before it lands too many blows. Try to avoid the other mobs for now.

TIP

Switch to Peaceful Mode to Get a Break

Getting mobbed by mobs? Click **Esc** to open the Options window and change your difficulty level to Peaceful. This despawns all hostile mobs and allows your health to regenerate.

Use these tips to survive and avoid mobs:

- Stay in the open as much as you can, and avoid heavily wooded areas if possible.
- Most mobs have a 16-block detection radar. If they can also draw a line of sight to your position, they will enter pursuit mode. (Spiders can always detect you, even through other blocks.) At that point, they'll relentlessly plot and follow a path to your position, tracking you through other blocks without requiring a line of sight. Pursuit mode stays engaged much farther than 16 blocks.
- Keep your sound turned up because you'll also hear mobs within 16 blocks, although creepers, as their name suggests, are creepily quiet.
- Avoid skirting along the edges of hilly terrain. Creepers can drop on you from above with their fuse already ticking. Try to head directly up and down hills so you have a good view of the terrain ahead.

- Mobs are quite slow, so you can easily put some distance between them and yourself by keeping up a steady pace and circling around to get back to your shelter. Sprint mode will leave them far behind.

CAUTION

Sprinting Makes You Hungry

Sprint mode burns up hunger points, so try to use it only in emergencies (and if you have food ready).

Hunger Management

Hunger plays a permanent role in Minecraft, much as in real life. While it's only possible to starve to death on Hard difficulty, hunger lowers your hit points, leaving you vulnerable, so it's always important to ensure that you have the equivalent of a couple of sandwiches packed before heading deep into a mine or going on a long trek.

Hunger is a combination of two values: the one shown in the HUD's hunger bar and a hidden value called *saturation*. The latter provides a buffer to the hunger bar and decreases first. In fact, your hunger bar doesn't decrease at all until saturation reaches zero. At that point, you see the hunger bar start to jitter, and after a short while, it takes its first hit. Saturation cannot exceed the value of the hunger bar, so with a full hunger bar of 20 points, it's possible to have up to 20 points of saturation. However, a hunger level of 6 points also provides only a maximum of 6 points of saturation, and that makes you vulnerable.

You'll find some key information about the hunger system here:

- On Easy and Normal Survival modes, there is no need to worry too much about hunger because your character won't drop dead from it. If you're close to home and pottering around in your farm or constructing some building extensions, you're fairly safe, but your health starts to drop. Eat something as soon as you can to fill your hunger bar and start rebuilding your health.
- Sprinting isn't possible when the hunger bar drops below 6 hunger points, or 3 shanks, as shown in the HUD.
- Keeping a relatively full stomach at 18 hunger points (9 shanks in the HUD) allows health to regenerate at 1 point (half a heart) every 4 seconds.
- Health depletes if the hunger bar drops to zero, increasing the risk of dying in one of the many imaginative ways Minecraft has on offer (see Figure 3.6).

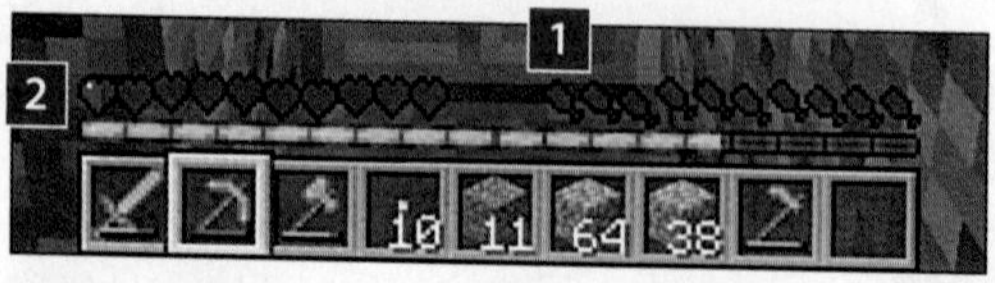

FIGURE 3.6 The effects of extreme hunger on Normal difficulty: Health depletes to just one point, or half a heart.

1. Hunger at zero
2. Health at one point

- Some limits apply to the amount that health can drop, according to the difficulty level. On Easy, health cannot deplete from hunger further than 10 points, or half the full quotient. On Normal, it drops to 1 point, which is an extreme level of vulnerability. On Hard difficulty, there are no limits, so don't ignore the hunger bar, or death from starvation could be just moments away. See "Getting Food on the Run," later in this chapter, to help avoid this.

Your Mission: Food, Resources, and Reconnaissance

Your second day is the perfect time to gather food and other resources and to take a quick survey of the landscape surrounding your first shelter. In particular, you want to find somewhere suitable for your first outdoor shelter. Keep an eye out for any of the following:

- **Passive mobs**—Chickens, pigs, rabbits, sheep, and cows all provide a ready source of food, raw or cooked, although cooked meat restores more hunger points than raw. Cows also drop leather that you can use for your first armor, and when you have an iron bucket, you can milk cows, and milk gives you an instant cure for poisoning. Chickens also lay eggs, so gather any that you find.
- **Natural harvest**—The harvest includes cocoa pods, apples, sugar cane, carrots, wheat, and potatoes (found in villages), as well as seeds. Knock down tall grass to find seeds (see Figure 3.7). When you plant the seeds, they mature into wheat within five to eight day/night cycles. From wheat, it's easy to bake bread, one of the simplest but most effective sources of food, especially if there are no passive mobs nearby. See Chapter 6, "Crop Farming," for more on agricultural techniques.
- **Construction resources**—You can mine plenty of cobblestone quite safely by digging into the terrain to expand your original shelter. But some other resources will definitely come in handy:
  - **Wood**—Wood is always useful, both for crafting and for fueling your furnace, where you can convert it into charcoal and then create torches.

- **Sand**—You can smelt sand into glass blocks, which you can then use as is or turn into glass panes to allow daylight into your shelter.
- **Coal**—Coal is used to fuel your furnace and make torches. You can often see it in veins on the surface of the walls of small caves or on the sides of cliffs. If you can safely get to it, make like a miner and dig it out.

FIGURE 3.7 Knock down grass to gather seeds to plant wheat, an easy crop to farm. You can then turn the wheat into bread—a handy food if you're stuck with no other options.

TIP

Making Use of Bones

The morning sun burns skeletons, leaving bones behind that you can craft into bone meal. Bone meal acts as a fertilizer, helping your crops grow faster—much faster! You can also use bone to tame wolves (changing them into dogs), which gives you an extra level of protection. Chapter 7, "Farming and Taming Mobs," has a lot more information on breeding and taming mobs in Minecraft.

Back to your mission. Start early, heading out with a stone sword at the ready, just in case. If you are low on wood, swing an axe at a few nearby trees.

Move carefully so that you don't lose your bearings. The sun rises in the east and sets in the west, and the clouds always travel from east to west, so you can always at least get your bearings. The sun also appears as a face (a recent addition) that is upside down in the east and right-side up in the west. Following a compass cardinal point (north, south, east, or west) using the sun and clouds as a reference can reasonably and accurately lead you away and back home again.

TIP

Finding Your Way

It's easy to become lost in Minecraft. Run helter-skelter from your base, chase a herd of livestock, discover a natural cave system, or take a shot across the sea like that famed Norseman Leif Eriksson. It's all part of the Minecraft charm. But don't become Columbus in the process.

A few quick tips:

- When you're able, craft a compass. It takes redstone and iron, and both are relatively easy to obtain with some assiduous mining. The only problem with a compass is that it's not a GPS; it always points to your original spawn point in the world. Think of that point as the magnetic north pole. Sleeping in a bed resets your spawn point but not your compass, so this method falls out of date as soon as you move to new dwellings and update your spawn point. You can also use a cheat code **/spawnpoint**, to reset your spawn point.
- Also, obtaining a compass is the first step in crafting a map. A compass is actually much more useful to your quest when crafted into a map; see "Mapping, or There and Back Again" on page 257.
- Don't forget that you can always use the built-in GPS that's available through the debug screen; see "Introducing the HUD" on page 51 earlier in this chapter.

Getting Food on the Run

If you are getting dangerously hungry, head to the nearest equivalent of a fast food outlet—a passive mob—sword at the ready. Your best bet is to look for cows and pigs. Each cow drops up to three pieces of raw meat when killed, with each piece restoring 3 hunger units and 1.8 in saturation, making for an excellent target of opportunity. Kill sheep to gather up to two pieces of raw mutton. You can also eat raw chicken and rabbits, but there's a 30% chance of developing food poisoning from them.

Rotten meat harvested from zombies is guaranteed to give you a stomach ache, but there is a quick fix. Cure any type of food poisoning by drinking milk obtained with a bucket from a cow. You can then eat any amount of poisoned meat, gain its restorative benefits, and cure the whole lot with one serving of milk. In other words, keep that rotten flesh the zombies drop just in case you need a quick top-up, and chase it down with a gulp of milk. (You can also feed rotten flesh to tamed dogs to keep up their health with no fear of them suffering any ill effects.)

Unless you are desperate, though, it is actually much better to take the time to cook all your meat first. There's less health risk, and you'll end up restoring more hunger and saturation points. It's therefore quite handy to always carry a furnace in your inventory, along with fuel. Think of it as a camping stove and cooler chest. When you've finished cooking, break down the furnace with a pickaxe, and it floats back into your inventory. If your tastes run to cookouts over an open fire, you can kill and cook pigs, chickens, rabbits, and cows in one blazing swoop by setting the ground beneath them on fire with a flint and steel. To do this, right-click on the ground, not the animal. Just take care that you don't do this anywhere near that fantastic wood cabin you just spent the last three weeks building. Fire can leap up to four blocks away.

NOTE

Fishing in the Sea of Plenty

Unlike hostile mobs, mobs such as chickens, cows, sheep, and pigs don't spawn on their own, so consider them a nonrenewable resource if you kill them in the wild. You're better off breeding them in a farm so they can be harvested and readily replaced. Fish, in contrast, are unlimited in quantity and very plentiful, especially if you fish when it's raining. By the way, your hunger bar never decreases when travelling by boat, making it the perfect opportunity to get in a spot of fishing. You also will never ever get food poisoning from chomping on raw fish. And they come pre-filleted. Sushi, anyone? Fishing is also something of a lucky dip, as you will pull up different types of fish and have a slim chance of hooking other valuable items such as saddles. See Chapter 7 for more information on saddles and slipping on some spurs.

TIP

Let Them Eat Cake

What's the quickest way to fill your hunger bar? Eat cake! Unlike in another well-known game, Minecraft's cake is not a lie. Each full cake provides up to 6 slices, each worth 1.5 hunger points, or 9 in total, and it's less resource intensive than creating golden apples. However, as in the real world, it won't last. The nutrients are lacking, so cake doesn't provide any saturation benefit. Make sure you eat some more nutritional foods such as protein as your hunger bar starts to top out to ensure that you also get that extra boost. A balanced diet is important in Minecraft, too!

Finally, if you simply cannot find mobs, your hunger bar has dropped to zero, and your health has plummeted to half a point, consider at least planting a wheat field and waiting it out in your shelter for the wheat to grow so you can harvest it and bake bread.

There's one final option if you're desperate: dying. If you are near your spawn point, place all your items in a chest and then find some quick way to die, such as drowning, falling, or mob baiting. You respawn back in your shelter with full health, a restored hunger bar, and all your possessions waiting for you. Get dressed, fully equipped, and head out there to try again.

Finding a Building Site

As you scout around, keep an eye out for a new building site. It doesn't have to be fancy or even particularly large. A 6×5 space manages just fine, and even 6×4 can squeeze in the basics. You can also level ground and break down a few trees to clear space. I did this in Figure 3.8. The site is located just up the hill from the first dugout, overlooking the same lake and river system.

FIGURE 3.8 A nice, flat, elevated building site after clearing some trees and filling some holes in the ground with dirt.

I usually prefer space that's a little elevated because it provides a better view of the surroundings, but it's perfectly possible to create a protected space just about anywhere. You may even decide to go a little hybrid, building a house that's both tunneled into a hill and extending outside.

TIP

Light Those Caves

Check for any caves or tunnels close to your site's location. If they aren't too big, light them up with torches to prevent mobs from spawning inside and wandering out during the day. Or you can just block their entrance for now.

So, what can you build on this site? Figure 3.9 shows a basic structure. It takes 34 cobblestone blocks that you dig out of the first shelter and 12 wood blocks for the roof, which you obtain by cutting down the three trees that were occupying the site.

FIGURE 3.9 The layout for a small cobblestone cabin using 46 blocks, roof not shown. The sharp-eyed will notice that it can be reduced in width one space further, but the extra space is worth the cost of the four blocks.

You can build the roof from almost any handy material, including dirt, cobblestone, or wood. Avoid blocks that fall down, such as gravel and sand. A two-block-high wall keeps out all mobs except for spiders. Spiders can easily scale two blocks, but an overhang on the wall keeps them out as they can't climb upside-down. However, it's easier to just add a roof, especially if there are trees nearby that the spiders can climb up and use as springboards to jump straight into your dwelling. (Yes, it's happened to me more than once. Having a large hairy spider drop on your head at night is not for the faint of heart.) Figure 3.10 shows the finished hut with a few torches on the outside to keep things well lit.

TIP

No Housing Codes in Minecraft

The roof in Figure 3.10 rests right on the lip of the inner wall. You can't directly build a roof like this from scratch. First, place a block on top of the wall and then attach the inner block for the roof. Remove the first block, and the inner block floats. Attach new blocks to that to build out the roof structure. It won't pass a building inspection in the real world, but it certainly works in Minecraft.

FIGURE 3.10 The finished hut—basic but serviceable. And it's spider proof. Although there is a large gap above the door, in Minecraft's geometry, the door fills the entire space, keeping the mobs out.

Building a wall even two blocks high can take a little bit of fancy footwork. Some basic techniques help:

- Place your walls one layer at time. Put down the first layer and then jump on top to place the second.
- If you fall off your wall, place a temporary block on the inside of your structure against the wall and use it to climb back up. You can remove it when you're finished.
- Use pillar jumping if you need to go higher. While looking directly down, press the spacebar to jump and then right-click to place a block underneath you. You land on that block instead of the one below. Repeat as often as necessary. To go back down, dig out the blocks from directly underneath you.
- Hold down the **Shift** key as you work around the top of a tall wall so you don't fall off. You can even use this technique to place blocks that are normally beyond sight on the side of your current layer.

See Chapter 8 for more building techniques and ideas.

TIP

Topping Your New Shelter

You might want to consider building a pillar and platform on top of your new shelter. This can help you survey your terrain and provides an easy-to-see landmark when you're further afield. Put some torches on top because mobs can spawn on any platform, even those that are quite small, and you don't want to poke your head up through the platform only to discover a creeper on a short fuse.

Using the Creative Mode Inventory

Minecraft's resources fall into several primary categories. Some of them are a natural early focus as you improve your position from first-night survival. Others come into more focus as you get further through the game, gear up for your exploration of The Nether and The End dimensions, and become more creative with all that Minecraft has to offer. You can view all the possible tools and resources by opening your inventory in Creative mode, as shown in Figure 3.11. The categories that follow correspond to the tabs running across the upper and lower sections of the Creative mode inventory.

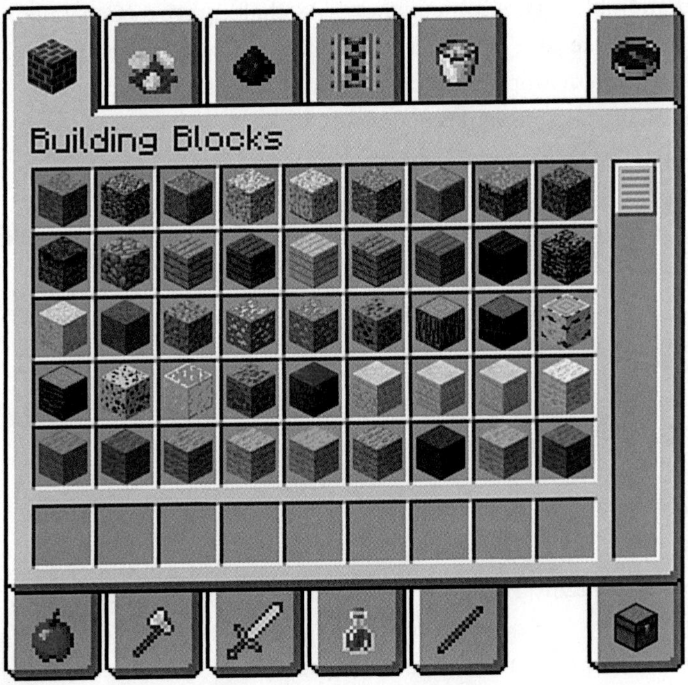

FIGURE 3.11 Creative mode inventory provides access to the full set of resources and tools.

TIP

Turn On Cheats

Turn on cheats when you start a new world to quickly jump between different gameplay modes. Type **/gamemode creative** (or **/gamemode 1**) and **/gamemode survival** (**/gamemode 0**) to move between the main types.

Here's a quick summary of the different resource categories:

- **Building Blocks**—Building blocks are used, as you might expect, for construction, including housing and almost anything else. Build a bridge for your redstone rail. Construct a dam. Elevate a farm above a level that won't get trampled by mobs or put up a fence. Build a skyscraper or reconstruct a monument. Minecraft provides a large number of primary blocks—such as cobblestone, gravel, wood, and dirt—that can be harvested directly, but things definitely become more interesting once you start creating secondary types of blocks from primary materials. You can store many items more efficiently (for example, by converting nine gold ingots into a single gold block) and climb more efficiently by crafting stairs instead of jumping up and down blocks on well-traveled routes. Building blocks are punny enough—the building blocks of creativity.
- **Decoration Blocks**—Decoration blocks are something of a catchall category. Generally, they are things you can use to make your constructions more interesting. Some of them are just visual, such as carpet, whereas others—such as crafting tables, chests, and the bed that keeps you safe at night—provide vital functions.
- **Redstone**—Redstone is an almost magical resource. You can use it to build powered circuits—quite complex ones—and then activate pistons to automatically harvest a farm plot, set up traps, open and close doors, and much much more. The limits are set only by your imagination. Redstone is also used to craft powered rail tracks and a range of other useful items, such as a compass and clock. See Chapter 9, "Redstone, Rails, and More," for more information.
- **Transportation**—Transportation is a small category but one that's a lot of fun and very useful. It includes powered and unpowered rails, minecarts, a saddle, a boat, and anything else related to moving yourself and other items around. There are enough options there to enable you to build everything from massive transportation systems to incredible roller coasters.
- **Miscellaneous**—Miscellaneous contains a range of useful and obscure items. You'll find the buckets quite handy for setting up new water and lava sources, and you can use the eggs to spawn most of the mobs, populate a farm, and more.

- **Search Items**—This category isn't for items, per se, but instead allows you to quickly locate particular items by using free-text search.
- **Foodstuffs**— This category contains the full range of edibles, including the enchanted form of the golden apple, the rarest edible in the game. Take a few of these with you the next time you think you'll be in a tight spot, and you may just be able to make it through that moaning zombie horde.
- **Tools**—Tools can be wielded as weapons, but not very effectively. They are, however, great for digging, chopping, and hoeing. You can use flint and steel to set Nether Gates on fire. You'll also find shears for stripping the wool from sheep, a fishing rod, and a few enchanted books that can add special powers to your tools.
- **Combat**—Combat provides your weapons and armor, as well as the remaining enchanted books that relate to combat items.
- **Brewing**—The Brewing tab contains all possible potions and a number of rare ingredients that don't fit into other categories. Potions are incredibly handy. Caught outside at night? The Potion of Night Vision triples the brightness to almost daylight conditions. You can learn more about brewing in Chapter 10.
- **Materials**—Materials is the final catchall category, along with the miscellaneous and decoration blocks. However, it differs because it is composed of secondary items that are derived from other actions. For example, killing a chicken can drop feathers, and you'll need those for the fletching on arrows unless you gather them from skeletons. Grow wheat to get bushels that can be used to tame horses, donkeys, and mules.
- **Survival Inventory**—Here is where you can equip your avatar with clothing and other items to take into Survival mode if you so choose. (Remember that you can do this from a Creative session by simply typing **/gamemode survival**.) Survival mode inventory also contains any items you were carrying when you switched to Creative mode. (It is empty if you started your world in Creative mode.) You can shift items between the Creative mode inventory and your Survival mode inventory. Any items you drag down to the hotbar are common across both inventories. Remove items from your Survival mode inventory by dragging them down to the square on the lower right that shows an *X*.

The Bottom Line

Congratulations! You've now learned everything you need to know to monitor your health, improve your tools for better longevity, avoid getting lost on your travels, and create your first mob-proof outdoor shelter.

These are the keys to Minecraft. Just remember to head back to your chest often to store the valuables you've gathered. Or build other chests further afield.

The next chapter is all downhill: It will take you deep into your first mine.

Mining

In This Chapter

- Learn the essentials you need for your first mining expedition.
- Find the most profitable mining layers.
- Avoid a speedy death with essential tips.
- Build an express elevator straight down to the diamond layer.
- Discover the most efficient mining techniques.

Mining is core to the Minecraft experience. Sooner or later, you'll need to take a few pickaxes in hand, supplies to satiate hunger, and a bunch of torches and a sword or two and start plumbing the depths. You will find resources down there: iron, gold, diamonds, redstone, and more. You'll find all the things you need to progress in the game. This chapter helps you find specific ores and develop efficient mining patterns that leave no stone unturned. Of course, it also gives you a few tips on how best to avoid an inadvertent respawn or at least recover with most of your hard-won resources and dignity intact.

Dig Deep, My Friend

Most of the desirable ores in Minecraft are located deep, close to the bedrock. Getting down there is a challenge in itself. There are two broad strategies:

- **Find an existing ravine, canyon, or cave complex.** These can also lead to abandoned mine-shafts. Some caves run on for hundreds of blocks, joining with the surface here and there, and occasionally running very deep. You'll usually see a range of exposed ores on their walls that make for easy pickings. The danger is that they are dark places, so in the larger caves, you will also run into a range of mobs. For now, even though this strategy will give you a bit of a head start, I suggest you hold off until you have armor, ranged weapons, and some sharp swords.

- **Create your own mine.** When you create your own mine, you can make sure it's well lit to ensure that there are no dark places for mobs to spawn, even over multiple nights, so you can go quietly about your business. For maximum convenience, you can even start a mine within your own shelter so there's no need to go outside. I focus on this strategy first. It is also likely that you will break out into cave complexes as you mine, so we'll take a look at that second.

Before you begin, ensure you have the right equipment for the job. At a minimum, you need the following:

- At least 20 torches, but bring more if you plan to go down for an extended period of time. Hold torches in your second hand to quickly swap between them and your pick-axe, or other primary tool.
- Wood blocks that can be turned into ladders, torches, tool handles, chests, and crafting tables. The only place you can find wood underground is in an abandoned mineshaft, so bring wood with you as often as you can. Fifteen or so blocks should do for now.
- At least three stone pickaxes to dig out iron ore and a shovel for digging out dirt and gravel. Bring some swords as well, just in case.
- Food. Nourishment is vital because a full hunger bar helps you heal from any damage you incur. Bring at least cooked meat, as well as bread if you've had the chance to build a wheat farm. In Chapter 6, "Crop Farming," and 7, "Farming and Taming Mobs," you'll learn how to ensure a consistent supply of food.

This will get you started. When you have found enough iron ore, you should also craft the following items:

- Two buckets (one already filled with water and one for gathering lava). You can use the water bucket to create pathways across lava pools and even to create waterfalls that you can safely descend and ascend over otherwise lethal vertical distances. The bucket of lava makes a great source of energy for the furnace. In a pinch you can also use it for fighting off mobs in cave complexes (though this isn't the best strategy because the lava can burn up any items that the mobs drop).

NOTE

Chicken or the Egg?

Actually, buckets present a "chicken and egg" situation for new miners. As you can see in the crafting recipe here, you need three iron ingots arranged in a V shape on your crafting table to create a bucket. To get those iron ingots, you first need to find iron ore and then smelt the ore into ingots by using our good ol' friendly furnace. Take heart—all this work is part of the Minecraft fun!

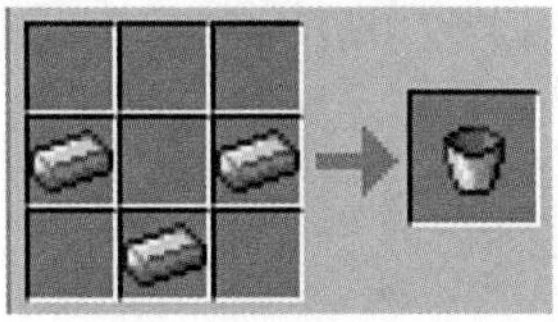

- An iron pickaxe for mining the more valuable ores, such as gold, redstone, and diamonds.

> **NOTE**
>
> **You'll Need Obsidian**
>
> You might not be lucky enough to find diamonds on your expedition, but when you do find them, you need to create a diamond pickaxe for mining obsidian—the only type of pickaxe that can do so. You need obsidian in order to build the portal to access The Nether dimension described in Chapter 12, "Playing Through: The Nether and The End."

The Mining Layer Cake Guide

Before you start digging, let's take a brief look at the ore layers in Minecraft. The Overworld has seven types of ore, as well as bedrock, and there is one more called Nether quartz that is found only in The Nether dimension. Figure 4.1 shows them all.

In addition, you'll find the following:

- Andesite (new)
- Diorite (new)
- Granite (new)
- Stone
- Gravel
- Dirt
- Obsidian
- Netherrack (Nether only)
- Glowstone (Nether only)

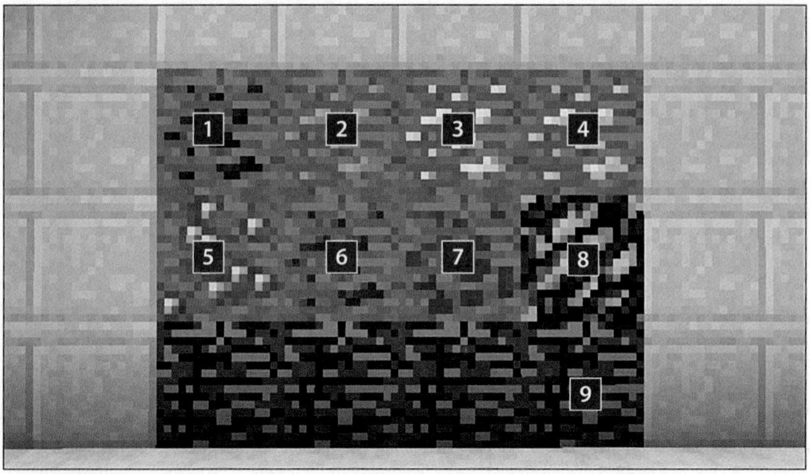

FIGURE 4.1 The most useful ores in the Minecraft world. Go get them all!

1. Coal
2. Iron
3. Gold
4. Diamond
5. Emerald
6. Redstone
7. Lapis lazuli
8. Nether quartz (Nether only)
9. Bedrock

TIP

A Word on Lapis Lazuli

Lapis lazuli is not only good for trading with villagers and making dyes, it's also a spell component for enchantments. So if you want that fancy glowing +7 sword, you'll need to get your hands on some of these gems. Remember to use a stone pickaxe or better to extract the ore.

World generation scatters various ores here and there in a statistical pattern that leads to a variety of striations. All the layers shown in Table 4.1 are counted from bedrock up. Layer 5, for example, is five layers above the lowest layer of bedrock, layer 0. (It might help if you think of layers as *altitude*.) To see your current height above layer 0, press **F3** to open the debug screen and check the value shown next to y.

TABLE 4.1 Ore Layers

Appearance	Ore	Most Common Layers	Less Common Layers	Used For	Mined With
	Coal	5–52	Up to 128	Torches and a fuel source	Any pickaxe
	Iron	5–54	Up to 64	Tools, weapons, armor, and other	Stone, iron, or diamond pickaxe
	Gold	5–59	Up to 23	Tools, weapons, armor, and other	Iron or diamond pickaxe
	Diamond	5–12	Up to 29	Tools, weapons, armor, and other	Iron or diamond pickaxe
	Emerald	5–29	Up to 29	Villager trading	Iron or diamond pickaxe
	Redstone	5–12	Up to 12	Circuits and powered items, clock, compass, and more	Iron or diamond pickaxe
	Lapis lazuli	14–16	Up to 23	Dyeing decorative items, enchanting	Stone, iron, or diamond pickaxe
	Nether quartz	The Nether	The Nether	Crafting redstone comparators and daylight sensors	Any pickaxe
	Bedrock	0–4	4	None	None

As you can see in the pattern of ore distribution in Table 4.1, there are a few layers where every ore can be found: layers 5–12. Although you can hit lava just about anywhere, including on the surface, it pools primarily in layers 1–10. This makes layer 11 a good target for mining. On your way there, you will definitely see plenty of ore, including coal and iron, and cartloads of dirt, gravel, and stone.

Getting there is a matter of luck and skill, and that can make for an exciting journey.

Lava Lakes and Other Pitfalls

Mining has its share of pitfalls, in both figurative and literal senses. Before you don your virtual miner's hat, check through the following list of dos and don'ts:

- **Don't dig straight down**—It's tempting, certainly. You could potentially dig all the way to bedrock using just one iron pickaxe. The problem with that approach is that you never know what lies beneath. You could break through the top of a cave's roof and face a fatal drop, fall into a nest of hostile mobs, or splash down in a lava lake and lose not only your life but also all your possessions.
- **Don't dig straight up**—It's easy to get lulled into a false sense of security after tunneling for a while, but you have no idea what may be on top of the block just above your head. You may tap an underground lake and flood a good portion of your mine. If you are mining higher levels, you could even tap straight into the bottom of the ocean. You could also tap into a lava flow, resulting in almost certain death. Fortunately, you should be able to spot some drips from lava or water when it is above you and separated by just a single block. A separate danger is opening up an avalanche of loose gravel or sand that can quickly suffocate you. Therefore, always mine up at least one block away from your current position so you have a chance to retreat and block off the tunnel if things go awry.

NOTE

The Golden Rule

The advice not to dig straight up or straight down constitutes what is known as the "golden rule" of Minecraft. Bear it in mind as you proceed on your adventures.

- **Keep some blocks in your hotbar**—Always have cobblestone or dirt at the ready to block off your tunnel in case you break through into a danger zone. Water probably won't kill you, but it can wash you back quite quickly and put out your torches. Lava oozes along much more slowly but is far more deadly. Be ready to block off any unexpected breakthroughs.
- **Be careful, be prepared, and always know your way out**—It's easy to get lost down there, especially if you break into a cave complex and decide to explore. Use torches, signs, cobblestone arranged into arrows, and blocks attached to a wall with a torch

facing the way out; they can all act like a trail of bread crumbs to help you find your way home. Read the sidebar "Signs, Signs, Everywhere" to learn how to make a sign.

- **Keep your mines well lit**—Any area you leave open and dark can be a place for mobs to spawn, and they will eventually come for you.
- **Block off any unlit areas**—These can include caves and fully explored tunnel branches. You can even knock your torches off the wall and collect them on your way out, as long as you remember to block off the entire branch when you get back to the main trunk so the mobs don't break through. If you do break into a cave, place a torch on the wall inside the cave and block it off, leaving no more than a one-block gap. (Okay, explore if you must but remember that you're on a mission.) You'll be able to see the torch or at least the light from the torch on the other side as an indication that you can come back and explore it later. Then head in a different direction.

TIP

Signs, Signs, Everywhere

To craft a sign, simply arrange six wood planks of any type above a stick, as shown in the associated crafting recipe. Then, once you right-click to place it, you'll have the opportunity to add text to the sign, as shown in Figure 4.2. Making and placing signs is an excellent antidote to getting lost in the Minecraft world, especially when you're mining deep underground.

FIGURE 4.2 Signs can help you navigate under and above ground. By the way, see that giant mushroom in the background? When you find one, try turning it into a treehouse.

Mining can be broken down into two parts: getting down and then cutting across to uncover as much valuable ore as possible. There are a few ways to do both.

Descending to Layer 11

The process of descending is also a process of discovery, and no two journeys will be the same. In all cases, follow any ore seams you find on the way down and then return to the plan. Check in with your layer level now and then by pressing **F3** and checking the y coordinate or just dig all the way to the lowest layer of bedrock you can find and then count 12 layers as you go back up.

The 2×1 Ladder Descent

The fastest way to descend is in a 2×1 pattern, placing ladders or vines as you go against one of the walls so you can climb your way out. Vines are plentiful in the jungle and in swamp biomes, but not elsewhere, and you will need shears to collect them. Ladders are crafted from sticks in an H layout across the crafting grid, with each set of seven sticks making three ladder blocks. Their advantage over jumping up and down stairs, besides being a fast method of vertical movement, is that they don't use up any energy, so you won't see any drop in your hunger bar as you traverse.

TIP

Use the Shift Key to Pause on Ladders

Hold down the **Left Shift** key to pause whenever you are ascending or descending a ladder. While paused, you can place torches and do anything else required, including placing additional ladder segments.

Dig out the block directly in front of you, as well as the one underneath. If all looks good, turn around and dig out the block you were standing on and the one underneath that, and you'll be down to a level pit. Place two ladder segments on the wall in front of you and repeat. Attach torches to the other wall every nine layers or so. You can also place blocks between the torches to break your fall. It shouldn't really be necessary because it's difficult to fall off a ladder, but staring down a 50-layer drop may induce feelings of virtual vertigo.

Figure 4.3 shows the view looking up to the sky from the bottom of a 53-layer pit.

FIGURE 4.3 Sunlight seems such a long way away when you're on layer 11, but ladders make for very fast ascents, and it takes only about 20 seconds to reach The Overworld.

TIP

Defying the Laws of Physics

Falling down the side of a shaft without a ladder is deadly, but like an acrobat at the circus diving off the high board into a saucepan of water, you can easily break your fall. Just dig out two blocks in the nonladder side of the shaft, pour a bucket of water against the side of the upper block, and survive shorter falls of around 50 blocks every time, as shown in Figure 4.4. You can also use this trick to make the world's fastest one-way express elevator to get down in a hurry. If you take fall damage, try increasing the water's depth. After a 250-layer fall you can splash down with zero damage in water just three blocks high.

FIGURE 4.4 Break an otherwise breakneck fall down a long vertical shaft with a block or three of thud-absorbing water.

The Straight Staircase

The staircase is one of the most natural designs, and it helps you move along quickly. To build a staircase, you'll need to break three blocks for each one down, so it's not quite as efficient as the ladder descent, but it's the simplest option available if you are short on wood for ladders and lacking in vines.

Start by digging down one block in front of you. Hop in the hole and then follow this pattern:

1 Dig out the block at eye level in front of you and the two underneath that.
2 Move into the hole in front of you.
3 Repeat.

As you go, don't forget to place torches every nine or so steps. If you hit any problems, either take a 90-degree turn to the left or right and continue or make a bit of space for a landing and do a 180-degree turn.

You can see a typical straight staircase in Figure 4.5.

FIGURE 4.5 A straight staircase is easy to descend and fast to ascend. You can improve it by crafting cobblestone stairs so that no jumping is required on the return journey.

The Spiral Staircase

A spiral staircase takes a little more care to build than a straight one, and you might get a bit dizzy going up and down with all the frequent turns, but it has a couple of advantages:

- A spiral staircase descends vertically, which makes for more methodical exploration. It's also easy to build if you don't have the wood needed for a vertical access shaft.
- A spiral staircase winds down around itself or a central core, exposing more surface area and therefore providing greater opportunity to discover seams of ore on the way down.

There are several different versions. The tightest staircase possible is the 2×2. You can build one by following the same steps as for a straight staircase. However, each time you drop down one level, just turn to the right or left 90 degrees and start again. Keep turning in the same direction to ensure that you drop down vertically.

A 3×3 version of the same staircase involves going down two steps straight, turning, going down another two steps straight, and so on. This leaves a single-column central core that you can remove to create an open light well, which gives you more illumination from each torch you place. It's also a bit easier to keep your bearings if you remove the central core as you go. Figure 4.6 shows the result.

FIGURE 4.6 A 3×3 spiral staircase provides a handy light well down the middle single-block core.

A 5×5 version is similar, but you go down four steps and then turn. This leaves a solid block of 3×3 in the middle. You can then dig out the central block in the pillar and place a ladder against the side when you're ready for faster ascents and descents. Open up blocks from the staircase into the core (except on the side reserved for a ladder) to bring light from the torches into the core. This style of staircase also exposes the maximum surface area, essentially mining out a block of 5×5 units all the way down. It is, however, a complicated method requiring that you keep careful count of the steps you dig on each side.

Layouts for Fast, Efficient Mining

There are numerous methods for mining, and some may lead to madness. You can wander around hacking at every rock in site, but you're going to miss a lot of ore deposits, and it's pretty easy to get lost in a maze of your own making. You can also go for grandeur, hollowing out halls as you go, dwarfing the Mines of Moria. Fortunately, Minecraft doesn't yet have a Balrog, although the Ender Dragon comes close.

A gigantic, modern underground lair with powered rails allowing you to zip back and forth in minecarts also has its charm (see Chapter 9, "Redstone, Rails, and More"). There's nothing wrong with that, and it does make for a fantastic creative challenge, but for your first serious dig, with what is probably still a quite limited set of tools, your aim should be to collect as much ore as possible with the least amount of effort and using the smallest number of pickaxes possible. That mine is called a *branch mine*.

Branch mines generally cover a rectangular surface area. You can choose any size you like, but you may also be limited by the terrain. Breakouts at layer 11 are quite common, and if you end up at a lava pool such as the one shown in Figure 4.7, you have little option but to treat it as the end of the trunk, or that particular branch. The good part is that lava pools provide a lot of light.

FIGURE 4.7 Lava lakes usually act as a natural barrier to further mining, at least in the beginning. Later you can use buckets of water to turn the lava into an obsidian bridge, but in the meanwhile just work around them.

So, what's the most efficient layout? The one I prefer is quite simple, easy to navigate, and effective. It relies on the fact that blocks of ore—yes, even diamonds—almost always appear in veins larger than a single block.

A branch mine uses a horizontal central trunk that's two blocks high by one block wide. Branches are then dug out perpendicular to the trunk, much like the branches of a tree—at least a strangely geometrical one.

Because each block of ore can be identified from any of its six sides, a distance of two blocks per branch exposes at least one side of every block to the side and also above and below you. In other words, move one space along a branch, and you expose a total of six blocks: two on each side, one below, one above, and the two in front of you.

Branch mining is the most thorough mining method available because it exposes every single block within the area the mine covers. But it's not the most efficient because ore veins usually spread across clumps of 2 to 16 blocks. Think of the goal, therefore, as being to uncover veins of ore, not individual blocks. If you find one block in a vein, you expose the next, and you can then follow the vein to its end.

Spacing each branch every fourth block, with three blocks in between, works best. Figure 4.8 shows a top-down view.

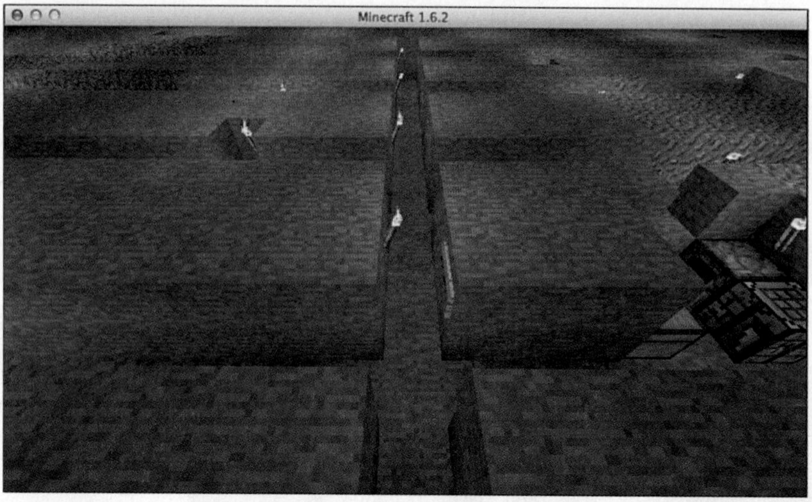

FIGURE 4.8 Space your branches every three steps, off a primary central trunk, and place a base camp for convenient crafting and storage.

NOTE

Spacing Your Branches

If your mining target is the more common ores such as coal and iron that occur in larger veins, you could even space your branches with four or five blocks in between. You might miss some smaller deposits but will intersect all the larger veins. This is an efficient technique that's useful in the higher levels.

When you've completed mining layer 11, head back up using the same spacing principal vertically that you did horizontally, leaving a gap of three blocks, or layers, between the roof of your first trunk and the floor of the next. As you work higher, you lose most of the chances for diamonds, but other ores are plentiful. And you can head down to bedrock the same way, taking extra care because there's a lot more lava about.

Staying Safe While You Mine

Your first mining expedition will undoubtedly turn up a lot of valuable ore. Don't risk losing it all if you die. Chances are you won't be able to make it back down from your last spawn point to pick up your valuables. Here are some tips that will help:

- Use the **Left Shift** key so that you can sneak around the edges of lava lakes and other hazards without risk of falling in.

- Build a small base to act as a staging point. It's easy enough to create a new crafting table and furnace, but if you've also been able to construct a bed and don't have wool for another, consider bringing your bed down with you from your Overland dwelling. You can break it up with any tool and pick up the floating icon so that it slots into your inventory. Set up your base somewhere central to your mine and sleep in the bed at least once to set a new spawn point. Figure 4.9 shows a minimal layout where everything fits into a six-block space.

NOTE

The Mobs Might Not Let You Sleep

You might need to try several base locations before you can successfully sleep in a bed. Any mobs nearby, even if blocked by walls, will prevent you from sleeping. Rather than search for and clear out caves, just pack everything up and find a new site somewhere else in your mine.

- Chests are easy to build, so place them in your base and anywhere you can access them with convenience in your tunnel system. Regularly return to a chest to drop off any valuable items you've found so that you can pick them up again if you respawn.

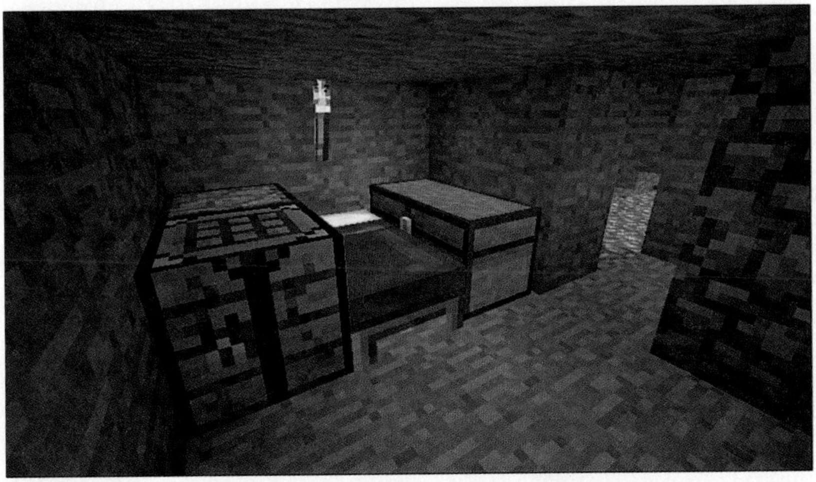

FIGURE 4.9 A mining base makes it easier to recover after a respawn. See the redstone in the upper-left corner? There's plenty down here, so I left it as decoration.

The Bottom Line

Mining is the only way to gather many key resources, including the diamonds required to mine obsidian and get to The Nether dimension. Don't make the mistake of mining too high, or you'll miss most of the good stuff. Once you hit layer 11, you'll be amazed at just how quickly you amass a huge range of useful resources. Mine your way in layers back up rather than starting at the top and working down, and you'll have a plentiful supply of iron for tools, coal for torches, and masses of cobblestone to expand your dwelling on the surface.

Minecraft places resources in 16×16 blocks that run all the way from bedrock to the sky. (These are known as *chunks*.) There are an average of just over 3 diamond blocks per chunk, and of course you'll find many times that of the more common ores. So if you don't find what you need, just dig across at least 16 blocks and try again. There's a wealth of material down there, and it won't be long before you can build an incredible powered rail system that can zoom you up and down from the surface as fast as a freight train, as well as carry resources for you.

You may have noticed something as you've toiled away at mining: Those caves you've no doubt uncovered look mighty tempting, with so much exposed ore just waiting to be collected. The next chapter helps you get battle-ready so that you can head back down, take on the mobs, and take home the spoils.

Combat School

In This Chapter

- Mobs: how to seize the day and enjoy your slay.
- Defend your territory with snow and iron golems.
- Wield a sword like a swashbuckler and deal extra damage with critical hits.
- Cover your flank with a shield.
- Happiness is a loaded quiver. Knock on the right doors and give hostile mobs the shaft.
- Grow a thicker skin by crafting armor and coloring it like your favorite sports team or superhero.

It's perfectly possible to live a peaceful existence in Minecraft. You can build a nice, safe mine; avoid cave exploration of any kind; create a self-sufficient farm that produces everything you need; protect your domain with mob-proof fences, keep it all well lit to prevent spawning inside; and retire at the end of each day with slippers on your soft, uncalloused feet in front of a warm fire, sipping a bowl of mushroom stew.

Ah, the serenity....But there's one problem: You'll miss out on most of the fun! Eventually, combat becomes a necessity. You don't have to incite a full-scale war, but having the right equipment, some key tactics, and a few fighting skills will let you progress much faster and further in the game than you will if you take a purely passive path.

I've introduced a few of the hostile mobs previously, but now it's time to get into the specifics of tactics, weapons, armor, and defense. It's a tough world out there, and most of it is trying to kill you. Learn the names and ways of all the things that go bump in the night, how to bump back, and a few other things that can do the bumping for you.

Introducing the Menagerie

Minecraft mobs might be a pain in the derriere at times, but you'll never get to Valhalla without 'em. Let's take a closer look at each of them and the unique tactics you can use to defeat them.

Remember that, in most cases, hostile mobs switch to pursuit mode if they are within 16 blocks and have a line of sight to your location. As soon as they switch, they'll track you even if you move out of direct sight. You can use this to your advantage, leading mobs to locations that are better suited for counterattack or escape, or even maneuvering them into a positions where they can be pushed off a cliff or into a lava pool. (But do ensure that you keep your own footing while doing so.)

Each hostile has specific strengths and weaknesses. Although any tool can do damage, you'll do best if you stick with a sword for short-range attacks and a bow for longer range. Mobs are also vulnerable to fire, so lighting the ground with a flint and steel can either weaken them enough that a final blow finishes them off or actually destroy them altogether.

This chapter introduces you to the mobs you are most likely to encounter in The Overworld. See Chapter 13, "Mods and Multiplayer," for complete details on the mobs that inhabit The Nether and The End dimensions.

Zombies

The first mob you encounter in Minecraft will probably be the humble zombie (see Figure 5.1). The sound of one of them trying to beat down your door can set hairs on end, but their bark in single numbers is worse than their bite. Zombies are slow, and while a poorly handled encounter can definitely kill you, if you're the aggressor, you'll stay on top.

FIGURE 5.1 Zombies are slow but have a habit of spawning in large numbers.

You can deal with zombies in a few different ways. If you encounter them close to a cave entrance and it's sunny outside, just lead them out as soon as they enter pursuit mode and watch them burn up in the light. Keep your distance, though, because they can still attack and cause you fire damage. Zombies can happily exist in daylight when it's shaded, overcast, or raining, or when they're wearing helmets. For a more direct assault, keep your crosshairs on them and hit first and hit often, clicking your left mouse button continuously. They'll only sometimes land a hit in return and will probably manage just one feeble attempt before they're overcome.

If you encounter more than one zombie at once, along with other mobs sprinkled in for good measure, hack through the zombies first and make your escape or retreat.

Now, there is just one problem: Zombies can call up their undead buddies as reinforcements, and they can also cause additional zombies to spawn upon their death. The resulting zombie apocalypse can make it tricky if you're caught outside at night.

TIP

Watch Your Back

Consider placing a wooden door at the entrance to a cave that connects back to your tunnel system. This will keep your base safe while you're exploring. The door also protects your retreat route in case you need to make a hasty exit, and you can always knock it down for retrieval and permanently block off the cave after the mobs have wandered off.

Zombies drop rotten meat when they're defeated. The meat is poisonous, but you can still eat it to build up your hunger bar. The best strategy here is to save up a few pieces and eat them all at once because you will still get only one hit of food poisoning. This is a great way to replenish your hunger bar from almost empty to full; your health will take a minimal hit from the poisoning and then start to replenish from the full hunger bar. Also, consider carrying a bucket of milk with you because drinking it instantly cures all types of food poisoning. You can also feed rotten meat to tamed wolves, as discussed later in the section "The Dogs of War," to keep up their health.

CAUTION

The Dead Stick Together

Zombies are the most "mobbish" of Minecraft's mobs. If you attack one, others nearby—even outside of the usual hostile range—might come swarming to help out their undead brethren.

Zombies sometimes (though rarely) drop items such as tools and armor.

Spiders

Minecraft has two types of spiders and a skeleton/spider hybrid.

You'll most often encounter the large spiders, shown in Figure 5.2. (See the sections "Cave Spiders" and "Spider Jockeys," later in this chapter, for more information on the others.) The large spiders are jumpy, literally. They can leap two to three blocks in a single bound and can climb walls unless there is an overhang or a layer of a block type they can't climb, such as glass. They're fast, aggressive at night and in dark places, and a little bit tougher to defeat than your average zombie.

FIGURE 5.2 Spiders are fast and able to climb walls, but they're easy to defeat even with a wooden sword.

NOTE

Building Spider-Proof Walls

Spiders can crawl up almost any wall unless it contains transparent blocks. Building these walls isn't always practical, though. An overhang provides an alternative defense. Position a single block on the outside of the third level of any wall such that the block forms an upside-down ledge. Spiders can't get through single-block gaps, so these overhangs only have to be positioned every second space, somewhat like the battlements on a castle keep's walls. See Chapter 8, "Creative Construction," for examples of this and other defensive construction techniques.

Spiders are, however, also very useful. Spiders drop string, a vital ingredient for crafting a bow. Every four pieces of string can also make one block (or bale) of wool. Gather three of those, and it's enough for a bed, which can then be used to reset your spawn point. That's *very* handy if there are no sheep nearby.

Sometimes a spider also drops one of its eyes. Treat spider eyes as a sort of extreme food if you can handle the concept, but keep in mind that they're poisonous along the same lines as rotten meat. Spider eyes are also a useful ingredient in some potions.

Spiders are just one block high and two blocks wide, so a 1×1 opening in a wall will keep you safe.

Their jumping ability gives them a slight edge in combat. The best strategy is similar to that with defeating zombies: Click fast and often to hit them as rapidly as possible. Also, walk backward at the same time, as long as you know what's behind you. This can help keep you out of range of their jump attack.

CAUTION

I Always Feel Like Somebody's Watching Me

Ever had the feeling someone's watching you? In Minecraft, that someone is probably a spider, watching you with all eight eyes, bright points of red in the dark. Spiders don't require a line of sight to enter pursuit mode, so they'll be on your trail as soon as you get within 16 blocks, and they'll do almost anything to get closer. Lock yourself in your shelter for the night to stay safe. But take care in the morning: If you hear the spider's hissing/slurping noise, it might be still waiting for you, hatred in every eye. Spiders have a habit of lurking in ambush on your roof, waiting for you to "tra la la" out the door the next morning without a care in the world, until their fangs sink into your back. Fortunately, the large spiders aren't poisonous, so just make sure you have your sword in hand, ready to fight back, and you'll be fine.

Skeletons

The sound of skeletons' rattling bones usually gives these mobs away a few moments before their arrow pierces your breastbone. They're sharpshooters, so the best approach is to stay out of the direct line of fire, ducking out to attack only when they're close enough. Do it commando-style, moving sideways to avoid the feathered missiles that will undoubtedly be coming your way. It's not an arrow-proof strategy, but it can help. Figure 5.3 shows a skeleton with its ubiquitous bow.

FIGURE 5.3 Skeletons are sharpshooters, so keep your distance until you can strike, and don't let them sneak up behind you.

If you can get close enough, you can use a sword to finish off a skeleton, or group of skeletons quite quickly. For this reason, a good strategy is to try to wait somewhere protected and let the skeletons get within reach. Skeletons also burn up in sunlight unless they are protected by armor or are wearing a pumpkin head, so luring them out into the sun won't always provide deliverance.

Skeletons usually drop arrows, and collecting them is an easy way to resupply your stock if you are also using a bow. You'll also often find arrows that have missed their mark sticking out of blocks, but you can't collect those, and breaking the block may cause you damage from the falling arrow.

Also, keep in mind that skeletons will try to circle around you and approach you from behind.

Cave Spiders

Cave spiders are invidious arachnids that you find in abandoned mineshafts. They're fast, small, and poisonous, and they make large spiders look positively passive.

FIGURE 5.4 Inhabiting only abandoned mineshafts, cave spiders aren't common, but they are definitely among the most deadly mobs.

Cavers, as they're often called, can slip through a gap one block wide and less than half a block high, so a 1×1 block hole in the wall offers no protection at all. You can easily spot them because of their blue coloring (see Figure 5.4).

Cave spiders don't spawn naturally. They're spewed out of a spawning device, a small fiery cage that shows a miniature version of themselves spinning around faster and faster until it seems they're flung out the side through centrifugal force. It's a bit like a washing machine's spin cycle gone mad. You'll also find other spawners busy dispensing other types of mobs such as zombies and skeletons. Slow them down or stop them completely using the tactics provided below.

If you are lucky enough to find an abandoned mineshaft, consider it a huge bonus. These massive structures sometimes come prestocked with well over a dozen chests with all kinds of goodies inside. Cave spiders and other mobs that may inhabit it can be a bit of a challenge, but go ahead and claim that mineshaft for your own. It's now *your* mineshaft. Just take care as you go and ensure you are well prepared for a challenging exploration.

Here's what you need to know:

- A bite from a cave spider won't kill you. Like all other poisonings, it can take you down to half a heart on Normal difficulty. It's the damage from the bite itself, not the poison, that can do you in.
- Cavers are easy to kill but are smaller than other mobs, so you need to aim your crosshairs with a bit more care and click frenetically.
- Fighting while walking backward works as well with cavers as with the large spiders, but cavers are faster so will be able to launch more attacks.
- A cave spider habitat is filled with spider webs. These will slow you down, but cavers can slip through those webs at normal speed.
- As you get close, place some torches down as close to the spawner as you can, or even on the spawner itself. This will prevent it spawning new mobs. You can then break it with a pickaxe, or more slowly with other tools. But keep your guard up, because there is often more than one spawner in close proximity.
- There's good news related to cavers: Abandoned mineshafts, where cavers live, are a treasure trove of resources waiting to be plundered. You'll find loads of chests, and the mine's structural reinforcements provide the only source of wood available underground.

Spider Jockeys

Sit a skeleton on top of a spider, and you get a spider jockey. A spider jockey jumps like a spider, shoots arrows like a skeleton, and is best given a wide berth. Fortunately, they're rare. If you see one, smash the skeleton if you can and deal with the spider next. You may not survive, but isn't that why you keep your valuables in a chest next to your spawn point?

Chicken Jockeys

What do you get if you sit a baby zombie on top of a chicken? A chicken jockey. They're fast and able to leap off tall buildings, cliffs, and so on without taking any fall damage. Fortunately, they are a very rare spawn.

Creepers

FIGURE 5.5 Creepers appear to be fairly docile until they get close and provide a taste of their truly explosive personality.

If Minecraft has an anti-hero, it's the creeper (see Figure 5.5). Think of creepers as walking improvised explosive devices (IEDs).

Don't panic too much when you first spy a creeper. You can survive a creeper attack unless you are caught totally by surprise, and a little armor can go a long way.

If you should turn a corner and there's a creeper right in front of you, do your best to sprint away. Your attack on a creeper needs to be well timed, and you need space to sprint in, thwack it, and move back out again so that its fuse resets. The force of your blow should usually be enough to knock the creeper far enough that this happens with reasonable surety. A sword with a knockback enchantment (see "Sprucing Up Your Weapons" on page 233) also helps a lot against creepers but actually makes things worse when you're fighting skeletons.

Unfortunately, if you see a creeper swelling like a balloon (something it does just prior to exploding), it's probably already too late.

Try to ensure that you don't become tangled in a fight with a creeper near an important structure. Just about the worst situation is stepping out your front door, straight into one. You'll end up with a crater where the front of your house used to stand. As one of the memes on the web reads, "I just undid in two seconds what you spent five hours building." You are generally safe if you can keep a distance of at least two blocks, but creepers move quite quickly.

Creepers do have an Achilles heel. If you lure one to water, you can easily deal with it by attacking from below. Creepers are also scared of ocelots and their tamed version, humble cats (see Chapter 7, "Farming and Taming Mobs").

As with most other mobs in Minecraft, creepers may seem somewhat formidable at first, but with a little practice, you'll find that you can dispatch them fairly easily.

Creepers drop gunpowder, a key ingredient in crafting TNT blocks and making throwable "splash" potions, described in Chapter 10, "Enchanting, Anvils, and Brewing."

Slimes

FIGURE 5.6 Slimes split into smaller slimes.

Slimes aren't too common because they generally spawn in swamps and (far less regularly) in other underground areas. But slimes can ooze up far from a swamp biome and spawn in any light level.

If any mob needs frenetic clicking, it's a slime. That's because each large one splits into up to 4 smaller ones and up to 16 tiny ones (see Figure 5.6). The tiny ones don't do damage but can be annoying as they swarm you. Just click and click and click until you've finished them all, and switch to your fists to finish off the tiny ones. All it takes to kill a tiny slime is one blow, and this will save durability on your sword.

Slimes drop slimeballs, a substance that makes ordinary pistons stickier than duct tape. You can also craft slimeballs into slimeblocks, the only blocks in Minecraft that can stick to other blocks—moving as they move or making them move when the slimeblock moves. Slimeblocks also act like trampolines: Try jumping on one from a great height, and you'll bounce back up part of the way without suffering any fall damage. In addition, you can use slimeballs to craft magma cream, which allows you to swim across lava lakes with impunity; this is very handy to use in The Nether. You can also use slimeballs for crafting leads, which makes passive mob management much, much easier. Slimeballs and slimeblocks are, in short, incredibly useful.

Endermen

The Enderman is a curious, otherworldy creature surrounded by a purple haze (see Figure 5.7). The Endermen call The End dimension home, and you'll see them there in enormous numbers, but they also appear in The Overworld quite often, so I've also included them here.

Endermen tend to teleport when attacked and have a habit of popping up behind you, which can make defeating them tricky. Your best bet, actually, is to ignore them. They're not hostile unless you put your eyes (crosshairs) on them, so popping a pumpkin on your head, while not offering any protection or winning you any beauty contests, essentially hides your eyes so that Endermen don't turn hostile.

FIGURE 5.7 Always look behind you when the Enderman you're attacking teleports away.

Endermen drop Ender Pearls, an essential crafting component for Eyes of Ender. These unusual items help find the strongholds that house the Ender Portals needed to access The End dimension. Although priest villagers also trade Eyes of Ender (see Chapter 11, "Villages and Other Structures"), attacking and defeating Endermen to gain the Ender Pearls and then using those to craft the Eyes of Ender is the quickest way to find strongholds. Attack an Enderman's legs to prevent it from teleporting away.

Incidentally, if you throw an Ender Pearl with a right-click, you'll teleport to its point of impact. You can use this tactic to escape hostile mobs or travel through difficult terrain. The only danger is that you will take a damage hit of up to five health points each jump, so use with care.

Zombie Pigmen

Like Endermen, these inhabitants of The Nether dimension are neutral unless attacked. As with wolves and zombies, attacking a Zombie Pigman causes them all to want to join in. If you get Zombie Pigmen riled up, you may find it best to try to make your escape. They'll calm down eventually. Figure 5.8 shows their interesting visage—a mug shot if ever there was one.

FIGURE 5.8 With a pack mentality, Zombie Pigmen are best left to their own devices.

Killer Rabbit of Caerbannog

The Killer Rabbit of Caerbannog is perhaps the most unusual mob in Minecraft. Every time a cute little passive rabbit spawns, there is a 1 in 1,000 chance it will turn into the Killer Rabbit of Caerbannog, a vicious although not particularly powerful hostile mob. (You'll recognize its name if you've seen *Monty Python and the Holy Grail*.) The rabbit does, however, have a fast attack, so either keep your distance and use a ranged weapon or attack with at least an iron sword so you can swiftly deliver 10 points of damage to kill it off. Or, if you are feeling Monty, run away, run away!

Guardians and Elder Guardians

These hostile mobs spawn in or around the huge ocean monument structures that appear in deep ocean biomes. The guardians shown in Figure 5.9 attack squids and players with an electrified beam and can be extremely difficult to defeat without enchantments such as Night Vision (to make it easier to see underwater), Depth Strider (to speed up movement underwater), and Respiration (to allow underwater breathing).

FIGURE 5.9 A guardian inside an ocean monument.

You'll also stand little chance of survival if you enter without a full suit of diamond armor and a diamond sword to inflict significant damage with every blow.

Elder Guardians are a stronger and larger version of guardians. Each monument contains three that will inflict you with mining fatigue, preventing the breaking of blocks. You'll need to defeat them before you can start to break up the temple and retrieve the eight gold blocks hidden inside each.

Attacking with a bow and arrow at close range and then ducking behind a block to hide can be an effective method for defeating both mobs, but swords can also work just as well if you have a high-level strider enchantment. You'll have several seconds to get out of the line of sight after first being targeted by each mob's beam before it actually fires and does damage.

Finally, attack guardians and Elder Guardians only when they don't have their spikes extended to avoid taking damage.

While ocean monuments don't provide too much loot at present, this may change in the future. You can read more about them in Chapter 11.

Defensive Mobs

Balancing out the host of hostile mobs are a couple of defensive ones that are unique because they are created by players, although not at a crafting table. To create a defensive mob, you need to stack their blocks where you'd like them to spawn, always ensuring that you leave the pumpkin block to last.

Snow Golems

Snow golems aren't the strongest line of defense because they don't cause damage to any of The Overworld mobs, but their furious rate of snowball throwing can be enough to keep zombies and other hostile mobs at a distance, making them useful around your home. Create your own snow golem with these simple steps:

FIGURE 5.10 Snow golems aren't particularly powerful, but who doesn't want a snowball-hurling automaton in their front yard all year 'round?

1 Gather at least eight snowballs by left-clicking any snow lying on the ground with a shovel.

2 Craft two snow blocks, using four snowballs for each.

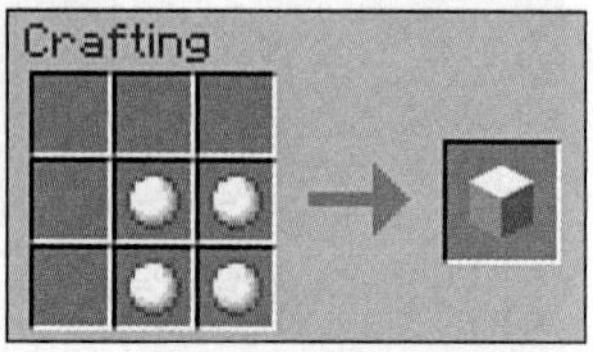

3 Create a stack of the snow blocks by placing one on top of the other.

4 Place a pumpkin or jack-o-lantern on top of the stacked snow blocks, as shown in Figure 5.10, to bring the snow golem to life.

Unfortunately, snow golems have a tendency to wander, so place them behind a fence or walled area for best results. But ensure that there's a roof over their head because like little Olaf in Disney's *Frozen*, they don't survive in rain or a desert.

Iron Golems

Iron golems exist to protect villages and their inhabitants. They're incredibly powerful, and you really shouldn't attack them. You also shouldn't attack any villagers because the iron golems will rush to their defense.

Iron golems spawn naturally in villages of sufficient size (approximately 21 houses), but you can also build one much the way you build a snow golem:

1 Build up a collection of 36 iron ingots. (These golems are incredibly expensive.)

2 Create four blocks of iron using nine ingots each.

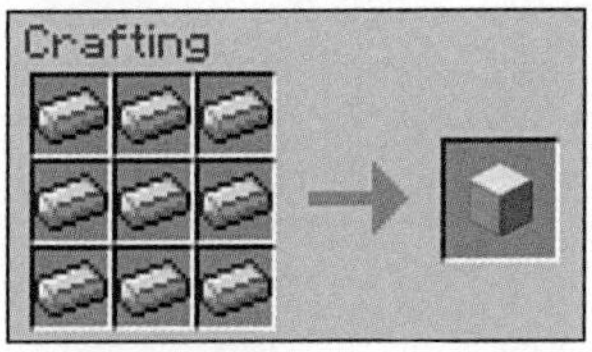

FIGURE 5.11 Iron golems aren't directly on your side, but if you set up your house inside a village, you'll be within their circle of protection.

3 Place one block of iron on top of the other and then attach two more blocks to opposite sides of the upper block in the stack. You are, effectively, creating a stack of iron blocks in the shape of a T.

4 Place a pumpkin on top of the middle upper block where the head would go.

Besides smashing the heck out of spiders, zombies, and most other hostile mobs, iron golems have the endearing habit of giving red poppies to village children (see Figure 5.11). Unfortunately, they don't really care too much about *your* well-being, so unless your strategy is to help protect villages, iron golems are not really worth building, especially given the enormous amount of iron required.

The Dogs of War

Would you like a loving pet that follows you around everywhere and mercilessly kills your enemies? You need a canine companion. Dogs are essentially tame wolves. You tame a wolf by offering it a bone. Offer it enough bones, and its eyes will change from small and fierce to big and loving, and a collar appears. (Note that you can dye the collars if you want to tell your dogs apart. You can even give them tags and name them.)

Once a wolf transforms into a dog, it acts like a dog. It will stay by your side, staring lovingly at you with its head cocked to one side whenever you have meat of any kind in your hand, and it will attack anything you strike or that strikes you. They are not, however, invulnerable. If one gets hurt, it makes a yelping noise and briefly flashes red. Give a dog a steak to help it heal. Its tail (and its hit points) will rise until the dog is happy again. When dogs get really happy, they run off in pairs, kiss, and make a puppy.

You can tame any number of wolves and raise as many puppies as you like. I once had more than 30 dogs following me around. I pity the poor hostile mobs that dared attack me back then. They never seemed to see it coming—and neither did I. I once saw my pack of dogs take down an Enderman in 2 seconds flat, before the meanie had the chance to think, "Ow! Ow! Better teleport out of h...argh!".

Dogs can help you save wear and tear on your weapons, too. Just thwack a hostile mob once, and the dogs will do the rest.

TIP

Give 'em a Bone

Dogs *love* skeletons (they are made of bones, after all) and will chase them without prompting from you. Skeletons do *run* away from dogs as fast as their rickety bones can carry them, but the dogs are faster and will eventually catch up.

Mob Target Practice

Provided that your game isn't set on Peaceful and you aren't playing in Creative mode, you'll eventually run across hostile mobs in the wild. However, if you're dying (pun intended) to practice combat sooner rather than later, then I have a recipe you might want to try.

Start by pressing **F3** and making a note of your avatar's current x y z position value. Next, press **F3** again to make the debug screen. Step a few paces outside that area.

As it happens, you can manually spawn mobs by using the **/summon** command. The basic syntax for the **/summon** command is as follows:

/summon ***mobname*** X Y Z

You can get fancier than this, though, going so far as to specify one or more datatags that describe additional parameters concerning the mob. If you want more information on **/summon** command syntax, consult the official Minecraft wiki: http://minecraft.gamepedia.com/Summon.

What's curious about the **/summon** command is that you can use it to invoke into your environment, in broad daylight, mobs that normally come out only at night. To prove this, use the **/time set day** command (if you're in night) to start a new day and then try invoking, say, a skeleton.

When you issue the **/summon** command, be sure to specify the location where you want the mob to appear, using the X Y Z syntax.

You can see the beginnings of one of my own practice combat sessions in Figure 5.12.

In Creative mode, you can also fetch spawn eggs for the mobs from the creative inventory and place them with a right-click to summon the mob. Position yourself where you'd like and then type **/gamemode survival** to switch back to a normal combat scenario.

FIGURE 5.12 By manually summoning hostile mobs, you can build combat experience and prepare yourself for "real-life" encounters. In case you were wondering: Yes, that skeleton just launched an arrow at my heart.

Weapons, Armor, and Shields

Out in the wild? Getting struck by skeletons? Zombies spawning everywhere? You can stand and fight, or you can decide to run. Either way, a decent set of weapons, a suit of armor, and a shield will help you survive to fight another day.

Minecraft has two primary offensive weapons: the sword and the bow. In a pinch, other tools will also do. None is as powerful as the sword, but if you run out of swords in combat, switch, in order of effectiveness, to an axe and then a pickaxe. If all else is lost, remember that you can also beat something over the head with a shovel.

TIP

Delivering the Winning Blow

Deliver a *critical hit* to cause up to 50% more damage. This works with every material and tool except the hoe. The trick is to make the hit as you are falling, and the easiest way to do that is to jump first, timing it right so that you have passed the apex of your leap by the time you strike. I'm not sure if it helps to yell "Hiiiiyaaa!!!" as you do so, but feel free to give it a try. You'll know you've succeeded when you see a little bloom of stars around the unfortunate recipient of your attack immediately after the hit.

Critical hits can be crucial for survival. You can use them to kill some mobs with a single blow, saving your sword's durability. Put in a bit of practice when you can, and the timing of the hit and the optional battle cry will become second nature.

The same techniques that work in many other combat games also work in Minecraft. Keep on the move; don't just stand like a statue and flail. Float like a butterfly and sting like a bee. Use the left- and right-arrow keys to circle around the enemy and dodge direct blows, ranged attacks such as from skeletons, and melee attacks, which essentially are full-body broadsides by slimes and the like. Always use height to your advantage when you're out in the open. It will help both with avoiding attacks and delivering critical hits.

It's worth noting that even though you can dual-wield weapons starting from v1.9, you can only attack with the item held in your main hand. (You can set the main hand to be your left or right hand in Minecraft's settings.) Use the **F** key to quickly swap items between hands.

However, you can use a bow held in your other hand, and you can carry torches or a splash potion. This makes it much easier to explore dark areas, carry out ranged attacks, and so forth. Replace that with a shield to attack and defend at the same time.

Dual-wielding really changes the nature of combat and combat tactics.

Swordcraft

The sword will no doubt become your go-to weapon. In a pinch, it's easy to quickly craft a sword from a few raw materials, and its damage and durability increase quickly as you upgrade from stone to iron to diamond and, later, add some enchantments on top. Table 5.1 lists the materials, damage inflicted, and durability of each sword material.

TABLE 5.1 Sword Materials

	Bare Fists	Wood	Gold	Stone	Iron	Diamond
Durability	Infinite	60	33	132	251	1,562
Damage points	1	4	4	5	6	7
Maximum critical hit points	2	8	8	9	11	12

The damage points represent the minimum damage from a successful strike. Critical hits increase that minimum by a random amount up to the totals shown in Table 5.1. Iron and diamond swords are obviously the most powerful, especially if you keep in mind that attack is actually the best defense. The quicker you can kill a mob, the less time it has to deliver blows in return. Dispatch them fast, and you can move on with your health mostly intact.

Sprinting while hitting also knocks back the target. This is a vital move for attacking creepers but not so good against skeletons because it gives them time to line up another shot. (If you've forgotten any controls, like how to sprint, make sure to refer to Table 1.1.)

The sword is unique among the weapons because it also provides a blocking move. Right-click to block any attack, either direct or ranged, if you can spot that arrow heading your way in time. This provides up to 50% of damage reduction, at the expense of dropping your speed to a crawl, so block at the last possible moment or in tight corners where there isn't enough room for the usual evasive maneuvers. Even better, successfully blocking a fireball will change its direction and fling it back toward its sender.

Bows and Arrows

A fully charged bow delivers more damage than a standard diamond sword, making bows very powerful weapons. Bows and arrows also enable you to attack from a distance, giving skeletons a dose of their own medicine and keeping you well clear of creeper detonation range. Figure 5.13 shows a bow in action. Bows can only be used from your dominant hand, although any arrows held in the other will be used before others in your inventory.

FIGURE 5.13 Archery target practice: Sorry, Porky.

Craft a bow from three sticks and three pieces of string and equip yourself with it in any quick access inventory slot.

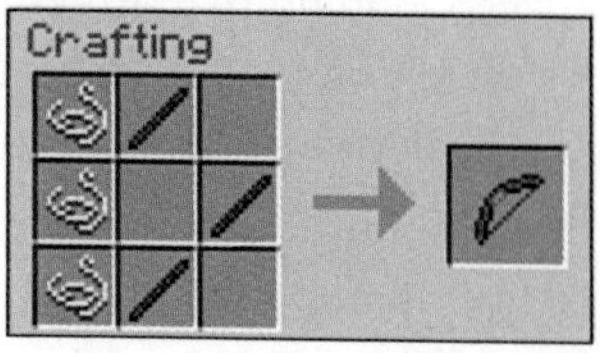

There is one other part to the equation: arrows. You can choose from several types, including the enchanted spectral arrow, which is crafted from a standard arrow surrounded by four pieces of glowstone dust. This arrow gives its target a glowing outline even when they are invisible. Even better, dip the arrow's tip into a potion for a long-ranged splash effect.

A piece of flint, a stick, and a feather will create a stack of four basic arrows. Four arrows isn't a lot, and you're going to need quite a few more to make having a bow worthwhile, but it's a good place to start.

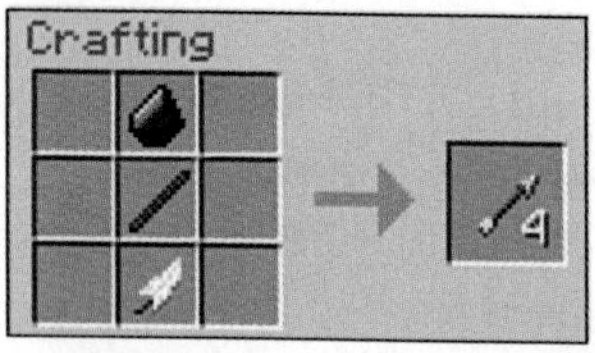

There are a number of ways to add more to your quiver. The easiest is to go for a quick scout in the morning when the sun comes up. Here's why:

- Skeletons often drop arrows when they burn at dawn.
- Zombies sometimes drop feathers at the same time.
- Chickens can die during the night, victims of wolves or cacti. You can also kill any random chickens you find during your travels to get both meat and often one or two feathers per chicken.

Sticks and feathers are easy enough to come by, but what about flint?

Every mined gravel block has a 1 in 10 chance of dropping a piece of flint instead of a block of gravel. It's a random process, but that also means that every block of gravel, if mined, placed, and mined again will eventually yield flint. You just need an efficient way to go about it.

Gravel usually seems to be a bit of an annoyance in mines because it's so common, and clearing the long vertical shafts can require a lot of effort. But where flint is concerned, gravel is actually quite a benefit. Gather all the gravel you can because it will yield flint, even if it takes a little while.

Dig out a nice big room somewhere convenient underground, light it with torches, and then fill in the middle with all the gravel blocks you've mined. Then have at them with a shovel.

Mining gravel with a shovel is incredibly quick, so it won't take long. Placing just 10 blocks is likely to yield 1 flint (enough for four arrows), and then you can reuse the other 9 gravel blocks. Add a new block to the mix and repeat.

TIP

Superfast Flint Mining

The quickest way I've found to recycle gravel for flint is to create a room with a set of four eight-block-long trenches that are two blocks deep with an additional step in the end so you can climb out. This creates a total of 64 gravel spaces—conveniently equal to a full stack of gravel in a hotbar slot. Keep another full stack of gravel in a regular inventory slot. This is the replenishment stack. With the hotbar gravel selected, jump into each trench, running up and down while holding down the right mouse button to place the gravel in a continuous stream. Switch to the shovel and do the same in reverse while holding down the left button to harvest the gravel and flint. Iron shovels provide the best durability without chewing up the much rarer diamond gems.

You'll get 6 to 7 pieces of flint each time you clear the room, which is sufficient to make between 24 and 28 arrows. Now replenish and repeat: Open your inventory window and hold down **Shift** while you left-click the spare stack of gravel. Just enough will be transferred from there to the hotbar stack to bring that back up to 64 units.

Ready for some archery practice? Follow these steps to shoot arrows with devastating force:

1. Make the bow the active item in your hotbar. Arrows can stay hidden in a regular inventory slot and are depleted automatically.
2. Use the crosshairs to aim at your target. You'll need to learn to account for the arrow's arc through the sky and to take into account your target's movement. Aim directly at nearby targets and increasingly above their head as they get farther away. If they are heading clearly in one direction across your line of sight, aim slightly ahead of that movement to make up for the time it takes the arrow to reach them. There's no hard-and-fast rule here; practice does make perfect.
3. Right-click and hold to pull back on the bow. Hold longer for a stronger shot. When it's fully charged, the bow shakes slightly, showing that it's primed for a critical hit with a damage bonus.
4. Fire the arrow by releasing the right mouse button. Fully charged shots leave a trail of stars behind the arrow as it flies.

Arrows deliver substantial damage and are the safest tool for dealing with skeletons, creepers, and other mobs that also deliver ranged attacks, such as ghasts and blazes.

Various enchantment effects can also greatly increase a bow's strength and versatility, as well as provide an unlimited supply of arrows.

Shields

With the new dual-wielding capability also comes the ability to craft and use shields. These replace the need to block frontal attacks with a sword, but they also block an attack from the side on which the shield is held, and serve to allow you to attack and defend at the same time. Try dual-wielding two shields to block all attacks in an arc around your front and sides. Perfect for a headlong charge through an attacking mob of mobs.

You'll need to right-click to hold the shield up to block attacks, and left-click at the same time to attack.

Craft a shield from one column of the same-colored wool, one column of any kind of planks, and a single iron ingot in the middle of the last column. Combine with a banner that uses the same base color as the wool to transfer its design (see Figure 5.14).

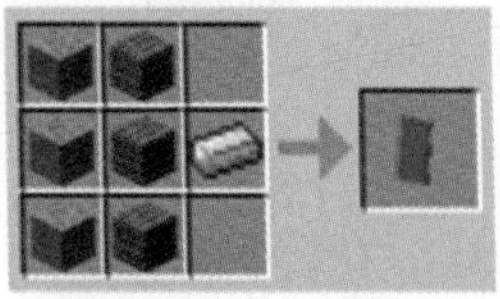

FIGURE 5.14 Customize your shield and get ready for action!

Shields take damage and can only be repaired at an anvil, although combining them at the anvil with an enchanted book of "unbreaking" will vastly increase their durability.

Armor-All

Armor is crafted from leather, iron ingots, gold ingots, and diamond gems. A fifth type of armor made from chain mail can't be crafted but is available as a tradable item in some villages, if you are lucky enough to find it (see "Emerald City: Your Ticket to Trade" on page 248).

A full suit of armor requires 24 units of source material, but the materials don't all have to be the same type. It's best to think of armor not as a complete suit but as its individual parts: a helmet, chestplate, leggings, and boots. Each can be made from a different material, depending on what you have on hand, and each adds to the damage protection value that protects your entire body, regardless of where you are hit. Your avatar is, to put it plainly, one giant hit box...like a punching bag that can also strike back.

As mentioned in Chapter 3, "Gathering Resources," each armor icon represents an 8% reduction in the damage you'll take, so a 10/10 suit of armor will reduce the damage you take by 80%, whereas a 1/10 suit will absorb only 8%. Armor becomes less effective the more damage it absorbs, although the rate at which it deteriorates also depends on its material, with leather being the weakest and diamond the strongest.

NOTE

Which Suit Suits You?

Finding 24 units of any of the materials that can be turned into a suit of armor isn't easy when you're starting out, but if you happen to have spawned near a few cattle, consider starting a farm, as described in Chapter 7 and breed the cattle rather than try to find more of them in the wild. You can also craft the hide from four rabbits into one piece of leather. Horses also sometimes drop two pieces of leather when they die. If you haven't found any willing bovines (or horses, perish the thought—it just seems wrong), and mining for an iron suit is the only reasonable option, ensure that you can build up enough of a stock of iron ingots for your tools before turning any into armor.

Your Heads-Up Display (HUD) shows the total defense points for your current armor. As with the other bars, each unit represents two points, and it decreases by half an icon as each point depletes.

Table 5.2 lists the maximum damage absorption provided by each armor material. Various enchantments can also improve the damage absorption of each type, with gold faring the best, followed by leather, diamond, and iron.

TABLE 5.2 Maximum Armor Protection Values

Material	Icons Displayed	Percent Protection
Leather	3.5	28%
Gold	5.5	44%
Chain	6	48%
Iron	7.5	60%
Diamond	10	80%

Having said that, not all the armor components made from one material provide the same damage protection. The chestplate always provides the highest protection, followed by leggings, the helmet, and boots. The ratios differ somewhat between materials but, generally, a chest plate is 3 to 3.5 times as effective as boots. Build your armor in chestplate-leggings-helmet-boots order for best results.

The crafting recipes for the different armor pieces are quite simple. I'll show them for iron, and you can just substitute whatever materials you have on hand. The same material must be used for each piece, but as mentioned earlier, you don't need to wear a full suit with each piece crafted from the same type of material. You can mix and match. For example, if you have been able to collect a lot of leather but only a handful of pieces of iron, consider using the leather for a chestplate and the iron for a helmet because this will give you the maximum damage protection from the available resources.

Here's what you need to craft each piece of armor:

- **Chestplate**—8 units of material

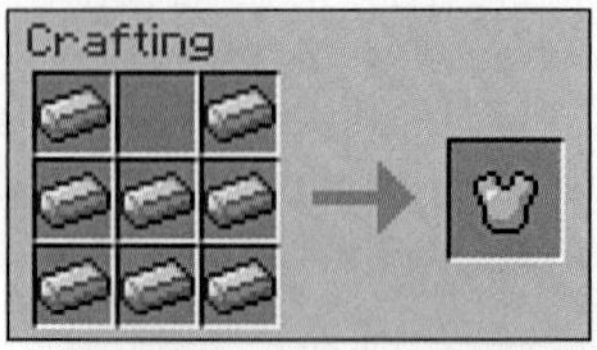

- **Leggings**—7 units of material

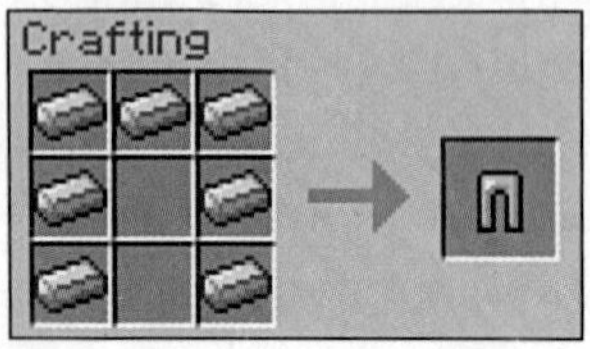

- **Helmet**—5 units of material

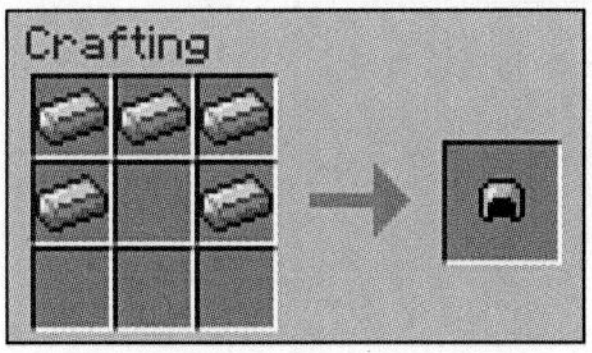

- **Boots**—4 units of material

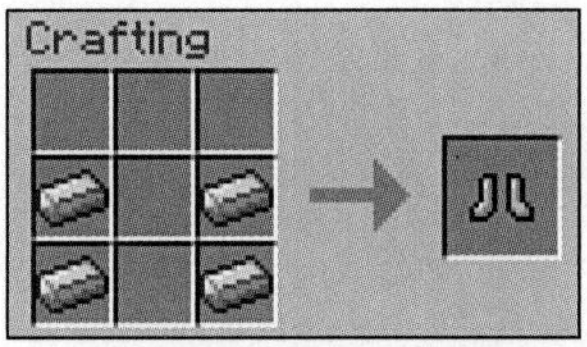

When you've crafted the armor, open your inventory window and Shift+click any piece to automatically put it in the correct armor inventory slot. You can also use an armor stand to keep your ready-to-wear suits out in the open instead of stuffed in a chest, or place the armor in four item frames on the wall.

Color-Coordinating Your Leather

Leather armor is the only armor that can be dyed. Although changing its color won't help one iota with damage protection, it's possible to step out in style by crafting up any of several hundred thousand different colors or color combinations for the different armor pieces. You could even make red, white, and blue armor to be like Captain America! Place the armor and different dyes in the crafting grid. Repeating the same dye more than once tends to weight the final color toward that dye. Figure 5.15 shows a finished example.

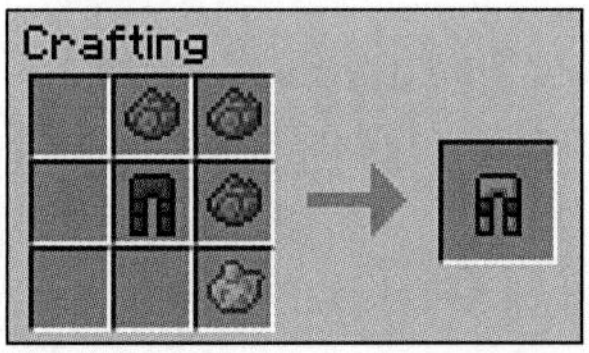

You may be wondering why you'd bother dyeing your armor. Well, it's certainly not necessary. But it's fun to differentiate your character for Multiplayer mode. Otherwise, it makes no difference. And it's also possible to change the entirety of your character's skin by logging in to your account at http://minecraft.net and clicking the **Profile** link. See Chapter 13 for more information.

FIGURE 5.15 Ready for some village trading, in colored leather chestplate and leggings, paired with an iron helmet and boots.

Taking Combat Damage and Healing

As this chapter comes to a close, it's time we have a heart-to-heart discussion about health, damage, death, and healing in Minecraft.

Recall that the HUD includes your health bar, which consists of a row of heart icons. Each heart represents 2 hit points, giving your avatar a total of 20 hit points. These hit points can be lost through combat damage, of course, but they also decrement through starvation; fall damage; touching fire, lava, or cacti; drowning; suffocation; or getting caught in an explosion.

We've discussed armor and the armor bar; the row of defense point shields represents the amount of damage your avatar's armor can sustain before you start losing hit points—that is, your avatar's life.

What happens as you're nearing death? You'll observe your health bar shaking. If the worst happens and your avatar is killed, you'll see the Game Over screen shown in Figure 5.16.

Notice in Figure 5.16 that when you die, you are presented with your game score and are given the opportunity to respawn into the current world or return to the title screen. You'll recall from earlier discussions in this book that the only option you have when you die playing Hardcore mode is to delete your world.

When you're in any mode other than Hardcore, and you respawn your avatar, you'll find yourself in the location in the world where you originally spawned when you started your game—or a place where you updated your spawn location. A nice pro tip for you is to issue the **/spawnpoint** command periodically to update your avatar's spawn location.

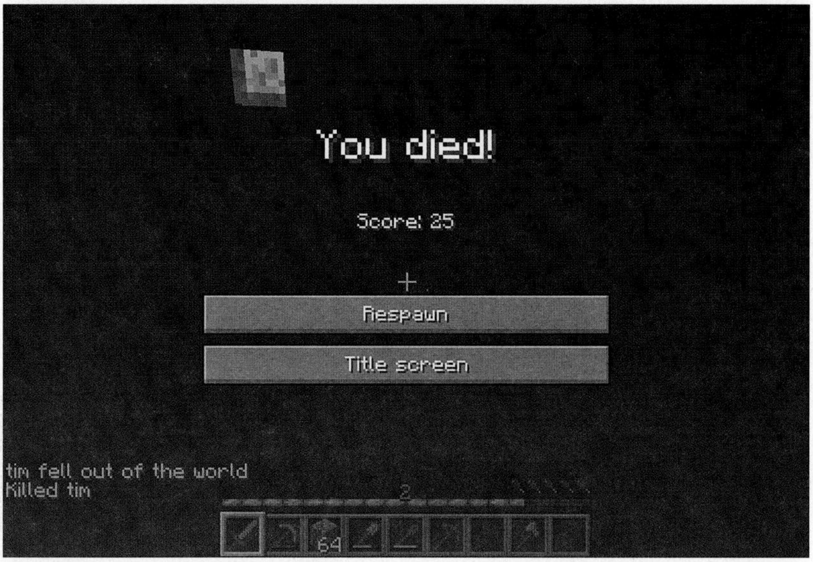

FIGURE 5.16 As long as you're not playing Minecraft in Hardcore mode, death does not signify a permanent end of the road for your avatar.

The Bottom Line

Minecraft's hostile mobs are quite a piece of work. Literally. They're creatively constructed, have unique behaviors, drop vital ingredients that allow you to continue your journey, and present an interesting range of challenges. You can't live with them and won't succeed without them.

There comes a time, my friend, when loins must be girded, weapons honed, and armor polished to a mirrored gleam, and all that is left is to: Go forth and conquer!

Of course, don't do it blindly. Practice around your base first while sharpening your skills. Don't carry too much with you; if you do, when you're killed in action, you'll have to race back for it. Also keep the area around your base well lit to prevent too many hostiles from spawning nearby. This will give you a nice stream of stragglers wandering by at night, but in most cases not too many at once.

One final tip: Until you have an excellent perimeter defense set up, lead any creepers away from your base and practice your attack runs there. If you die, so be it; death happens, and it may happen often, but at least you'll keep the side of your house from looking like it was hit by multiple rocket-propelled grenades.

In time, you will succeed, and picking off hostiles will seem like a walk in the park—maybe Central Park at 3 a.m., but a park nonetheless.

Crop Farming

In This Chapter

- Become self-sufficient with your first crops and optimize your farm.
- Learn the secrets of hydration; it doesn't take much to do a lot.
- Harvest your farm with one click of a button.
- Build a fully automated water harvester.

Farming is fun. There, I said it. I'm not talking about turning your Minecraft character into Farmer Joe and chomping on a stalk of wheat while slopping out a pigsty. I mean farming the Minecraft way.

Farming in Minecraft refers to any system that creates renewable resources. This concept goes well beyond a simple wheat field. It includes growing a host of different crops that all have specific purposes and creating fully automated hands-off harvesting systems. This chapter takes you through the elements of a crop farm and how to transform harvesting from a multi-click chore to one push of a button or twitch of a lever.

Choosing a Crop

Given that you can farm just about anything, you might be wondering where to start. Let's talk about the basics first because you can easily branch out from there.

Wheat is the most useful crop to farm initially as three wheat sheaves crafted into bread forms a useful food staple, and wheat is also used for breeding cows, sheep, and mooshrooms, as well as for taming horses. It's also easy to get started for two reasons:

- You can find the seeds just about anywhere by knocking down tall grass. Besides planting wheat fields, you can also use seeds to breed chickens.
- Wheat will grow quite happily without water, although it does grow faster with hydration available.

First find your seeds. You don't need many. When harvested, all growable crops drop up to three times as many seeds as they take to plant. This means you can start with a small stock and quickly expand your plantation as the plants mature. Just harvest, replant, and repeat until the crop reaches your target size. Under optimal conditions, the crop will reach maturity in two to three day/night cycles.

Before you get started, here are some tips to keep in mind:

- All crops except cocoa beans grow faster when planted near water.
- All crops except cocoa and sugar cane need their soil prepared with a hoe, to convert dirt or grass blocks into *farmland* blocks.

CAUTION

Watch Your Step

Walking on farmland soil blocks can cause them to revert to ordinary soil, unless you're sneaky. Planting a raised bed makes harvesting easier because you don't need to worry about stepping on the soil and can therefore run down the aisle, quickly lopping off the produce.

- The hoe is your mainstay farming tool, so we should quickly review its crafting recipe. Essentially, a hoe is simply two sticks combined with two wood planks (any variety), cobblestone, iron ingot, gold ingot, or diamond.

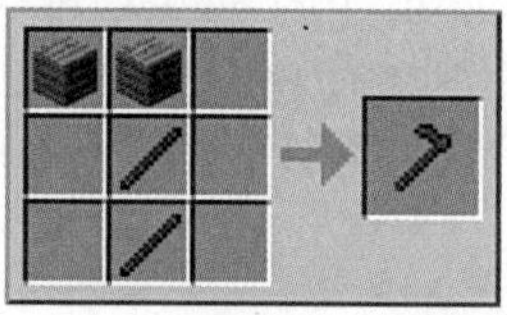

- Use a perimeter fence at least one block high—or two of any other type of block—to prevent mobs from overrunning your farm and trampling your carefully grown produce. The fence won't keep out spiders, but they don't trample crops.
- All crops grow better in light. Use torches to keep the area well lit at night and to prevent mob spawning.
- Crops can also be grown underground, as long as you provide plenty of light.
- You don't need an enormous farm to become completely self-sufficient. Figure 6.1 shows an example of a farm with every possible crop planted, as well as pens for chickens, pigs, cows, and sheep. It's about as close as you'll get in Minecraft to having your own supermarket.
- Once a farm is established, it doesn't require constant tending. Mature crops don't rot or decay and can be harvested any time you need to top up your pantry.

FIGURE 6.1 A farm this size provides more than enough produce and has every component required for every Minecraft recipe.

Each Minecraft crop has some unique characteristics. Table 6.1 provides a full rundown of them all. (Minecraft v1.9 has added a beetroot crop, and you'll find it in village farms. Harvest and replant it the same way as wheat. Beetroot cures hunger, but not health.)

TABLE 6.1 Crop Types

Crop	Obtain Seeds By	Growth Conditions	Used In
 Carrot	Directly replanting. Occasionally dropped by zombies but more commonly found in village farms.	Plant on a farmland block with hydration.	Consume as is to restore 4 hunger points and to tame and breed rabbits, although dandelions also do the trick.
 Cocoa beans	Harvesting mature cocoa pods yields cocoa beans that are directly replanted.	Must be grown on jungle wood blocks.  The blocks can be stacked with pods planted on each face.	 Cookies, and also for creating a brown dye.

Crop	Obtain Seeds By	Growth Conditions	Used In
 Melon	 Placing melon slices, obtained by harvesting melon, in a crafting slot. You might also find seeds tucked away in chests in various dungeons.	Plant with clear space around each block to allow the melon to grow.	 Melon slices (each block provides three to seven slices, with each slice restoring 1 hunger point). Also used to create glistering melon, an ingredient for brewing potions. Nine melon slices can be re-formed into a single melon block and used for construction.
 Potato	Directly replanting. Occasionally dropped by zombies but more commonly found in village farms.	Plant on a farmland block with hydration.	 Consume as a baked potato by cooking in a furnace (restores 6 hunger points). You can also eat it raw and restore 2 hunger points.
 Pumpkin	 Placing a pumpkin block in a crafting slot.	Plant with clear space around each block to allow the pumpkin to grow.	  Pumpkin pie (restores 8 hunger points) and to create a jack-o'-lantern.
 Sugar cane	Breaking the top blocks of sugar cane when harvesting and replanting. Leave the lowest block for regrowth.	Must be planted on sand, grass, or dirt that is directly adjacent to water.	Use to craft sugar and paper. Sugar is used in cake, pumpkin pie, and some potions. Paper is used to make books, bookshelves, enchantment tables, and firework rockets.
 Wheat	 Left-clicking tall grass.	Best with hydrated soil, but any farmland will do.	 Bread, and with other ingredients also used in cakes and cookies. Wheat is also an important tool for farming animals.

Cooking with Minecraft

Minecraft provides numerous recipes that deliver varying levels of hunger restoration. Tables 6.2 through 6.6 provide a complete guide that will help you optimize your efforts so you aren't left on the verge of virtual starvation.

Minecraft Bakery

Who doesn't love the smell of fresh baked bread? You can cook up your own without an oven, surprisingly, using just the crafting table.

TABLE 6.2 Crafted Fresh Daily

Food	Food Points Restored	Effect	Obtained By
Bread	2.5	—	Crafting Found in dungeon chests
Cake	1 per use (6 total)	—	Crafting
Cookie	0.5	—	Crafting
Pumpkin pie	4	—	Crafting
Rabbit stew	10	—	Crafting

Minecraft BBQ

There's no need to dial down the heat on your furnace after a bout of smelting. Just pop in the raw meat and you'll get a juicy and nutritious cooked meal in less than a minute.

TABLE 6.3 Grill It

Food	Food Points Restored	Effect	Obtained By
Baked potato	3	—	Cooking potatoes
Cooked chicken	3	—	Cooking raw chicken or killing a chicken with fire
Cooked fish	2.5	—	Cooking a raw fish
Cooked mutton	6	—	Cooking raw mutton or killing a mutton with fire
Cooked pork chop	4	—	Cooking a raw pork chop, killing a Zombie Pigman, or killing a pig with fire
Cooked rabbit	5	—	Cooking raw rabbit or killing a rabbit with fire
Cooked salmon	3	—	Cooking a raw salmon
Steak	4	—	Cooking raw beef or killing a cow with fire

Alchemy Eatery

Add that magical touch to your carrots and apples to gain beneficial effects.

TABLE 6.4 Golden Chef

Food	Food Points Restored	Effect	Obtained By
Golden carrot	3	—	Crafting
Golden apple	2	Provides very fast health regeneration for 4 seconds	Crafting and found in dungeon chests
Enchanted golden apple	2	Provides health regeneration for 30 seconds + fire resistance (5:00) + damage resistance (5:00)	Crafting and found in dungeon chests

Raw Food Diet

Ever considered going raw? There's a Minecraft equivalent ready for the taking.

TABLE 6.5 As Is

Food	Food Points Restored	Effect	Obtained By
Apple	2	—	Found in strongholds, found when destroying leaves
Carrot	2	—	Found in villages
Melon slice	1	—	Harvested from melon blocks
Potato	0.5	—	Found in villages
Raw beef	1.5	—	Dropped by cows
Raw fish	1	—	Fishing
Raw mutton	2	—	Dropped by sheep
Raw pork chop	1.5	—	Dropped from pigs
Raw rabbit	3	—	Dropped by rabbits
Raw salmon	1	—	Fishing

Eat at Your Own Risk

Sometimes a bite of something bad can save you from starvation. Use these food items as a last resort.

TABLE 6.6 Diner Beware

Food	Food Points Restored	Effect	Obtained By
Poisonous potato	1	60% chance of dealing 2 hearts of damage	Rarely found when harvesting potatoes
Pufferfish	0.5	Hunger III and Nausea II for 15 seconds, Poison IV for 1 minute	Fishing
Raw chicken	1	30% chance of inflicting food poisoning	Dropped by chickens
Rotten flesh	2	75% chance of inflicting food poisoning	Dropped by zombies
Spider eye	1	100% chance of inflicting poison	Dropped from spiders

Establishing a Farm

The first step in building a new farm is choosing a suitable location. You'll probably want something fairly close to your house, and in a reasonably flat area, although you can also adjust the landscape as required by removing any stray blocks. Figure 6.2 shows the outer edge of the same farm from Figure 6.1. The entire rear quarter of the farm is essentially suspended on a floating platform one block deep.

FIGURE 6.2 In difficult terrain, farms can float using just a one-block-deep dirt platform.

CAUTION

Stay Close for Growth

As you may have noticed, Minecraft worlds are enormous. If the game kept the entire lot in memory at once, and kept all the different crops, mobs, and other blocks updating...well, let's just say you'd need a wicked-fast computer (so tricked out you might find it getting coopted by the Meteorological Bureau to run its weather simulations).

Instead, Minecraft keeps just a small section of the world active in memory at one time—and that's the part that's around you to a distance of a few hundred blocks, although this does vary depending on your movement speed and the render distance selected under Video Settings in the Options menu. (In Multiplayer mode, the default setting keeps a swathe of 441 blocks active around each player.)

This chunk updating therefore becomes quite important for farms. You could build a gigantic, fantastic grow-everything farm on a nice flat piece of land, but nothing will grow if you wander too far away because that area will be unloaded from memory, although there are some mods that will keep distant chunks ticking away. Until you install those, keep your friends close and your farms closer.

To begin, mark out an area sufficient to fit your wheat farm. (Don't worry, we'll expand it to other foods later.) A single block of water can hydrate a 9×9 square of farmland blocks, if it is positioned in the middle (see Figure 6.3). You end up with 4 blocks of farm space in each direction from the water block, which means you have a total of 80 farmable blocks (remember that the one in the center is occupied by the water). Each block provides 1 bushel, or a total across the plantation of 26 loaves of bread each harvest. That's a lot of produce—more than you need—so you might consider starting with something a little smaller. A benefit here is that a smaller area is also easier to fence.

In Figure 6.4, I've laid out a smaller field of 35 farmland blocks. The lake provides hydration down one side, extending in a total of three rows from the fence bordering the lake. The single water block on the other side hydrates the rest. Placing a path up the middle isn't strictly necessary because there's no reason you can't trample up and down the field during the harvest, working your way in from the edges while holding down the left **Shift** key to sneak across the fields, but I prefer touches like this for aesthetic reasons. Also, particular blocks will mature earlier than others, and the path ensures access to mature blocks in the middle of the field so you don't have to walk over planted ground to reach them.

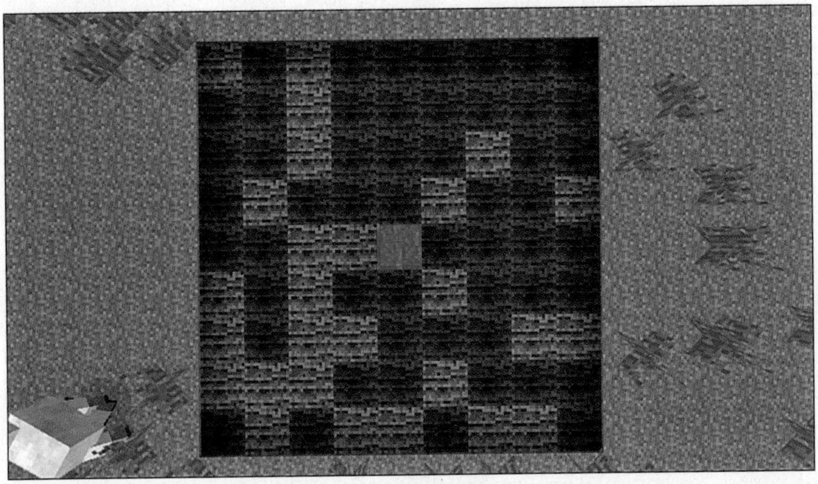

FIGURE 6.3 Hydration from a single water block extends out four blocks in each direction.

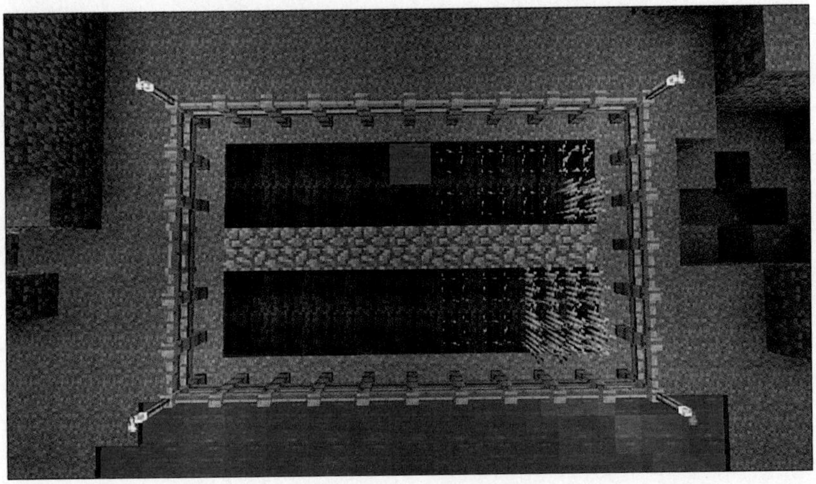

FIGURE 6.4 The seeds that come from harvesting crops allow a plantation of almost any size to quickly multiply. There's no need to plant every block when you're starting your first field.

The first harvest in this 35-block farm provides a total of 16 bushels of wheat and 27 seeds. The bushels produce 5 loaves of bread, with 1 bushel left over. The 27 seeds are almost sufficient now to plant the entire field; just 8 blocks are still vacant. They'll be planted with the seeds from the next harvest, shown in Figure 6.5.

The steps for creating your own field are quite easy:

1 Find a suitable area, or create your own by flattening the landscape and adding dirt blocks where needed.

2 If a water source isn't available nearby, craft a bucket from three iron ingots, place it in a quick access slot, and then fill it from a source. You'll need to right-click the bucket on a water source block to successfully fill it.

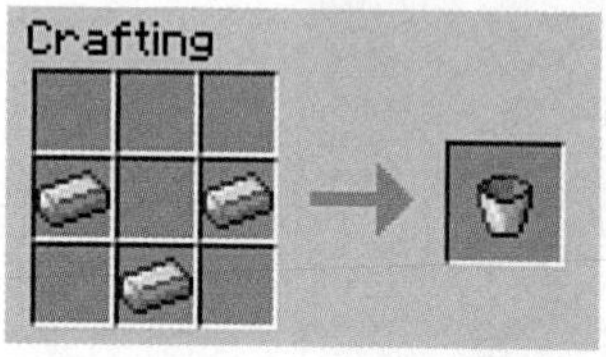

Water source blocks are present anywhere there is water, but water can also flow seven blocks from the source, so you may need to try clicking several times to get to the actual source block. You also need to be playing in Survival mode because buckets don't fill in Creative mode.

TIP

Creating a Permanent Watering Hole

Give yourself a constant source of water by digging out a 2×2 hole and filling the two diagonally opposite corners with water. The water source becomes self-sustaining, replenishing indefinitely no matter how many times you fill your bucket. This trick does not work for lava.

3 Use a hoe to till any grassy or dirt blocks into farmland.

4 Put up a fence or erect any other barrier two blocks high to keep out mobs. To create a fence that's three panels, you need a set of two sticks and four planks. While it can be difficult to spot the visual difference between a gate and a fence, especially if you're making a dash for safety, fences and gates take on the color of the wood from which they are made, so try using one material for fences and another gates. You can also build fences from stone, including mossy blocks for that slightly rundown look.

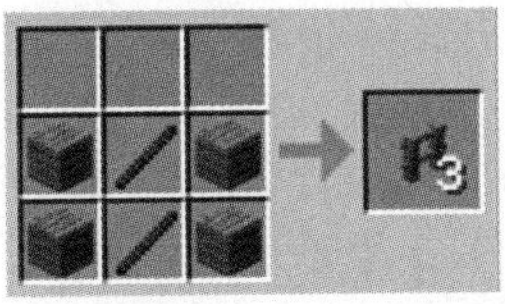

5 Fences are actually 1.5 blocks high and so can't be jumped. Add a gate for easy access.

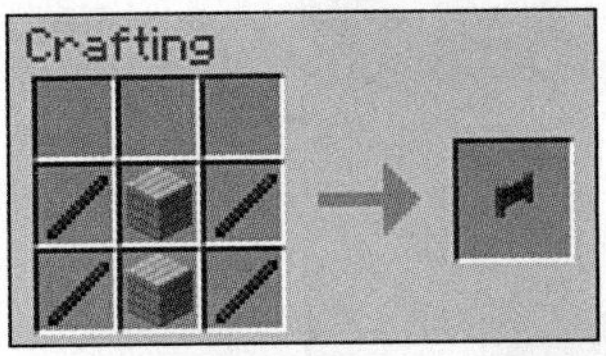

6 Add some torches to the perimeter to ensure that mobs don't spawn inside the field and also to keep the crops growing through the night.

7 Plant the seeds you collected previously by right-clicking on the tilled blocks.

Give the crop a little time to grow. It can take a few day/night cycles, depending on light conditions, although it might take just two if lighting and hydration are optimal. Wheat bushels are only produced from mature wheat crops that have reached their final stage of growth. When the tops of the crop turn brown, they're ready.

TIP

Grind Dem Bones

Bone meal, crafted at the table by placing regular old skeleton bones, gives almost every crop a boost. The growth spurt won't take a crop instantly from seedling to mature plant, but it does push the crop forward one or more stages. Although bone meal can help melon and pumpkin plants grow to maturity, it won't speed up their crop formation. However, one dose of bone meal on a grass block will encourage tall grass to grow in a 10×10 space. This is a great way to collect all the seeds you need to start a wheat field. A little bit of fertilizer can go a long way.

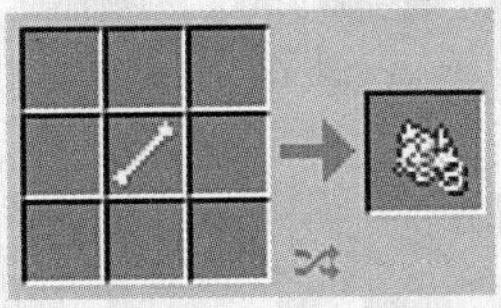

You can use any tool to harvest the wheat because harvesting does not impact durability. Just left-click each crop block and pick up the results.

Figure 6.5 shows the second crop ready to harvest; it produces 27 bushels and 43 seeds.

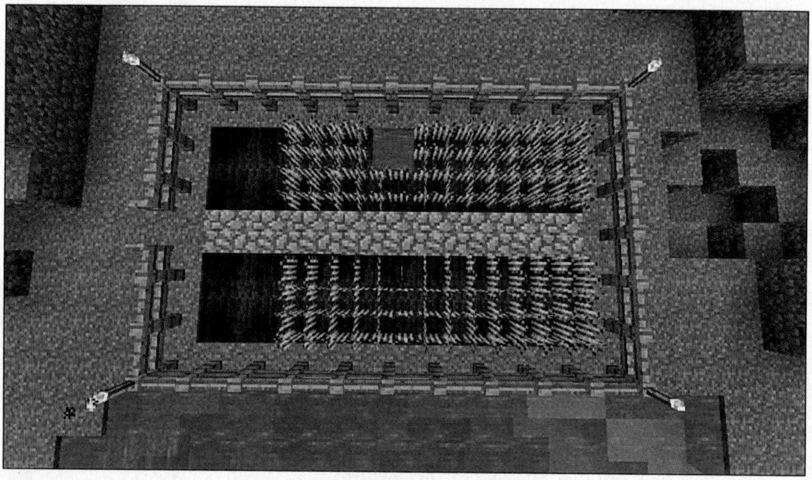

FIGURE 6.5 The wheat field now produces enough seeds to be self-sustaining, allowing the complete field to be planted and leaving plenty left over for bread and other uses.

It won't take long until you are producing more than enough wheat and seeds. Keep them handy. You can use wheat to lure and breed cows, sheep, and mooshrooms, and you can use seeds to do the same with chickens. See Chapter 7, "Farming and Taming Mobs," for more information.

TIP

Tread Lightly to Save Your Crops

Walking across a crop bed can destroy those crops or turn tilled dirt to dust. If you need to get to the other side, tread lightly by holding down the left **Shift** key as you move so that you *sneak* over your crops. It will work a lot better than hurtling across in the usual stampede.

Figure 6.6 shows an alternate farm layout with two raised beds to make harvesting easier. You can just run up and down the aisle with the left mouse button held down, quickly collecting the wheat. When planting, do the same with the right mouse button held down. The central water troughs collect any harvested bushels and seeds that fall into them and sweep them to the end of the rows for easier collection, although you'll need to run around to pick up any strays that didn't get knocked in. Arranging this system correctly is quite important. Follow these steps:

1 Make two raised beds, each 17 dirt blocks long, leaving a single row in between. I generally make the beds 2 blocks wide.

2 Place 2 blocks on top of each other directly in the middle—that's 9 blocks from the end—and attach a torch to each side of the top block that faces water. Leave the other sides free so that you can plant crops on the two adjacent farmland blocks. The additional light will help your crops grow. In Figure 6.6, I've also placed a jack-o'-lantern on the center block because lanterns throw out a bit more light than torches, and if you squint hard, they look a tiny bit like a scarecrow's head.

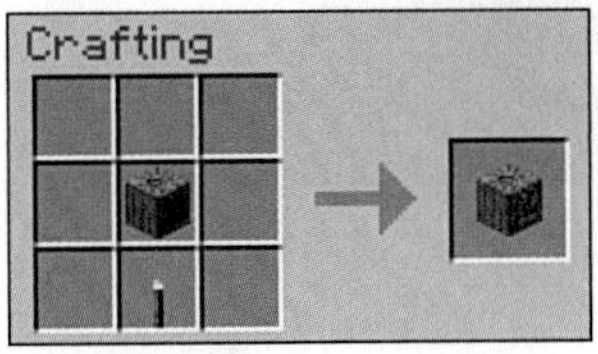

3 Place a water source on either side of this block. Each water source creates a river that runs down the central channel, ending after exactly 8 blocks, directly aligned with the end of each row.

TIP

Leveling Up Your Hydration Skills

Water can hydrate one level down but never up, so always ensure that your water flows either on the same level as your crops or just above them. In both cases, it will still hydrate up to four horizontal blocks away, even with a gap in the middle.

3 Build a nice cobblestone path all the way around, as shown in Figure 6.6, if you like. It's not necessary but nice to do it. For a more rustic look, you may want to use pressed dirt, introduced in Minecraft v1.9.

4 Fence the area any way that works for you and hoe and plant the blocks. You'll find it easiest to work on the inner section of each bed, first running along the edge, holding down your left mouse button to till the blocks and then, with seeds selected, using your right mouse button to quickly plant them.

5 When harvest time comes, use any tool to quickly knock out the wheat and seeds. Most that are flung away from you will wind up in the water and wash down toward each end of the beds. Because the beds are hydrated, you can also run up and down them to pick up any seeds or wheat left behind without too much worry about reverting the beds to dirt blocks. Dry beds revert much faster than hydrated ones!

6 Knock the mud out of your shoes (just kidding) and go make some bread.

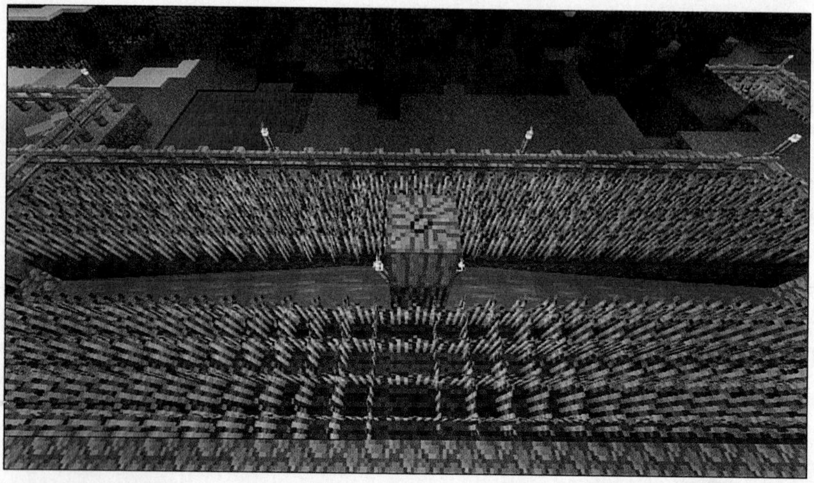

FIGURE 6.6 Raised beds make it easier to plant and harvest, and the central water supply never dries up and conveniently washes harvest crops down to collection points at either end.

> **TIP**
>
> **Greenhouse Effect**
>
> Want a farm that's protected from trampling by mobs yet gets all the sun and water it needs? Try building a greenhouse. All you need is sand, which is plentiful, that you smelt into glass blocks in your furnace. Add a door, a path between the crops using whatever is readily available, and water...and your food supply is safe. You can even forgo the door and instead add an underground path.

Automated Farms

Automated farms can save you from a lot of the tedium involved in harvesting crops, even if they don't help with the planting. There are an essentially endless number of ways to build these, with some variations according to the crop, but each primarily relies on one of three methods:

- Pistons cut across the top of the crop, sweeping the harvest into a channel of water that carries it to a convenient central collection point.
- Pistons move the block on which the crop stands, shaking the harvest loose.
- A torrent of water floods the entire crop, carrying the harvest down to a single location. The water can be controlled using pistons or a water dispenser and, if set up in a farm

adjacent to a village, receives the added bonus that villagers will replant the crop for you with a combination of wheat, potatoes, and carrots.

NOTE

Want to Be Moved? Use a Piston

Pistons are one of the most useful features of Minecraft's redstone system. I show you how to use them here for farming, but you'll also find a lot more detail on these and all the other juicy redstone equipment in Chapter 9, "Redstone, Rails, and More."

Figure 6.7 shows a piston farm that uses the first two methods mentioned earlier: using a piston to cut the top of the crop and shaking the farmland itself to break loose the harvest.

FIGURE 6.7 This wheat farm uses two types of piston farming to automate the harvest.

1. A row of standard farmland block, hydrated by the water flowing from a water source block positioned up the far end of the central channel
2. Collection point for the harvest
3. The raised row of farmland blocks
4. Lever that provides an on/off switch and power to the pistons
5. Redstone dust placed on the ground to deliver power to the pistons
6. Pistons placed on their side that are powered by a raised block behind them that carries the redstone current the rest of the way
7. A row of sticky pistons

The principles used in Figure 6.7 are simple. Pulling the lever with a right-click of the mouse causes the sticky pistons to extend (see Figure 6.8). This pushes the raised farmland across the top of the lower rows, harvesting those crops by scraping them into the central water channel. At the same time, the movement of the raised farmland causes its crops to shake loose. Return the lever to its off position, and the pistons retreat. Because they are *sticky*, they also pull the attached farmland block back to its original position.

FIGURE 6.8 The happy harvest. It's a bit messy, but it gets the harvest done more or less instantly.

The only problem with this method is that a lot of the harvest falls outside the collection channel. Also, as you can see from Figure 6.9, once the pistons retract, the entire lower section has to be hoed again, and the upper farmland blocks revert quite quickly because they're not hydrated. There's a fairly easy fix, though: Strategically position water blocks at each end of the upper rows, as shown in Figure 6.10.

NOTE

Semi- and Fully-Automated Farms

Automated farming doesn't mean quite the same thing for every crop. Melons, pumpkins, and sugar cane can be farmed in a fully automated manner because the stem of the plant stays behind. With a timer-delayed circuit, you can just set it all up and walk away. It will operate indefinitely. All the other automated farms (those for wheat, carrots, potatoes, and cocoa pods) really only handle the harvesting for you. You'll still need to replant seeds for the next crop if the farm isn't adjacent to a village, and you'll have to break out the hoe to repair any farmland that has reverted to standard grass or dirt block after harvesting.

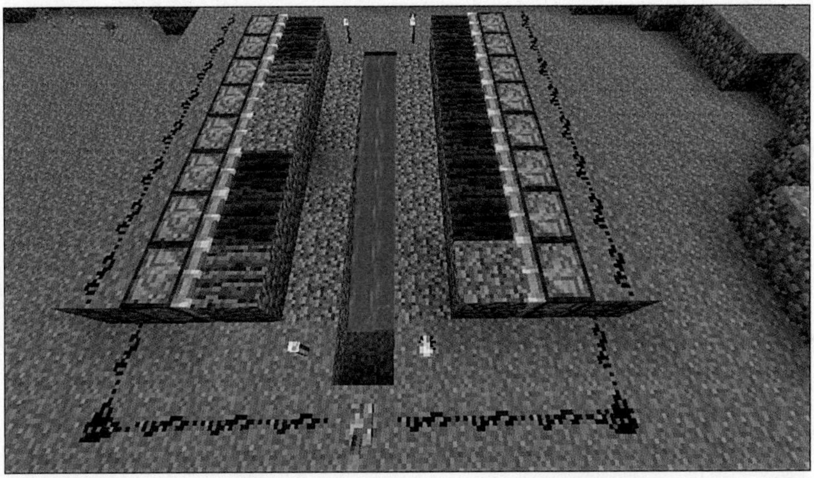

FIGURE 6.9 After harvesting, a lot of the farmland reverts to dirt or grass blocks. The water harvesting method described here solves this issue.

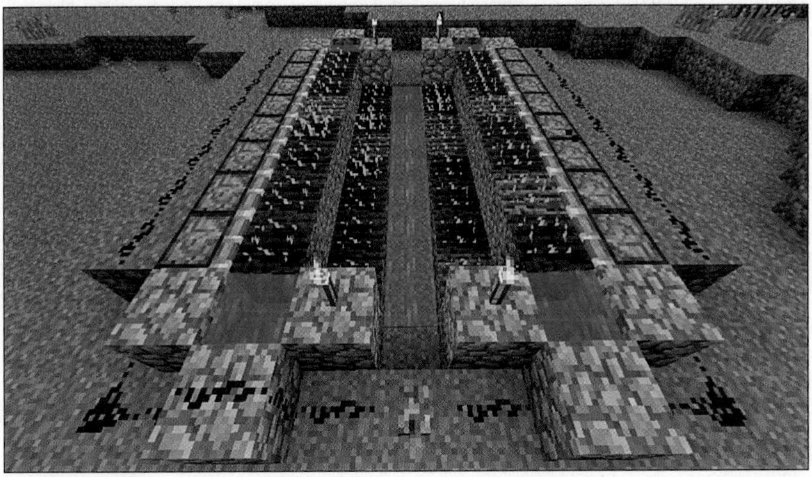

FIGURE 6.10 The corner water blocks help hydrate the upper farmland rows. In this layout, water in one corner is able to hydrate the nearest raised blocks on the other side because they are still just four blocks away. The gap in the middle is ignored.

Building an automated farm can be quite resource intensive. The basic piston used for cutting a crop requires three wood plank blocks, four pieces of cobblestone, an iron ingot, and one redstone. If you've mined extensively and knocked out enough wood, you'll likely have plenty of materials at your disposal, but it may get trickier when you build the sticky piston used for pushing farmland. You build this from a standard piston and a block of slime. If you haven't come across any slime mobs during your travels, you'll need to find a way to get to a swamp biome for the slime spawning grounds or head into a cave structure where you may be lucky enough (if fighting a giant blob of slime can be considered such) to find a few oozing their way across the floor.

However, building an automated farm can also be a great way to learn about some of Minecraft's advanced features. It may all seem a bit confusing at first, but once you have the basic moves down, the rest is really just a repetition of those building blocks. It won't take you long to start developing some quite amazing layouts. Let's look at the different methods step by step.

TIP

Getting Creative with Farming

Practice makes perfect, right? Automated constructions can definitely take some time to build and understand. If you're low on resources but really want to try building the examples shown in this chapter, consider starting a new world in Creative mode and run riot with the unlimited resources. You can then switch back to your current world and continue in "Survivor or Bust!"

If Minecraft automation deeply sparks your interest, you'll want to check out my book *Advanced Strategy Guide to Minecraft* (ISBN 9780789755735) as well. In that book, I delve into automation broadly and deeply.

Creating a Piston Harvester

The simplest piston harvester is quite easy to build. Figure 6.11 shows a push-button-operated harvesting piston. Levers and redstone provide a way to connect multiple systems so they all operate together, but let's take a look at this first design.

FIGURE 6.11 Automated farming can be quite simple, schematically speaking. No need to get up to your ears in an electrical engineering degree. Maybe next chapter....

1. Water hydration and collector
2. Farmland with crop
3. Piston facing the crop
4. Cobblestone block, although almost any block will work
5. A wooden push-button crafted from a wood plank block

Building this is easy, and it's a great way to get a basic understanding of how all this automated stuff works. Just follow these steps:

1 Dig a hole for your water supply and fill it from a water bucket.

2 Hoe the grass or dirt block to turn it into farmland and plant some seeds.

3 Create a standard piston. Minecraft always places pistons so that the face of the piston points toward you, snapping toward the closest of the six possible degrees of orientation, so place this one by standing on the block next to the water supply, facing the farmland block. Right-click to place the piston on the far side of that block.

4 Place a dirt, wood, cobblestone, or other kind of solid block behind the piston.

5 Craft a wooden button from wood planks and right-click to place it on the side of the block behind the piston.

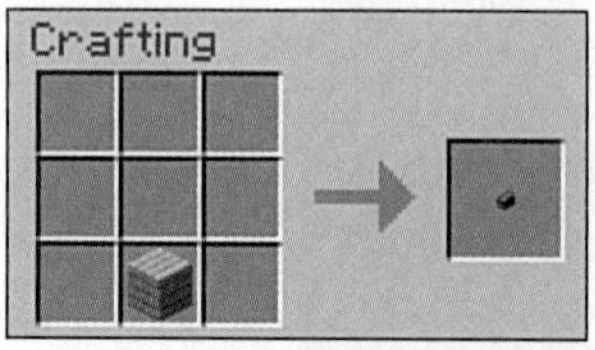

Position yourself close to the button and right-click it to operate the piston. The piston powers up, sweeping the crop off its farmland block. The harvest may spring directly into your inventory, depending on how close you are standing, or it might float around waiting for you to collect it. The piston automatically retracts after a brief delay because buttons send just a brief pulse of power.

Well done! That's all there is to creating a simple piston harvester.

One piston an automated farm does not make, but it's remarkably easy to extend this design into one that is much more effective. Follow these steps:

1 Replicate the same pattern right next to your first harvester, minus the button on the side of any but the first block.

2  Run a little trail of redstone dust (right-click on the top of each block with redstone selected in your quick access bar) to create a circuit that links each from the first to the last. Figure 6.12 shows what this ends up looking like.

3 Click the button again to push the pistons out in unison.

4 For extra props, create the sticky piston harvester and add an extra block of harvesting to each piston on every click of that button.

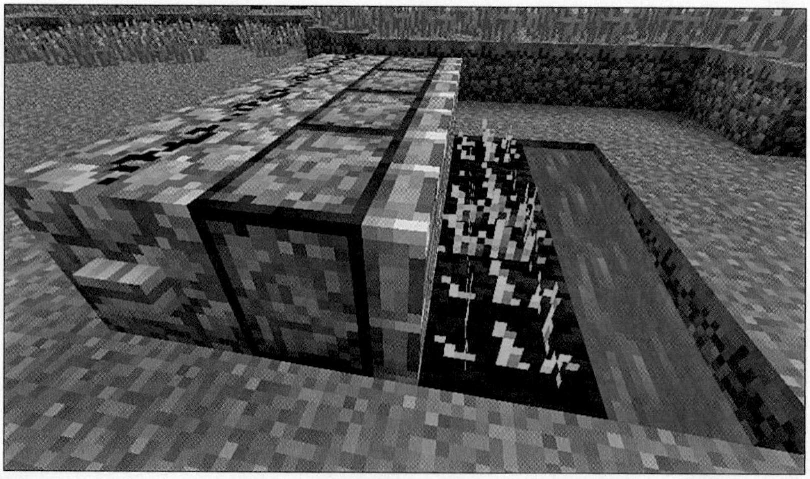

FIGURE 6.12 Set up a row of pistons with a line of redstone dust to create a synchronized one-click harvesting row.

Sticky Piston Harvesting

Sticky piston harvesters work on the same principle as the simple piston harvester, but they offer one key advantage: The harvesting power of the piston is doubled because it can also push and pull back a farmland block to shake its harvest loose (see Figure 6.13).

Start by crafting a sticky piston using a standard piston and a slimeball (the sticky part). Then follow the same routine as for a simple piston harvester but place an additional dirt block directly in front of the piston, hoe it to turn it into farmland, and plant seeds on it and the farmland block in front.

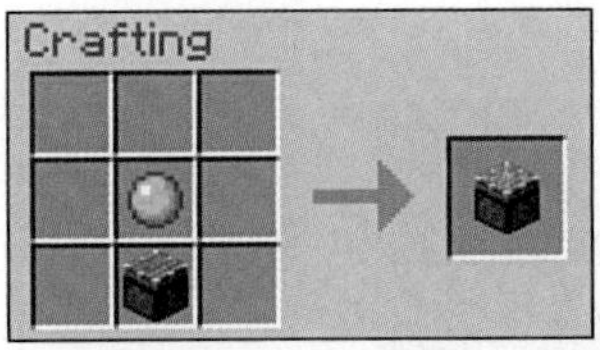

FIGURE 6.13 A sticky piston sticks like glue to the block in front, keeping it attached as the piston moves back and forth. This means using sticky pistons is an easy way to construct sliding doors, windows, and all kinds of other fascinating machines. More on that in Chapter 9.

There's just one problem with using the button system. It's fine for a single row of crops, but it can't handle an entire farm's harvest. What if you wanted to create a system where the entire farm's harvesting is automated with a single click?

Running redstone along the ground provides a central control panel and a coordinated system across multiple crop rows. It has many benefits and takes only a few more steps.

Just decide on a central point, put the button on a block, and run a redstone trail back to the pistons from either side of that block. Redstone currents run for only 15 blocks. Insert redstone repeaters if the trail is longer.

Creating a Water Harvester

Using water to harvest wheat has a major advantage over using a regular piston harvester: The water washes away the crops but doesn't revert the farmland to a regular dirt block.

There are two basic methods:

- Use a piston to drop water from a raised water source so that it flows out over the farmland.
- Use a dispenser containing a filled water bucket to send out a stream of water.

Figure 6.14 shows a farm built using the first method.

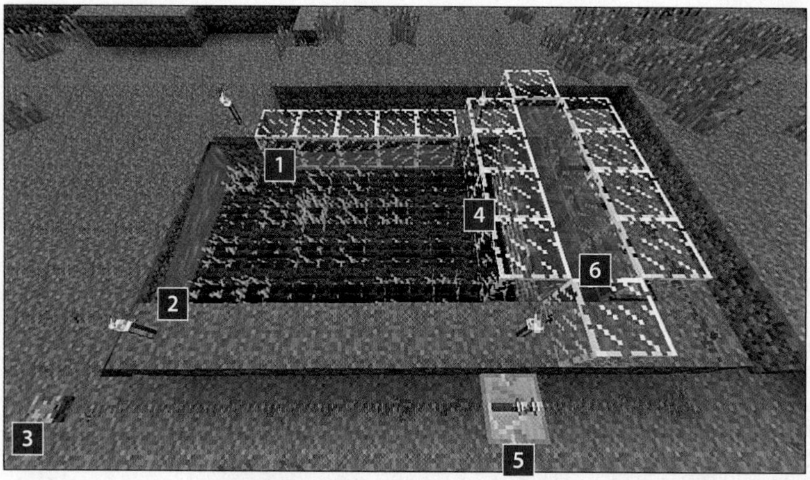

FIGURE 6.14 A water-harvested wheat farm; the glass blocks are just for illustrative purposes and can be replaced with dirt, cobblestone, or any other type of block.

1. Hydration source
2. Collection stream
3. Lever set to On because this type of harvesting drops water only when the power goes off
4. Row of pistons in their extended position, holding back the water
5. Redstone repeater required to amplify the power due to the length of the circuit
6. Water source used for harvesting, suspended by the extended pistons

The layout of the piston system is a little difficult to detect in a completed working farm, so Figure 6.15 shows a simplified view. The water source is held in place by the surrounding blocks. In Minecraft's geometry, the extended piston beneath also prevents it from flowing down. However, as soon as that piston is retracted, the pathway through the block under the water opens, allowing the water to flow out over the crops.

FIGURE 6.15 Close-up of the piston and water source block.

Levers work better than buttons on this type of layout because you want the water to keep flowing until the crop has been washed away. Make one with a block of cobblestone and a stick.

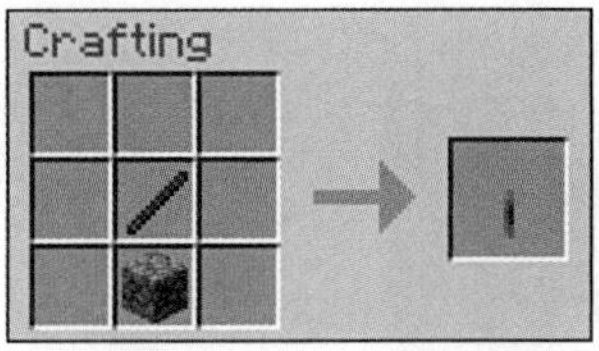

When creating this type of farm, make sure you build up all the surrounding components, including the pistons—powered and therefore extended—before you place the water sources in the upper reservoir. Otherwise, you have to wade through a constant flow of water, fighting the current, as you build the rest of the farm. You also can't place redstone dust in water, and that can make the wiring somewhat challenging if any water has escaped to places it shouldn't.

The other method described earlier relies on a dispenser block. Figure 6.16 shows a simplified view that you can easily extrapolate into a complete farm.

The dispenser layout is easier to build than the water-drop used previously but also more resource-intensive because dispensers require redstone, an undamaged bow, cobblestone, and, in this case, a bucket filled with water.

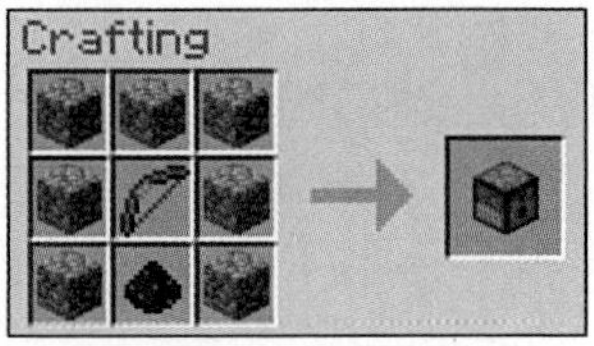

Place the dispenser with its outlet facing the crops. Then right-click the dispenser to open its own inventory window. Place a full water bucket in one of the slots. Your dispenser is locked and loaded!

TIP

More Fun with Dispensers

Dispensers are a lot of fun. You can load them with all kinds of items and then shoot out arrows at mobs, pump out lava or bone meal, or shoot fire and fireballs. They're great for traps because they can operate with trip wires and pressure plates—a popular feature in jungle temples, where they're pretty good at transforming anyone in mere moments from intrepid explorer to something more akin to a skewered kebab.

Finally, rather than using a lever, I've used a wooden button attached to the side. Just right-click the button to start the flow of water and right-click again to stop it. Connect a number of dispensers in sequence by running redstone dust along the top of each block. That single button still controls them all.

FIGURE 6.16 Simplified layout for a water dispenser harvester.

Harvesting Other Crops

Sugar cane, pumpkin, melons, and cocoa pods all work best using a slightly different and nondestructive method of farming.

Harvest sugar cane using a standard piston raised above ground level (see Figure 6.17). This piston is operated from a lever made from cobblestone and a stick.

The piston shears off the sugar cane, leaving the original stalk still planted so that it can grow again.

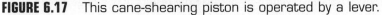

FIGURE 6.17 This cane-shearing piston is operated by a lever.

Harvest any other crop by placing pistons beside the main stem's growth blocks. As with sugar cane, the piston shears off the crop, leaving the original plant untouched.

TIP

Underground Farming

If you prefer to spend most of your time building a mine, try creating an underground farm. The principles are the same as for an aboveground farm. The only real difference is that you need to hollow out a large enough space, as shown in Figure 6.18, and place plenty of torches to keep things well lit and to prevent mobs from spawning. Underground farms have the advantage that they can be properly secured from hostile mobs so that you can tend the crops day or night without fear of being sniped by a skeleton over the fence or straying too close to a lurking creeper.

FIGURE 6.18 Underground farms can keep you thoroughly supplied. This one is next to my massive mine down at layer 11.

The Bottom Line

Crop farming is an important part of Minecraft because the results play a huge role in crafting, brewing potions, and satisfying hunger. A full hunger bar restores health, so you absolutely shouldn't contemplate venturing out for extended periods without also carrying a good supply of food—and maybe even some potions for a faster fix.

Start farming with very simple layouts, choosing the crops according to whatever you can gather from nearby biomes. If there's no tall grass for wheat seeds, look for a nearby village and pinch some potatoes and carrots while you're there. Avoid food poisoning by baking your potatoes in a furnace before consuming them—unless you are in desperate straits. Only poisonous potatoes are dangerous, and you can usually tell the difference, but why take the chance? Melons also provide a steady source of nutrition, although they satisfy only 1.2 hunger points per slice. Cocoa beans, pumpkins, and sugar cane all require at least wheat to become food grade, so it's best not to start with them.

Of course, cows, pigs, rabbits, and chickens are all good sources of food, and there is one other natural harvest worth mentioning: fungi. Find some small red and brown mushrooms or break up a couple of the giant ones that pepper the landscape, and you can make a hearty mushroom stew that also provides a huge 7.2 points of saturation. First create a wooden bowl from three wood plank blocks (bonus: you'll get four bowls from this) and then arrange the mushrooms and bowl on the crafting table. Yum!

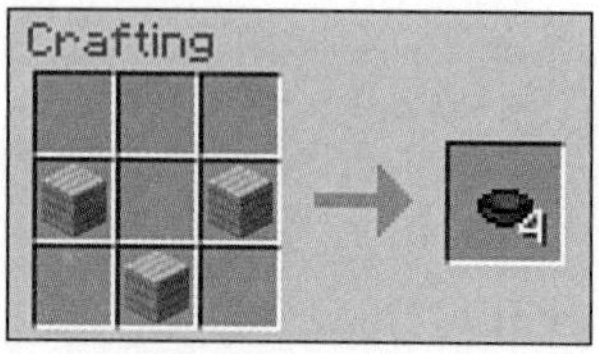

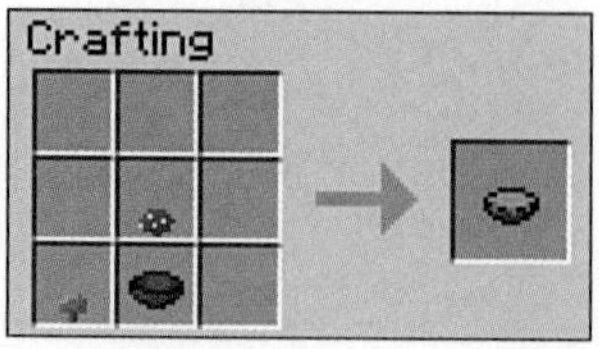

Farming and Taming Mobs

In This Chapter

- Create a passive mob farm for a constant supply of eggs, meat, and more.
- Tame ocelots to scare off creepers and use wolves for self-defense.
- Gallop across the world by taming and riding horses and use donkeys and mules to cart supplies and resources.
- Fancy a spot of fishing? Tap one of Minecraft's unlimited food resources.

Although historically, domestication of animals came before agriculture, in Minecraft it's best to start with the green stuff. After you've mastered farming, then you might want to look at ranching.

Crops are nice and easy to grow, and there is very little hassle involved. If you wanted to live a vegan life, crops can provide everything you need, but animals provide other resources besides meat.

Minecraft's passive and neutral mobs (all those that don't actively seek to kill you) can provide food, ingredients for crafting, decorative items, transport, and, very handily, defense and attack assists. While they may not wander up for a quick cuddle, consider them, at least, as friendly as mobs get.

In this chapter, you learn how to make the most of Minecraft's animal kingdom.

Farming and Working with Friendly Mobs

Mob farms create replaceable resources through breeding. Each animal is a little different, so I've compiled a list of characteristics in Table 7.1.

Figure 7.1 shows a mob farm with the most useful creatures (excepting rabbits)—a working farm with sheep, chickens, cows, and pigs. Fortunately, all the animals are self-sufficient and never starve to death. All you need to do to keep the numbers up is breed one pair for every one that you use up.

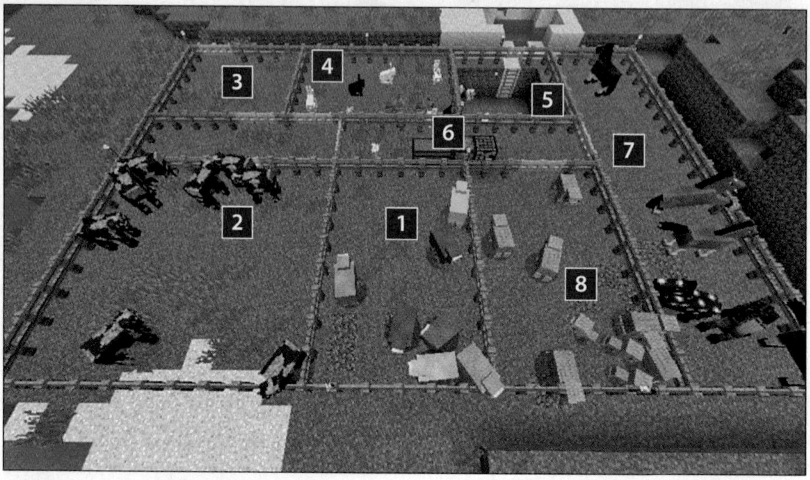

FIGURE 7.1 A passive mob farm.

1. Sheep pen, with sheep dyed in a variety of colors
2. Cattle pen
2. Chicken yard dug down two blocks to prevent them from escaping
3. Double gates in the corral to aid entry and exit
4. Rabbits being wascally
5. Chicken yard with access gained from a ladder against the wall just below the gate (chickens haven't yet mastered ladder climbing)
6. Workshop and storage
7. Horses—stables would make a nice addition
8. Pigs in a pen

Farming involves a few basic steps that I'll take you through in more detail as this chapter progresses:

1 Do like Noah and collect at least two of each creature.

2 Lure them back to your farm, either with food or, even easier, dragging them by the end of a lead.

3 Ensure that their enclosure is secure, with a fence or a two-block-high wall. (Chickens need a two-block-high fence or a three-block-high wall.)

4 Breed the animals using the specific food for the species.

5 In 5 minutes, when they're be ready to breed again, repeat step 4.

6 Wait 20 minutes (24 Minecraft hours), and the newborn will have matured.

You'll have the farm fully established in just a few day/night cycles.

There's no need to go all Texan and build a giant cattle yard. If this is just for your needs and not a cooperative multiplayer game, two breeding pairs of each type provides plenty of resources.

TABLE 7.1 Passive Mob Leading and Breeding Guide

Animal	Lead or Tame With	Breed Using	Provides
Cows 	Wheat	Wheat	Leather, raw beef when killed, and milk
Sheep 	Wheat	Wheat	Raw mutton and wool that can be dyed different colors
Mooshrooms 	Wheat		Mooshroom stew (by milking) and red mushrooms from shearing (found only in mushroom island biomes)
Pigs 	Carrots (or wheat on Xbox)	Carrots (or wheat on Xbox)	Pork chops; pigs can also be ridden with the help of a saddle and a carrot on a stick
Chickens 	Seeds	Seeds	Chicken, feathers, and eggs
Horses, donkeys, and mules 	Right-click with an empty hand to tame; wait until thrown off and then repeat	Use a golden apple or golden carrot with horses and donkeys; breed a horse with a donkey to create a mule	Ride a horse to gain super-fast transport; equip donkeys and mules with a chest for cross-country transportable storage
Wolves (dogs) 	Tame by feeding them bones	Pork chops, raw beef, steak, chicken, and rotten flesh	Tamed wolves will follow you (unless told to sit) and attack any mob that attacks you or any that you attack, or any skeleton that comes within range

Ocelots (cats) 	Approach carefully to no closer than 10 blocks with a raw fish in hand. Wait for the ocelot to approach and don't make any sudden movements; slowly target it with your crosshairs once it is within 3 blocks and feed it the fish (You may need to repeat several times.)	Raw fish	Tamed ocelots turn into cats; both wild and tame cats scare the creeps out of creepers
Rabbits 	As with ocelots, approach carefully with a carrot in hand and follow the same tips as above	Carrots and dandelions	Breed tamed rabbits to create a supply of meat, pelts, and the rabbit's foot that is used in some potions

Farms take a little bit of planning; otherwise, they turn into an exercise in herding cats. (See the ocelots info in Table 7.1.) Ensure that all animals have to go through a corralling yard to actually escape. This is a double-gate system, with the same purpose as an air lock, and can be shared by all pens. It can be quite tricky to get out and close a fence gate with the herd wandering around at random. Herds have a habit of (or perhaps a secret strategy for) preventing you from closing the gate before one or two have slipped through. The second yard stops those that do make a run for it from escaping the farm entirely. You can try to lead them back by enticing them with food, but that just attracts the rest of the group, making for double trouble. Using a *lead* makes it easier (see the next section, "Using Leads"), or you can just treat any escapees as volunteers for the chopping block.

Farm animals don't need to be fed, but wolves do. Their tail acts as a health indicator. If a tamed wolf's tail sticks straight out, it's in full health—its tail gradually drops down as its health decreases. Any sort of meat will do, cooked or not, including the rotten flesh that zombies drop, although they get more hunger points restored from the cooked stuff (just like you do).

TIP

Puppy Power!

When more than one dog (wolf) gets very happy, you get puppies. As of v1.8, you can speed up the growth of puppies—or, indeed, any other animal—by feeding it the breeding item. So, in this case, any kind of meat except cooked mutton will make for happy tails and, soon, a full-grown wolf/dog.

NOTE

Your Farm Is (Mostly) Safe from Hostiles

None of the hostile mobs intentionally attack farm animals, although collateral damage from creepers exploding near you is always a possibility, and if you are caught off guard by a skeleton firing arrows over the fence, you could—I'm not saying you should—use a cow for cover. Keeping wolves around will keep the skeletons away. Heck, they're made of bones! Both wild wolves and tame dogs chase skeletons without provocation, and the skeletons run from them. Wolves also have quite a taste for rabbits and sheep. They'll stalk them in packs if they can and will even cross water to sink in their fangs. Ocelots, on the other hand, enjoy snacking on chickens.

Using Leads

You can always entice a friendly mob to follow you by using the items listed in Table 7.1, but mobs tend to stray after a while, and you will have to constantly backtrack to fetch them. A surer method is to craft a lead from four pieces of string and a slimeball. Right-click to attach the lead to the mob and, if possible, it will follow you, as shown in Figure 7.2. You can also right-click to tie a lead to a fence or post—which is handy to help prevent them from wandering off during the night if you haven't had a chance yet to fence them in. Leads can stretch a maximum of 10 blocks before breaking.

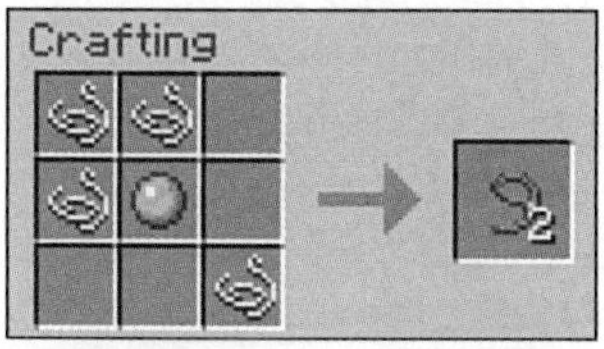

TIP

When Pigs Fly

In Creative mode, any mob you have attached to a lead can also take to the skies as you fly. It looks a little like a fire-fighting helicopter carrying a water hopper, but it can be done. Just ascend gently so the lead doesn't break. A mob will sustain damage and quite possibly die if dropped heavily onto land, and it is difficult to do this gently as they bounce up and down on the end of the lead like yo-yos. It's much easier and safer to drop a mob down into a body of water instead of onto a hard block (so they don't sustain any damage).

FIGURE 7.2 A wild horse on a lead. It doesn't look very wild. In fact, it waits indefinitely, hitched to a fence post, while you go looking for that elusive saddle. While horses don't much like water, they'll happily cross ice.

Breeding Animals

Breed animals by right-clicking on them while holding their favorite snack. You'll know you're on the right track when you see the floating love hearts appear above them (see Figure 7.3). To create offspring, feed two of the same species that are standing close together. Minecraft is genderless, so any two will do. They'll quickly find each other and create a mini-me, although if you continue to hold their food source in hand, they'll be a little distracted, so switch to something less enticing in your hotbar after you've fed them. Infants take 1 Minecraft day, or 20 minutes of real time, to reach maturity.

FIGURE 7.3 Love is in the air for this Miss (or Mister) Piggy.

Breeding two sheep with the same dyed wool results in an offspring of the same color. (If the parents are different colors, the new color is randomly chosen from one of the parents, although there are some combinations that produce a new variant.) Use dyed wool to create colored carpet. While you can do this just by breeding the right sheep, dyes on their own are also incredibly useful—for staining leather armor, dog collars, hardened clay, glass, and banners, as described next.

Dying for Dye?

There are 16 dye colors in Minecraft, made from a combination of original materials and crafting:

Bone Meal	Dandelion Yellow	Light Blue Dye	Orange Dye
Cactus Green	Gray Dye	Light Gray Dye	Pink Dye
Cocoa Beans	Ink Sac	Lime Dye	Purple Dye
Cyan Dye	Lapis Lazuli	Magenta Dye	Rose Red

For example, place a rose on the crafting table to get rose red dye. A dandelion produces yellow dye. The lapis lazuli ore produces a deep blue dye, and cocoa beans produce brown dye. Combine lapis lazuli dye with bone meal to create a light blue dye. While wool and stained clay are limited to the 16 dyes available, armor can be stained using any combination of dyes. An internal formula mixes them up to produce a new color. Recent updates to Minecraft have added new flowers for dyes. Lapis lazuli is also a required component for creating enchantments, so ensure that you conserve some for later. Fortunately, it's easy to gather in large amounts while you're mining close to bedrock.

As just one example, add any dye to a block of white wool to obtain some nice coloration.

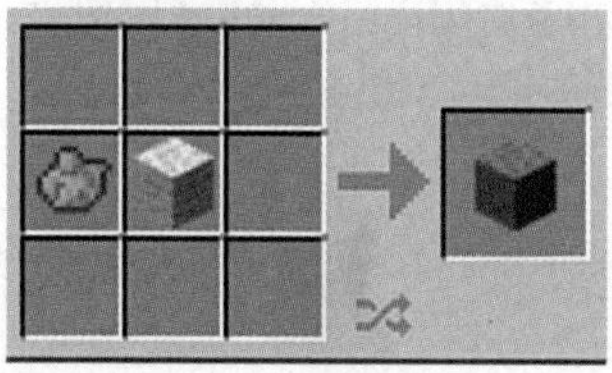

Dyeing is easy. You'll find a comprehensive chart of all the possibilities at the official Minecraft wiki. Jump to http://bit.ly/1khXRGz to view. However, perhaps the most impressive use of dyes and other items is for creating banners. You'll learn all about them in Chapter 8, "Creative Construction."

Taming and Riding Horses, Donkeys, and More

The equine contingent in Minecraft provides the fastest transport available, besides flying in Creative mode. Horses are first past the post in the flying hooves race (660 blocks per minute), and with a speed potion they will run even faster. Donkeys and mules are pack animals, so they plod along a little slower, but they are still quite speedy. You can do anything you would normally do while riding any of these beasts, including fighting mobs, mining, and collecting dropped items. Their additional length also means that you can fly over single-block holes in the ground without fear of falling, and if you time the jump just right, you can leap over much longer gaps.

There is just one associated challenge: You need a saddle to stay on any of the animals for any useful amount of time, and saddles are not easy to come by. They can't be crafted, so instead try looking in the chests located inside dungeons, desert temples, and Nether fortresses, or try trading for one with a villager, as described in Chapter 11, "Villages and Other Structures."

When you're properly equipped, follow these steps (which are identical for donkeys and mules, as shown in Figure 7.4) to acquire your own equine transport system:

1. Find a horse in the wild. This might take some time. When you do find one, assume that you've been smiled on by the mob-spawning gods. Approach it with an empty hotbar slot—in other words, empty hands.
2. Right-click the horse to mount it. You'll more than likely be thrown off , but being bucked off won't bruise you. Keep persevering. It may take four or five tries, perhaps even more. You can sweeten the deal for the horse by feeding it wheat, sugar, apples, or bread between attempts. When the horse displays the love-heart animation, you know it is finally tamed.
3. Open the inventory window while you are mounted or right-click with something held in your hand and transfer the saddle to the horse's own saddle slot in the top left of the inventory window.

Now you have a fully steerable mount. Use the standard movement keys to ride and press the left **Shift** key to dismount.

Donkeys and mules aren't as fast as horses, but they can carry items in chests hanging from their sides. Each chest holds 15 items, so this is a handy mob that can help you bring home your haul.

The heads-up display (HUD) changes when you're riding, as shown in Figure 7.5. A jump bar replaces the experience bar, and the hunger bar and oxygen bars make way for one showing the animal's health.

FIGURE 7.4 From left to right: a horse in iron armor, a mule with chest panniers and saddle, and a camera-shy donkey with the same.

FIGURE 7.5 A jump bar almost fully charged. I find it easiest to release the spacebar when it reaches the end of the blue section. Usually, due to my reaction time, it then hits the fully charged point.

Jumping is easy, but as they say, timing is everything. As you run forward on the horse, hold down the spacebar, charging the jump bar until it peaks all the way to the right. Actually, Figure 7.5 shows the maximum charge with the bar fully lit up. It takes some practice to perfect this, so you might find it beneficial to build a little equestrian park using fences and mounds to create barriers over which you can leap until you have the timing just right.

Horses, donkeys, and mules vary somewhat randomly, and some can't jump as high or as far as others. Horses are the strongest, and the best of them seem to be able to clear a wall 5 blocks high, which is actually quite amazing, given that every other mob except spiders can clear only a single block. Horses can also leap across up to 12 blocks (or so) when running at full speed, although a slower mount won't make it so far.

TIP

Leave the Barn Door Open?

A gap of less than two blocks wide will keep a horse in a pen, but you will need to widen that if you want to ride the horse out and gallop in style.

Although riding a horse at full speed can be exhilarating, avoid doing that in deeply wooded areas where it's easy to become entangled in low-lying branches. It's even hard to ride a horse through deep woods. Hacking through low branches can take some time, and the branches could even kill you. Learn from my mistake! Riding through a thick forest, I got my head caught in a tree and quickly died. Whether I was smothered or concussed, I'm not sure. Once respawned, I had to go retrieve my items *and* search for my horse, which had, naturally, wandered off somewhere. Make sure that your path is tall enough for you *and* your horse!

Armoring Your Horse

Horses differ from donkeys and mules in that they can wear armor, as shown in Figure 7.6. Armor can't be crafted and can only be found in the same places as saddles. Equip a horse with armor by mounting the beast and opening the inventory window. Then transfer the armor to the slot just below the saddle.

Loading Up the Pack

Attach a chest to a donkey or mule to access additional inventory slots. You need to dismount to do this. Right-click while holding something and then transfer the chest to the animal's inventory slot.

As pack animals, donkeys or mules can't be beat; they transport everything you need from one location to another. Figure 7.7 shows an example.

FIGURE 7.6 A horse in full iron armor. There are three types of armor, in increasing damage resistance: iron, gold, and diamond.

FIGURE 7.7 A donkey loaded with all the essentials for an expedition, including crafting table, chests, a furnace, and a boat.

Riding Pigs

Pigs can't fly in Survival mode, but they can be ridden; for a long time, in fact, they were the only rideable entity in Minecraft, and remain the mount of choice for zombie pigmen. There's no need to tame them; just place a saddle on a pig's back and right-click it with an empty inventory slot selected. The pig will move randomly at first, but if you craft and hold a carrot on a stick, you can steer the pig as you would a horse.

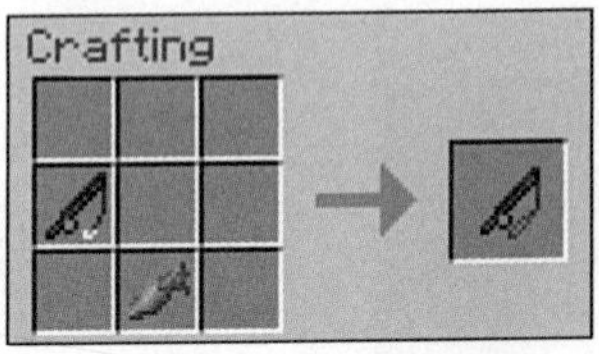

Now that the larger beasts are available, there's not a lot of use for rideable pigs, except for one small trick. Place one in a minecart and jump on its back, and the pig powers the minecart for you. This is another way to get around quickly, especially if you don't have the gold available for powered rails. (See Chapter 9, "Redstone, Rails, and More," for more on railed transport.)

Fishing

Fishing is a great way to ensure a steady supply of food, and it gives you the raw fish required to tame ocelots to turn them into rather cute house cats.

First, build a fishing rod from three sticks and two pieces of string.

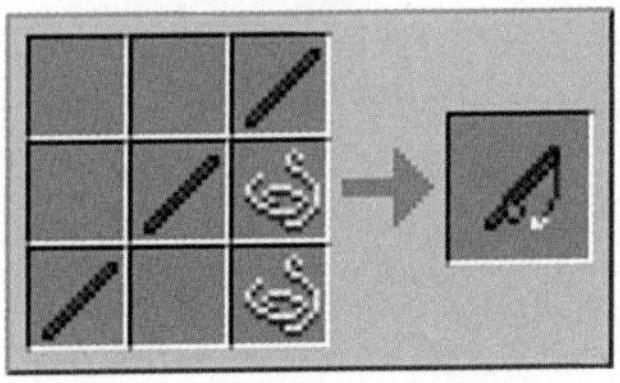

Any body of water will do, but casting in a way that hits a solid block doubles the decrease in your rod's durability, so always try to cast into deep water. You can do this standing on land or in water, or even sitting in a boat.

Watch the bobber carefully. The soon-to-be-ensnared gives itself away with a trail of bubbles leading right to the hook. Right-click as soon as you see the bob dip below the surface to catch the fish.

It's generally best to fish in the rain. You'll catch an average of 4 fish per minute. Otherwise, expect to catch around 2 per minute. Each rod can catch 65 fish before it breaks, and because it's possible for fish to fly back over your head so that you lose the catch, it's usually best to fish with your back against a tall wall.

A safer way to fish is from a boat, as shown in Figure 7.8. The key advantage is that boats provide protection from land-based mobs, and the guardians don't venture far from their quite rare ocean monuments. However, if you do get attacked, you should be able to quickly speed away. Craft a boat with five wood plank blocks. Place it in a body of water and right-click to jump in. Use the **W** key to move forward and steer by pointing the cross-hairs in the direction you want to go and **S** to slow down. Avoid solid blocks while you travel because they cause damage to your boat. Break up the boat with any hand tool when you've finished fishing to pull it back into your inventory.

FIGURE 7.8 After a hard day's mining, why not relax in a boat doing a spot of fishing? Boats also offer very fast transport—which is great if you're near an ocean biome.

Ah, the Squid

There is one other friendly mob: the squid. It can't be bred, so farming is out of the question; but if you kill one, you'll find that its ink sacs do make for a mean black dye. Figure 7.9 shows a squid in the wild.

As of Minecraft v1.8, killed squids drop experience orbs. Other than the experience point bump and the dye sac, the squid provides little other than some animated "color" to your Minecraft world.

FIGURE 7.9 I felt bad about sacrificing this harmless squid, but I really needed the black ink to dye my super-cool leather armor.

The Bottom Line

Friendly mobs are more than just field dressing; they're an important part of Minecraft's gameplay.

If you're lucky enough to spawn in a place with more than a few friendly mobs, go out and hack and slash for some fast food. Then work on pulling in the rest. If you don't see very many nearby, try to resist giving your sword arm a workout. Friendly mobs don't respawn, so the numbers won't increase, and they can go on the endangered list all too quickly. Work on bringing some in and set up a farm.

You'll find sheep and cows heading toward well-lit, grassy areas. Horses do much the same. Ocelots prefer jungle biomes, and chickens seem to be, well, just about everywhere. Oh, and perhaps the oddest friendly mob in Minecraft, the mooshroom, can be found hanging around its namesake: the extremely rare mushroom biome.

Creative Construction

In This Chapter

- Time for a block party! Build your first aboveground base.
- Decorate your pad with chairs, tables, and paintings.
- Chill out Zen-style with flowing water, pools, and fountains.
- Warm things up with a fireplace or two—and don't forget the barbecue.
- Follow the steps to build an underwater abode.
- Protect your perimeter and take potshots at mobs with a water trap.
- Stage a fireworks display to celebrate your completed construction.

This chapter is packed to the brim with construction ideas, from a few starting tips on finding sources of inspiration to a detailed list of all the things you can add that go beyond the basic functional elements.

Construction is easy—basically just put one block on top of another. But take heed: Once you start, it's hard to stop. Every step is like opening another door, and you'll soon find your imagination running riot.

Even if you have no particular architectural talent—and I must confess that I am absolutely astonished by the incredible feats some have achieved with soaring Gothic cathedrals and entire cities that are nothing short of wonderlands—construction starts with a single click.

Leaving the Cave

If you've been busy mining, farming, and doing all the other Minecrafty things that get you established, you probably haven't had the time to build a glorious aboveground structure or to decorate your home with nonfunctional items. Well, now's as good a time as any to take a bit of a break. Unleash Minecraft's bevy of building blocks and unlock your creative potential.

Some of the incredible structures players have already created include:

- Models of famous locations and buildings, including cathedrals, towers, castles, palaces, and cultural landmarks. Think the Reichstag, Taj Mahal, Louvre, Westminster Abbey, Sydney Opera House, Empire State Building, and much more.

- Fictional locations either as faithful replicas or as near as can be achieved, including Tolkien's Middle Earth, Caribbean pirate towns, and, in the ultimate homage, levels and locations from other video games, movies, and TV series, including, of course, *Game of Thrones* (see Figure 8.1).
- Giant pixel art depicting almost anything at all: statues and sculpted creations that are glorious explorations of the maker's creative capabilities.

FIGURE 8.1 King's Landing from Game of Thrones, built in Minecraft with incredible attention to detail. (Image courtesy of WesterosCraft)

The list could go on, but I'll curtail it here. Suffice to say that anything is possible—and probable.

NOTE

Get a Whole New Look with Resource Packs

In a standard installation, Minecraft has an organic, pixelated appearance, but it's possible to completely change the look of every block. Resource packs (which used to be called texture packs) make this easy and can change the way your creation looks from the default to rustic, realistic, modern, hi-tech, or even cartoon-like. Hundreds of resource packs are available. More on this and some handy download links can be found in "Resource Packs: Change Your World" on page 296. If you can't wait to see how these look, click over to http://www.minecrafttexturepacks.com to get a feel for them now. I recommend the Faithful 32×32 for a higher-resolution world with crisper textures and, therefore, a smoother look. Another fun one I like to use when in superflat worlds is one of the many *TRON*-themed resource packs. Try a few, but be warned: Quality varies.

Each Minecraft block is 1 cubic meter, so many replicas are built to a 1:1 scale—even the entire center of historic Beijing, from the ancient city walls torn down by Mao all the way back toward the Forbidden City, with, it seems, every *hutong* in place.

Many of these creations are too much for one person, so they have sprung up on multiplayer servers. Others, though, represent thousands of hours of effort by dedicated individuals who will often then share their maps as free downloads.

So, having set the scene, what's the easiest way for you to get started without necessarily budgeting the next six months to a building project?

You can take several approaches:

- **Extend your current shelter**—Keep all the basics in place while building out and up a little at a time.
- **Start from scratch aboveground**—Pick a location close to your current spawn point or strike out to a better location with your bed in hand to reset your spawn. Figure 8.2 shows an example.

FIGURE 8.2 Home, sweet home, perched far above the madding crowd.

- **Head to the nearest village**—A village is a handy location to set up a home if you don't mind the villagers' constant creaky grumbling that makes them sound like they require a squirt of WD-40. There's often at least one villager happy to swap wheat for emeralds, which you can then trade for more valuable items. You can also harvest their fields of wheat, potatoes, and carrots—and wipe the sweat from your brow while the villagers get busy replanting.
- **Dive**—Not all shelters need to be aboveground or deep in a cave. I've included a tutorial on building underwater later in this chapter.

TIP

Floating Blocks

Minecraft ignores basic physics on almost all the standard blocks except for sand and gravel. This enables the creation of gravity-defying structures. Stack them as high as you like and build a platform to create a structure floating in the sky.

Imagine a fortress connected to the ground with just a single block. It's perfectly possible. You don't need to build up from the ground to start, either. The new **/fill** command is a huge time saver. Its syntax is **/fill XX1 YY1 ZZ1 XX2 YY2 ZZ2 *blockname***, and you can use it to a maximum of 32,768 blocks (32×32×32). You can see the ***blockname*** options under the Name column by opening this link http://goo.gl/QYTVb3.

For example, start a world in Creative mode and then start flying by pressing the spacebar twice, and teleport to a central location by typing **tp/ 0 200 0**. Then type **/fill 1 201 1 32 232 32 minecraft:planks** to create a gigantic 32×32×32 block of planks in the sky. The **/fill** command replaces any other blocks with its own if they intersect its coordinates. Try replacing **minecraft:planks** with a smaller amount of the block **minecraft:tnt** at ground level, and then set it off with a flint and steel, fly up, and enjoy the destruction.

Note that too much TNT will bring your PC to its knees, and once the explosions stop, you may need to back out and reenter your world for it to correctly update the display.

There are as many approaches to building aboveground as there are different worlds in Minecraft. The easy way is to go for a box design. It doesn't take much effort and is something of a natural starting point. You could also go for a walk around your actual neighborhood, grabbing photos with your phone or camera. If you'd prefer not to have a run-in with Neighborhood Watch, check out some online real estate sites. They often have multiple photos and architectural plans. YouTube also hosts numerous videos that players have created to show off their amazing creations.

NOTE

Multiplayer Construction Rules

Multiplayer servers implement different sets of rules around construction with blocks that may be locked down to prevent *griefing* (a.k.a. wanton vandalism by random visitors). Knock a block out, and it immediately pops back. Trusted, or *whitelisted*, players typically gain greater access to allow for cooperative builds, or to build on their own lots. Gaining this trust can be as simple as registering your email address or as complicated as submitting the equivalent of a résumé to prove that you have the necessary construction credentials prior to being let loose. For more information on Minecraft servers, a great resource to consult is *The Ultimate Guide to Minecraft Server*, by Tim L. Warner (9780789754578).

Building a Custom World

Before you learn how to make a world your home, let's examine how to create your own custom world in the first place. Minecraft v1.8 gives you a new world type called Customized, in which you have great control over all aspects of world/biome structure and composition.

Because these world customization options are so comprehensive, it helps to start with one of the seven environment presets already provided. From the title screen, click **Singleplayer**, **Create New World**, **More World Options**.

On the Create New World screen, change the **World Type** to **Customized** and then click **Customize**. You'll see the first of four Customize World Settings screens, as shown in Figure 8.3.

FIGURE 8.3 In Customized mode, you can control just about every environmental aspect of a new Minecraft world.

Click **Presets**. Here you can avoid getting bogged down with making a number of granular choices concerning the presence or absence of strongholds, mine shafts, ravines, and the like. Instead, you can decide on one of the following premade world environments:

- Water World
- Isle Land
- Caver's Delight
- Mountain Madness
- Drought

- Caves of Chaos
- Good Luck

Each of these presets does a good job explaining the kind of biomes you can expect from each.

The Good Luck preset, shown in Figure 8.4, is particularly interesting for experienced players. Minecraft's developers made this world as inhospitable as possible for all but the most diehard (pun intended) players.

FIGURE 8.4 Talk about inhospitable! The Good Luck world customization preset includes tough terrain and huge lava oceans.

Should you decide to forgo using one of the presets, you can turn to the four settings pages that give you full management of world options. Here are some of the major choices, along with their value ranges:

- Sea level: 1–255
- Strongholds: Yes/No
- Mineshafts: Yes/No
- Ravines: Yes/No
- Dungeon Count: 1–100
- Water Lake Rarity: 1–100
- Lava Lake Rarity: 1–100
- Biome: All/individual biomes

- Caves: Yes/No
- Villages: Yes/No
- Temples: Yes/No
- Dungeons: Yes/No
- Water Lakes: Yes/No
- Lava Lakes: Yes/No
- Lava Oceans: Yes/No
- Biome Size: 1–8

You'll also notice that the Basic Settings page has a handy **Randomize** button, which gives you a "roll the dice" approach to world generation. If you've decided to let Minecraft generate your world according to its natural order, click **Defaults** and be done with it.

Cool! Now that you know how to generate a world that is more to your preference, it's time to turn your attention to how you can inhabit that world with style and grace.

Unleashing Your Interior Decorator

Not everything in Minecraft has to be functional. Figure 8.5 shows all kinds of components that can be put together in different ways to create a homey ambience, both indoors and out. While it's a little frustrating that you can't sit at a table or relax on a lounger, furniture stills makes a very nice addition to any home.

FIGURE 8.5 An open-concept living area with a wide-screen TV, modular lounge with coffee table, sun bed, dining table, and fireplace. There's also a kitchen tucked in the back-right corner.

I've put together a collection of different ideas for you, but this is also one of those areas where your own creativity and experimentation come into play. Try out some of these in a world set to Creative and let the juices flow:

- **Chairs**—Chairs are made from staircase blocks. Craft a staircase from six wood blank blocks. The chairs can be as long or as short as you want, from single seats to a modular lounge. Place signs or trapdoors (in their open position—right-click to toggle them) on the sides to create armrests. Extend the base of the chair with a slab to create a deck-chair effect that's perfect around a pool or on a sun deck. Figure 8.6 shows a view of chairs around a dining table (see the next bullet).

NOTE

Placing Signs

Signs placed against a block attach to the side of that block. Signs placed on top of a block become freestanding, with their orientation fixed so that they face toward you when placed.

- **Dining table**—Create a table by placing a single fence block, which becomes the stand. Then place a pressure plate on top of the post to form the table's surface. Pressure plates don't create a seamless surface, so for larger tables, consider using squares of carpet instead. Surround the table with a few chairs to complete the picture. If you make a giant dining table, use regular blocks and then place pressure plates or carpet as placemats. Remove some squares of the table's surface and pop some cake down in their place to finish the picture.
- **Beds**—Think of the standard Minecraft bed as just the starting point. Put two side by side for a double, or make a king size bed out of three and some blocks behind for a headboard. Then place some slabs at the foot to get the proportions right.
- **Bedside table**—Use a standard construction or wood block or a bookcase—anything that matches your color scheme. Then put a torch on top, in the middle of the block. The torch will burn permanently, but if you put a redstone torch in the middle and then a lever on the side of the block, you'll have a light you can switch on and off. Replace the redstone torch with a redstone lamp for much brighter lighting.

FIGURE 8.6 A dining table with Marie Antoinette–approved centerpieces. Let them eat cake.

- **Indoor plants**—Choose a plant such as a flower, sapling, cactus, or leaf block cut from a regular tree with shears or a tool enchanted with silk touch. Pick a base block such as grass, dirt, or sand, plant it, and attach signs or trapdoors to its sides to give it a nice boxed look, as shown in Figure 8.7, or create a flower pot from three bricks. Smelt clay to make bricks, arrange them into pots, and plant flowers, saplings, ferns, and mushrooms (see Figure 8.8).

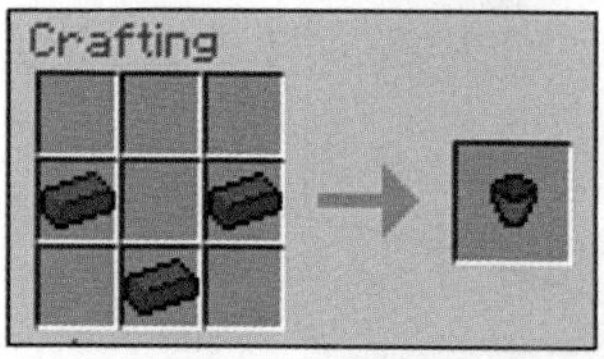

- **Hedges**—Leaf blocks also work well in decorative construction. Use them to build hedges lining a path or parkway. You can even use them for the walls of a tree house. The blocks won't decay, unlike regular leaf blocks that are no longer attached to their trunk. Gather leaf blocks from trees by snipping them with shears.
- **Fantasy trees**—Use wood and leaf blocks to create unique trees dotted around your estate. You can even place them inside a giant atrium to create your own Crystal Palace.

FIGURE 8.7 Planter boxes and hedges add a leafy touch to rooms and balconies. It's safe to plant saplings indoors because they won't grow without empty blocks above.

FIGURE 8.8 Flower pots are decorative planters. Place them on almost any surface.

- **Item frames**—Crafted from eight sticks and one piece of leather, item frames serve a decorative and practical purpose as single-item storage. Place a frame on any wall and then take the object you'd like to store in hand and right-click the frame to place it inside. Store that enchanted diamond sword you plan to save for later combat, or maybe a diamond pick for when you need to retrieve more obsidian. Left-click the frame to retrieve both it and the object later, or right-click the item in the frame to rotate it through eight possible orientations. Use an item frame and a clock to create a wall clock, or place a map in the frame for permanent reference. The map updates to show the locations of all other item frames containing maps, making it the only way to actually place a "pin." Make a grid of multiple frames and maps to create a single seamless picture of your entire explored domain.

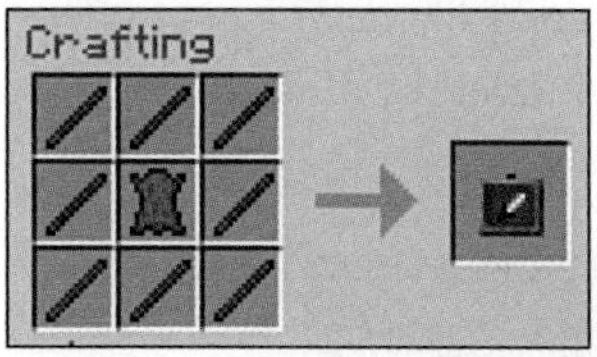

TIP

Opening the Door to Style

Minecraft has six types of wooden doors, as well as one made from iron. The standard door is made from oak, but you can also use spruce, acacia, dark oak, jungle wood, and birch. Choose the right material to match the door to your building's style.

- **Paintings**—These are purely decorative. You create them with the same recipe you use for an item frame, but with the leather swapped for any piece of wool. Placing paintings is a little bit random because Minecraft tries to scale up to suit the flat space available, with some limits. There's a built-in inventory of 26 pieces of art in different shapes and sizes, although the art itself varies with different resource packs. One way to try to force a painting to be sized a particular way is to first surround the target area with other blocks and then click in the lower-left corner of the target space and remove the additional blocks. It doesn't always work, but this is a little less random than other methods, although there's nothing wrong with placing, removing, and repeating until you've found the best image and fit.

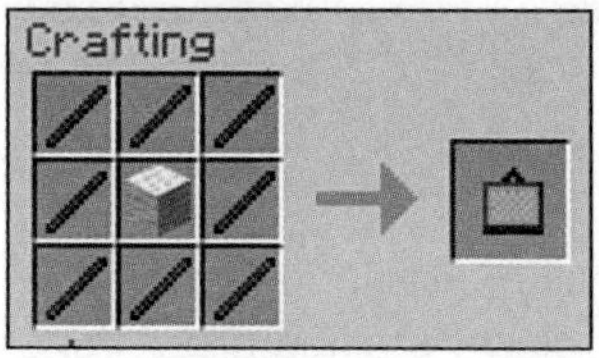

- **Fountains**—Build fountains as simple or complex as you like. Place a water source on top of any other structure. Glass blocks work quite well for this, but any block will do. Create a hollow fountain by removing the blocks after you've placed the water. The original water source will stay elevated in its original position. Also, don't forget to put a surround around the base so the cascade doesn't turn into a flood. Figure 8.9 shows an example.

- **Ponds and pools**—As long as water drops one level every seven blocks, it can flow on forever from a single source. Take advantage of this to create water features that flow down and through your house into a pond. Add a few floating lily pads to complete the effect. Pools are a nice touch that can look good surrounded by almost any smooth blocks, especially with the addition of deck chairs, mentioned above.

FIGURE 8.9 This small indoor fountain feeds the swimming pool located on the recreation level of the house.

- **Netting and wisps**—Cobwebs gathered with shears or silk touch can stand in as netting between two posts. Tennis, anyone? Use redstone to draw lines on the court. Cobwebs can also suggest smoke billowing from a chimney, or you can use them for lashings and cargo nets on ships.

TIP

Getting Colorful

Minecraft includes a collection of stained objects that are all craftable in Survival mode and easy pickings in Creative. These include stained glass, stained glass panes, stained clay, colored carpet tiles, and colored wool blocks. Use these to add a dash of color to every structure.

- **Bookshelves**—Although bookshelves have an official use for enhancing enchantments (see Chapter 10, "Enchanting, Anvils, and Brewing," for the full details and crafting recipes), they're also excellent decorative items. Stack them up where needed to build a library or add some interesting ambience to any living room. Slabs also work well and are easier to make than a bookshelf item. Stack them up to create multiple shelves and dress the sides with regular blocks or just run them straight to the wall to make them appear as built-in shelves.
- **Raised and lowered floors**—Slabs are half a block high, making them ideal for creative flooring and embedded fixtures. Although items placed on a slab seem to float, two sets of slabs can lead down to a sunken lounge or an indoor pool. And if your design extends to the bathroom, create a slab floor and leave a one-piece hole against the wall. Place a cauldron in it and fill it with water to make a recessed sink, then attach a lever to the wall with the handle facing down to simulate a spout. Using slabs is also a useful way to hide redstone wiring. They'll float one block up, with the redstone running underneath and out of sight, saving an additional layer of trench digging. More on this in Chapter 9, "Redstone, Rails, and More."
- **Fireplaces**—You need to know just two things about fireplaces. Netherrack (a block from The Nether) burns forever. Set it on fire with a flint and steel and bask in the glow. The other thing, perhaps slightly more important, is that fire is catching. Don't surround your fireplace with wood blocks. As a matter of fact, don't have anything flammable within at least two blocks—or more, just to be sure. Use nonflammable materials such as cobblestone and bricks. A fireplace looks great with a glass pane in front of it (see Figure 8.10). Fireplaces also make pretty decent firepits or barbecues (see Figure 8.11). S'mores, anyone?

FIGURE 8.10 A modern fireplace set inside a wall with a glass pane in front. The fire provides a dynamic animation, making a room feel warm and alive.

FIGURE 8.11 This barbecue is made from a mix of brick blocks and staircases. Note that the trapdoor, like a door, doesn't burn, so it is safe to position it above the fire. You can also use iron trapdoors for the grill if you prefer that look.

NOTE

Baking Your Own Banners

A banner is like a coat of arms that you can design yourself—a heroic heraldry, if you like, or just a statement or personal mark. You can plant banners on almost any block, facing in any direction, or hang them from walls and even transfer them onto shields. They are crazily customizable, and once you have created your own design, no matter how many steps it took, you can copy it quite easily to new banners. Figure 8.12 shows a variety of them, but the possibilities are almost endless. For inspiration, check out the ever-changing list at http://www.planetminecraft.com/banners, along with step-by-step instructions on completing each. You'll be amazed at the creative possibilities.

Blank banners are crafted from six blocks of wool and a stick. Dyeing the wool first by combining white wool with dye or breeding colored sheep also changes the banner's background color.

Build a banner from that starting point by adding various patterns and graphical adornments. You can add up to six additional layers by using the flag again each time in the crafting grid.

The additions include a wide range of block-type patterns that can form stripes, crosses, and so on, and more specific graphics from a selection of in-game items. Look to http://minecraft.gamepedia.com/Banner for the full compendium of banner recipes.

FIGURE 8.12 Banners provide a uniquely personalized decoration to Minecraft. You can hang them, have them freestanding, or even add and rotate them within an item frame.

Construction is one of the indulgent pleasures in Minecraft. In Creative mode, you'll have access to the full range of available materials, but there is also something to be said for building an amazing structure in Survival mode. Having to find the materials first really adds to the experience.

Building Underwater

There's not a lot of justification for undertaking the effort to build an underwater house, except for that most important of reasons: because you can! It's a fun challenge. An underwater house provides great visibility, is immune to hostile mobs, including the creeper, and, well, is just pretty darn cool. Building this type of house can take a little bit of extra work, but it's fairly easy, and you can let your imagination take you anywhere you want to go, from the equivalent of a reversed aquarium, with you as the soul internee, to a full remake of Bioshock's Rapture. Figure 8.13 shows a small underwater base.

Building underwater is a methodical process. The trick is to consider it the inverse of mining. Instead of removing material, you actually want to fill in the entire shape of your structure to displace the water, place the final shell of the building around that (for example, glass blocks), and then remove the internal material to create the living area. There's no method of pumps or pipes to suck water out or pump air in, so this displacement system is the only viable method.

There are a few ways to go about it. In Creative mode, it's pretty much a matter of taking the time and a bit of care. You can stay underwater as long as you need.

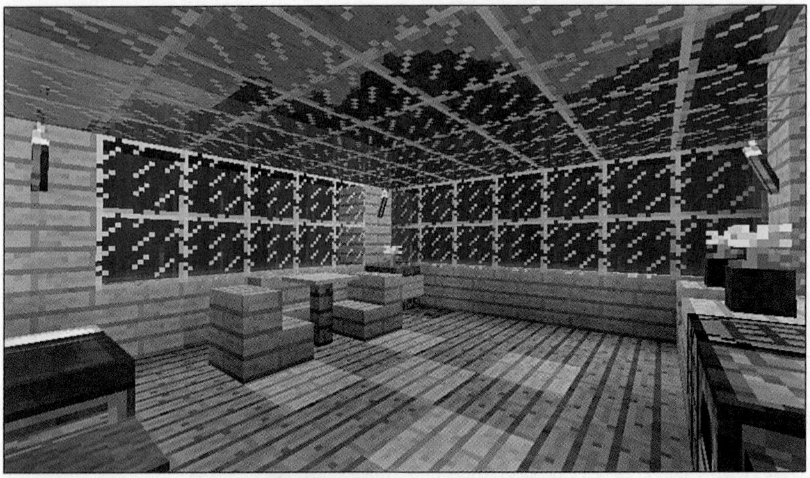

FIGURE 8.13 Make like a dolphin and head underwater to build your aquatic base.

Survival mode adds a twist because running out of air is a constant risk. It becomes vitally important to keep a close eye on your oxygen bar and health bar. Swimming up from the bottom of a lake *always* takes longer than expected, causing hits on your health, so the real trick is to find a way to create an air supply down below.

At a minimum, ensure that your kit includes these items:

- **One bucket**—Crafting a bucket takes just three iron ingots and provides you with the equivalent of a limitless tank of air.

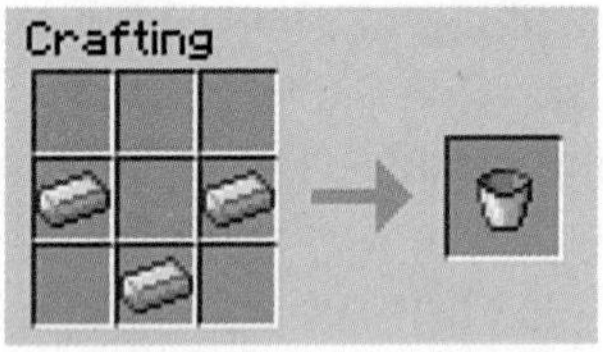

- **Doors, ladders, and signs**—These blocks displace water but leave space for you to stand and grab a breather. You can make do with just one of any type, but it's best to pack a few.

- **Light sources**—Torches go out in a soggy fizz as soon as they hit water. Jack-o'-lanterns work best and can be smashed up and repositioned as required. Glowstone from The Nether also works well. See the "Light Up Your (Underwater) Life" tip, later in this chapter, for another option.

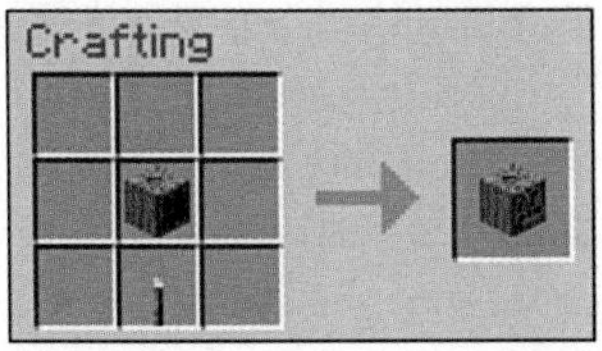

- **Construction equipment**—Bring the usual suspects—a couple of shovels for digging sand, dirt, and gravel, as well as some pickaxes for the harder stuff. Having an axe also makes it easier to reposition other equipment, such as doors.
- **Soft blocks**—You need several full stacks of dirt, sand, or gravel as temporary filler material to remove the water from your construction. By the way, I use the term *soft blocks* to refer to the temporary blocks you'll use during construction—those you can remove quickly with a shovel while underwater.
- **Construction materials**—You need lots of glass blocks for the outer shell, as well as any other material you want to use.
- **Food**—It's important to keep a full hunger bar underwater so that your health recovers quickly if you run out of air.

TIP

Survive with an Island Spawn Point

Underwater construction can be a hazardous business, so place a bed nearby and take a nap before you begin. If your spawn point is nearby, you can get back down quickly enough to pick up any dropped items should you suffer a watery demise. If you are building too far offshore, use a boat to return quickly or build an island platform on the surface, perched on top of a single block tower. It just needs to be big enough for a bed and a torch to prevent mob spawns at night. Alternatively, find a good location and type **/spawnpoint** to reset your spawn to your current position.

Getting Started

There are plenty of methods for getting started, including tunneling in from the side of a lake, but these aren't always practical. The most comfortable I've found is to jump right in. Here's how:

1 Find a location. You need a body of water that is at least four blocks deep. This gives you two blocks of standing room, a glass roof (because it looks awesome), and one block of water over the top, but you may also want to go deeper. There are no practical limits; the only concerns are having sufficient air and light, but keep the structure on the conservative side initially. Figure 8.14 shows the exterior view of the structure you already saw in Figure 8.13.

FIGURE 8.14 Keeping your initial structure to a conservative size helps you get used to building underwater while providing plenty of room to breathe. This one is 9x9x3 high.

2 Keep the bucket handy in your hotbar, along with a door or three. If you are using ladders or signs, have some soft blocks and either of those at the ready.

3 Head to the bottom and keep a close eye on the oxygen bar. It depletes in 16 seconds. As it drops, take a practice breath. Right-click with the bucket selected to create a brief pocket of air. If it doesn't work on the first go, click again. Once you start the cycle, it takes one click to empty the bucket and one more to refill it, so as soon as you get used to the double-click, you shouldn't have any problems grabbing a quick gasp to fully reset the oxygen bar in a split second.

4 Place the door as soon as you reach the seabed (see Figure 8.15). If you are using ladders or signs, create a stack of two blocks and then put the ladder or sign on the top block. Any of these actions creates a permanent air pocket you can step into to breathe. Incidentally, jumping into a lake with any of these items at the ready is also a good way

to escape hostile mobs at night, and you can poke at the bottom sides of any curious creepers that swim by. What's not to like?

FIGURE 8.15 Doors create a two-block-high breathing space. The jack-o'-lantern provides a waterproof source of light.

TIP

Light Up Your (Underwater) Life

Things get gloomy in the deep. Anything over seven blocks down comes close to pitch black, even during the day, and torches need a full block of clear air to stay lit. How can you light up the murky mire? Jack-o'-lanterns and glowstone both work well, as does the sea lantern found in ocean monuments. Another option: Change your screen settings. Press **Esc** to open the Options menu. Select **Video Settings** and shift the **Brightness** slider all the way to the right.

Light tunnels also work well. Place blocks and ladders above your first air-pocket block until you reach the surface. The light flows down the tunnel, brightening up the sea floor, and provides a convenient access shaft for your submaritime traversals, as shown in Figure 8.16.

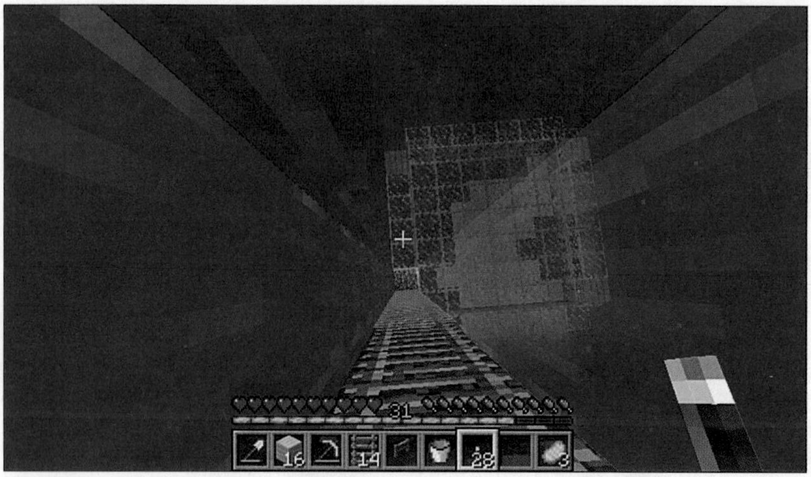

FIGURE 8.16 Looking down a long access ladder from the sea's surface to the undersea dwelling.

Building the Structure

Now that you have a survivable location on the seabed, it's time to get started on the structure. Building underwater takes a few steps and a lot of care:

1 Plan the perimeter. I find it easiest to create an air tunnel around the edges by using dirt blocks and ladders at eye height, and I fill in the interior as I go. Figure 8.17 shows an example. All the ladders are recoverable later, and I generally put them on the interior wall so that I can work on the exterior without worrying about removing a ladder and getting swamped by an inrush of water.

FIGURE 8.17 A one-block-wide tunnel and ladders keep the water at bay. I've removed all the stray water sources in the lower half of the tunnel by swamping them with sand blocks dug out earlier.

2 As you fill in the interior, also start building up the external shell on the outer side of the tunnel. Use your final construction materials such as glass blocks because this will form the permanent structure. Keep some soft blocks at the ready to plug up any water breakthroughs. The wall only needs to be two blocks high. Given that you're on the bottom of the sea, you can always dig down later to create more height. Place some torches as you go to create additional light, although know that they won't attach to glass.

NOTE

Flooded In? Head to the Source

It's quite usual to find your tunnels still half flooded even after all the walls are done and every ladder is in place. The damp ankles are caused by water source blocks that still exist on the floor of your perimeter tunnel. To remove them, place any kind of soft block wherever you can see anything that looks like the head of the water spring. This kills the water source, and you can then quickly shovel out the soft block. Repeat until all the source blocks have been extinguished and your tunnel has dried. The sponge block found in ocean monuments (and dropped by the monument's elder guardians), or in the Creative inventory, also makes it easy to soak up water across a larger area. In Survival mode, a used sponge becomes a wet sponge that must be dried in a furnace before reuse.

3 With the interior full and the external wall done, attach the ceiling. This is easy. All you need to do is jump out of the tunnel into the water and run backward across the interior fill, placing blocks as you go. Unless you've planned an enormous structure, it's easy to do a row or two without having to stop for air, but keep your bucket handy just in case. Fill in any gaps you spot in the interior as you go. You're almost there!

4 Dig out the internal material to fully open the space. Breaking up the soft blocks dislodges the ladders so they can be scooped up into your inventory and perhaps used to create a laddered pillar all the way to the surface.

5 Make an access point. You can place a door or just use a pillar and a ladder outside the wall. Add some finishing touches to the interior, and you're done!

Once you've built this one room, the rest is even easier. Place a bed down in your new home and sleep in it to reset your spawn point to the ocean floor. Then you can take it bit by bit. You should have just about all the materials you need, except maybe wood. And you are on the ocean floor, so there's plenty of sand for glass, and there's nothing stopping you from digging straight down and mining other materials as required.

NOTE

Underwater Enchantments

Several enchantments and potions help with underwater work. The most important is the respiration enchantment, which applies to helmets and increases the length of time you can breathe underwater while also reducing suffocation damage. In addition, like the night vision potion, it improves your underwater vision. The second is water affinity, a speed boost for tools when they're mining underwater. Finally, the depth strider enchantment applied to boots enables much faster walking when underwater.

One of the key advantages of underwater dwellings is that they don't require protection against mobs, at least not until the squids launch their revolution. But houses on land do. Let's look at some key strategies for protecting your other perimeters.

Protecting Your Perimeter

There's nothing worse in the Minecraft world than stepping outside your front door only to hear the quick hiss of a creeper's fuse running down and finding two seconds later that a massive crater has replaced half your house. (Creepers can take out a dirt block that measures 5×5×5.) If the explosion doesn't kill you, the next influx of hostile mobs probably will. In any case, rebuilding will be a painful experience, especially if you've gone all out with a delicately aesthetic blend of textures and materials. (A cobblestone wall—okay, that's not so bad, but that's the Building 101 course.)

There is an easy way to step out in the morning and enjoy a breath of fresh air without a pang of fear interrupting the ritual. It's the perimeter—your stake in the world. Varmints, be gone!

Become a Ditch Witch

Ditches provide protection without interrupting the view. They were even a feature of English country gardens, known as the *invisible fence*, designed to keep the sheep from trampling the peonies without the fence line blotting the landscape.

In Minecraft, no mobs can cross a ditch that is two blocks deep and just one block wide except for cave spiders, but they usually exist deep underground. However, creepers can still detonate when close. Build three blocks deep, and they won't trouble you unless you fall in. Or dig two blocks deep and put a fence around the inside edge of the ditch. You won't need to worry about an inadvertent stumble, and creepers will stay nicely defused.

So what about spiders? I don't worry about them too much. They're easy to kill, don't explode, and provide string for bows, fishing rods, and, with sufficient numbers, enough string to make the wool for a bed—handy if sheep aren't around.

TIP

Mobs Go with the Flow

Place water sources in strategic locations in the ditch to wash the mobs downstream, away from critical areas (see Figure 8.18). This can help you build a smaller perimeter because you can force the hostiles to bunch at the far end of your property.

If spiders still give you the shivers and you want to keep your AAA insurance rating, build a ditch for all other mobs and then a wall behind it, with an overhang. Get a little fancier by making the middle layer of the wall iron bars or a glass pane so you can still look out on the marauding hordes.

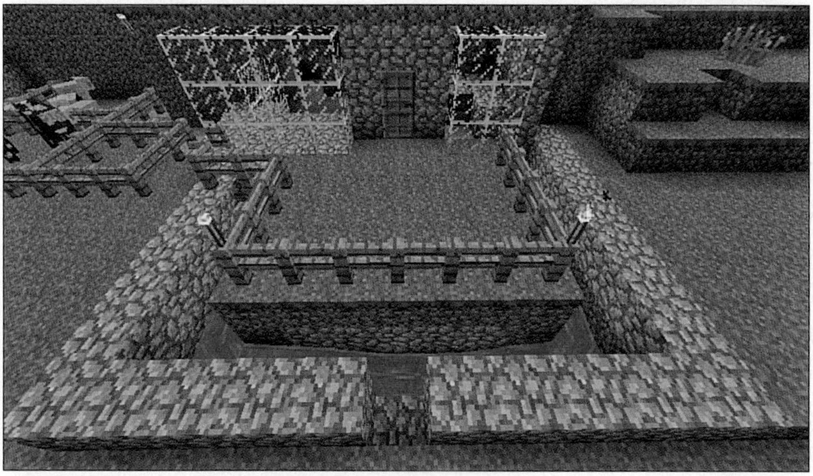

FIGURE 8.18 A ditch with water flowing to a central point (the middle front here) sweeps any mobs away from the entrance so they can exit through the gap in the front.

CAUTION

Knobble Their Knees

The ditch gathers all kinds of mobs. Some, such as zombies and skeletons, burn up during the day, but others, such as creepers, stay put. Leave an easy egress of steps out of the ditch to the exterior if you want your ditch to self-clear and aren't using the mob pit and water-clearing method described later, in the "Mob Pitfalls" section. Or cut in a tunnel under the wall at eye level for you and knee level for the mobs so that you can hack at their feet to collect their drops while being safe from attack. This works best if the tunnel is two steps back from the edge of the ditch so that creepers don't detonate. Your sword can still reach them just fine.

Alternatively, put your house in an unassailable position atop a small stone tower. Enter through a door in the base, build a stairway or ladder going up at least three blocks (or many more, if there's a good view!), and create as large a platform as you like. The overhang from the platform keeps spiders at bay. Use other perimeter fences to provide protection for farmland if you don't want to build them all in the air.

CAUTION

Don't Forget the Torches

It's easy to forget, while focusing on the defensive perimeter around the house, that an unlit roof also provides a mob spawning platform at night. If you're wondering how that spider surprised you in the bedroom, it could be that it simply dropped from the sky and climbed in through that opening you left leading out onto a sunny morning verandah. Always place a few torches on your roof to keep things clear. Torches can also help you spot home when you're out exploring.

Mob Pitfalls

Mobs may be a nuisance, but they're also a boon as they carry all sorts of useful items, from enchanted weapons to food. Why not reap the benefits of their fall?

Here's how to do it:

1. Dig a ditch two blocks deep and nine blocks long around your perimeter.
2. Create a vertical pit in the ninth block. The most effective height is a drop of 22 blocks because this leaves spiders, skeletons, and creepers with just one point of health—enough to dispatch them with a single punch and gather the resultant experience points that help with enchanting and anvil repairs. However, if you don't mind using weapons instead, the pit can even be just two blocks lower than the water flow.
3. Place a water source at the other end. It flows for 8 blocks, pushing mobs toward the pit. You can also place a second water source coming in from the other direction, providing a total of 19 blocks of coverage around your perimeter, and the water can flow around corners if required.
4. Choose a safe location inside your perimeter or even inside your house and tunnel down toward the bottom of the pit so that your eye height ends up at the same level as the lowest part of the pit. Any mobs that stray into the ditch gradually wash down toward the pit, fall in, and gather at the bottom. Head down the access tunnel to safely finish them off and collect the spoils. Figure 8.19 shows a trapped creeper.

FIGURE 8.19 Creeper knobbled: The water keeps it in place while attacked, and the water washes its drops (gunpowder in this case) toward you.

> **TIP**
>
> **Ding! Your Zombies Are Ready**
>
> For extra points and convenience, add a pressure plate to the bottom of your pit, connected to a redstone lamp sitting somewhere in normal sight. When a mob hits the bottom of the pit, the pressure plate sends a signal to the lamp, lighting it up. Be sure to use normal wooden or stone pressure plates. Weighted pressure plates only react to items, not mobs.

If you have no particular interest in collecting mob drops, fill the pit with lava. Keeping a mob's feet to flame will see the mob off quite quickly, but it also burns up any items. You can also use cacti in the ninth hole of the ditch to serve up death by a thousand cuts. Just place a cactus block instead of digging the pit but keep in mind that cacti can also destroy any dropped items.

Thick as a Brick

The defenses previously mentioned are designed to keep mobs at a distance, but the final line in the sand, or cobblestone, will be your own building's walls. This is also an aesthetic choice. Design your castle's keep, so to speak, more than one block thick. A direct creeper hit can take out a couple of layers of cobblestone and up to five layers of other materials. If you really do want that log cabin look, consider creating a sandwich of wood outside, an internal cobblestone section, and then a wood interior. Switch these around to suit your own needs. A couple of layers of external cobblestone with a wood interior is much safer than a single layer of wood. Sandstone has little blast resistance, so definitely create a three-ply if you like the sandstone look.

Keeping with the concept of a castle's keep, attack is also part of any defensive strategy. Knock out a 1×1 block in a wall and then fill with a slab, leaving just a half-block gap. Fire arrows at targets through the slit. You'll have an excellent field of fire, and skeletons will have a much more difficult time getting a clear shot at you.

Finally, obsidian is the toughest material you can mine in Minecraft. It's a little difficult to collect, but you'll find a guide that makes it easy in Chapter 10.

Making Fireworks

What better way to celebrate your construction than with a grand opening replete with fireworks?

Fireworks are easy to make and even more fun to set off (see Figure 8.20). They're created through crafting: You first make a firework star and then turn that star into a rocket. You can add optional colors, effects, and a shape for the burst at the same time, and then you can include an optional fade with the firework in a further crafting operation. There are numerous combinations of ingredients, so I'll provide a quick decode here. Table 8.1 shows the prototypical examples for each step. Each recipe is shapeless, meaning the ingredients can be placed in any position on the crafting grid.

FIGURE 8.20 Fireworks are a perfect addition to any celebration. Hello, July 4?

The firework star uses a basic recipe of gunpowder and any combination of up to eight dyes. Build in either or both of the two explosive effects at the same time that you're creating the firework star, using the following:

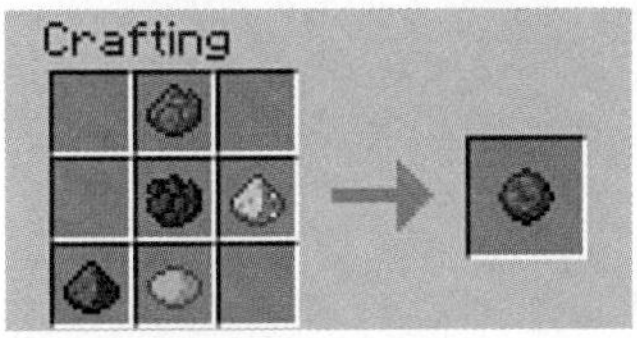

- **Trail**—Add a diamond gem to the base recipe to create a trail behind the burst particles when the firework explodes.
- **Twinkle**—Add glowstone dust to the base recipe to cause the particles to crackle before the firework fades.

Adding one further ingredient to the same recipe gives the firework a shape other than the default small ball:

- **Large ball**—Add a fire charge to give the firework's explosion a much larger radius.
- **Star shape**—Add a gold nugget to give the explosion a star shape.
- **Burst**—Add a feather to give the explosion a random effect.
- **Creeper shape**—Add a mob's head (you can find them in the Creative inventory) to make the firework explode in the shape of a creeper.

If desired, place the completed firework star and any dye on the crafting grid to add a fade effect with a secondary color.

Transform the completed firework star into a rocket by adding up to three gunpowders and a piece of paper. To launch the firework, right-click on the ground at night, in an open area, with the rocket held in hand. Or you can load it into a dispenser facing sideways or upward and then activate the dispenser, or an entire string of them. Add repeater delays between dispensers and various timed loops to create your own fireworks display. See Chapter 9 to learn more.

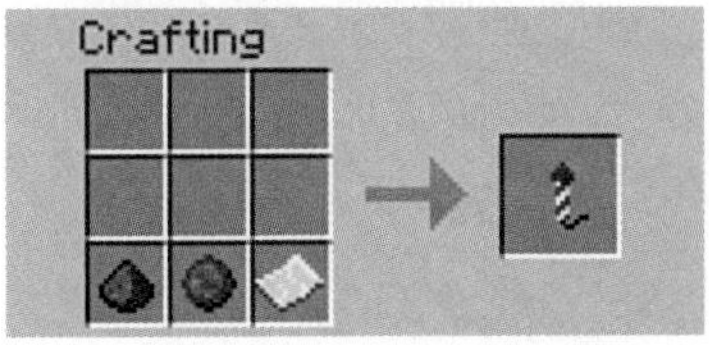

TABLE 8.1 Firework Recipes

Type of Firework	Ingredients	Recipe	Description
Firework star	Gunpowder and up to 8 dyes	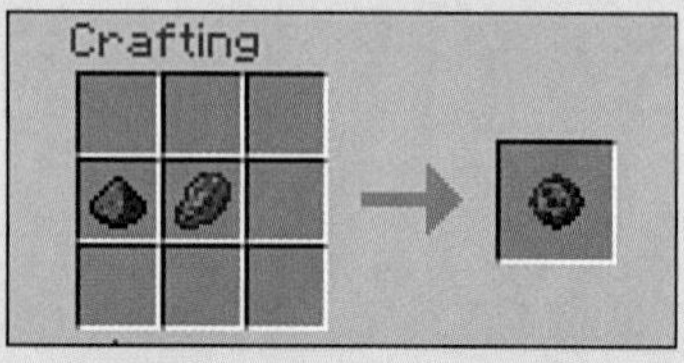	Creates a basic firework star that will explode with the selected colors.
Firework star with effect and shape	Gunpowder and any dye, as well as items required for effect and shape	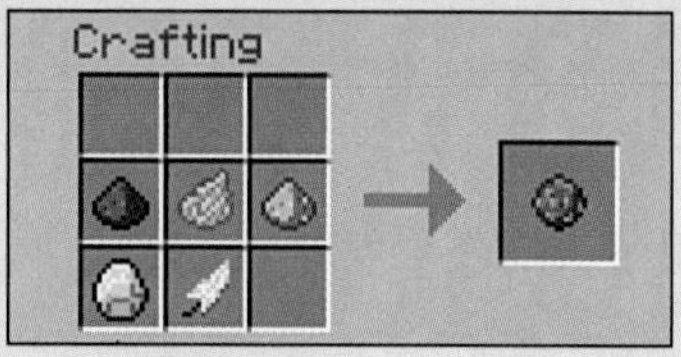	Creates firework star with an effect and shape such as a firework star with a yellow color, trail and twinkle effects, and a burst shape.
Firework star with fade color	Firework star and up to 8 dyes	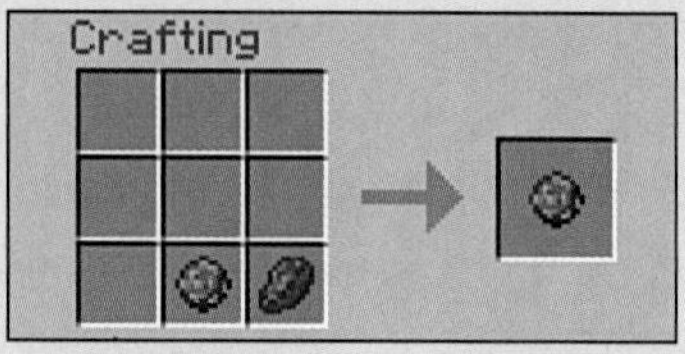	Adds a fade effect to the firework, into the colors indicated by the placed dyes.
Rocket	Paper and up to 3 gunpowders	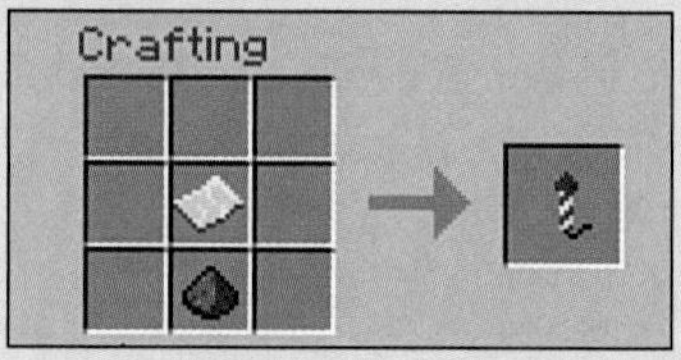	Creates a basic rocket that will fly into the air, leaving a trail, but without any firework explosion. Add additional units of gunpowder to make the rocket fly higher.
Firework rocket	Firework star, paper, and up to 3 gunpowders	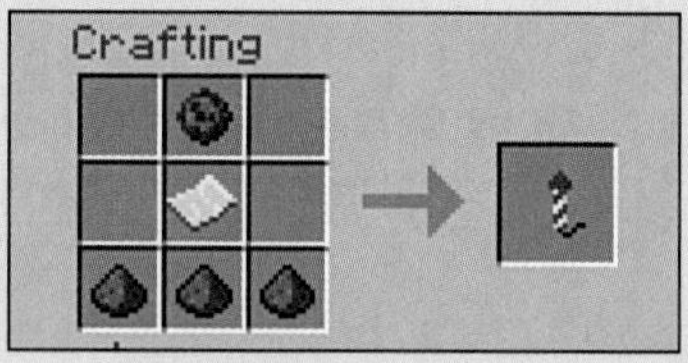	Creates a firework rocket with the effects of the included firework star. Increase the explosion height by adding more gunpowder. 1 or 2 gunpowders is usually sufficient, and 3 gunpowders gives a height that is quite difficult to see from the ground.

The Bottom Line

It takes a little bit of time to build a beautiful home, but it does provide a pleasant interlude between mining, farming, and fighting mobs. Enjoy the time. As you master the different techniques, you'll no doubt develop your own and create soaring, graceful masterpieces in the sky—or under the sea.

This chapter has been about letting your imagination take flight. In the next, you'll explore a completely different side to Minecraft: redstone and transport. It may be enough to make you think about all construction from a different perspective.

Redstone, Rails, and More

In This Chapter

- Create automated contraptions with redstone power sources and components.
- Build cool circuits with redstone wiring.
- Understand different types of power to avoid wiring problems.
- Create perimeter warning systems, piston-powered doors, repeater loops, and more.
- Learn to use AND, OR, and NOT gates.
- Use redstone to build powered rails for a minecart transport system.
- Hop into hoppers to automatically load and unload items from containers and carts.

Redstone and rails create an entirely new Minecraft experience.

- *Redstone* is one of the ores you probably have seen in mines. When dug out and placed on the ground, it provides a way to transmit power between different devices, like a strand of electrical wire. It's used for operating pistons, controlling doors, and doing all sorts of other neat tricks.
- *Rails* are tracks on which minecarts run, and when those rails are powered by redstone, they provide a system like an electric train track that can transport goods between different areas and also give you, sitting in a minecart, quite a thrill ride.

It's a brilliant, almost magical system that makes some real-life parallels with electrical circuits but is different enough to be absolutely confusing, even baffling, at the same time. It will challenge you to rethink everything you already know. Is it worth the effort? Absolutely.

The trick to understanding redstone is to try your very best to not bring any real-world assumptions with you. It's a different type of energy than electricity. For example, it runs on a single strand so doesn't have positive and negative wires, and it can be created by many types of devices, even a lever stuck in the ground, or a wooden button attached to the wall. Redstone has its own rules, its own behavior, and its own results. Some of those are almost beyond imagination. I'm betting when the folks at Mojang started thinking about adding a few logic circuits to redstone, they didn't think someone would spend possibly months of his life building a simulacrum of a computer, complete with a 1,000-pixel graphical display, the entire system filling hundreds of acres and using tens of thousands of components.

In the same way that the building blocks of Minecraft deliver an architecturally infinite construction playground, redstone adds a whole new dimension. In some ways, it harks back to the genesis of the electronics industry, simulating the breadboarding of electronics with wires and vacuum tubes. Very retro.

This chapter is an introduction to redstone and transport. It teaches you the essentials, and you won't need an engineering degree to succeed. Even if you're not switched on by some of the more complex aspects of this extraordinary system, it is definitely worth coming to grips with a few core techniques. They go well beyond the water harvester from Chapter 6, "Crop Farming," and you'll have fun exploring this creative new world.

Seeing Red: A Beginner's Guide

Certain aspects of Minecraft are completely intuitive and can be understood through the usual process of discovery. Redstone is different, but getting a handle on it isn't so hard. The complete redstone system is made up of just a few core concepts: power sources, wire, modifiers, and output devices.

TIP

Use Creative Mode

I recommend that you test and explore this chapter in a world set to Creative mode and perhaps even Superflat, using the Redstone Ready preset. It's just so much easier as a learning exercise to place and wire up components, including the more exotic ones, this way.

Once you get a grip on redstone essentials and start to figure out how to put these building blocks together into more interesting systems, you will never think of Minecraft the same way again.

Power Sources and Signals

Power sources provide the energy to power devices or to signal that an event has occurred, such as a mob (or someone in Multiplayer mode) stumbling over a tripwire. Figure 9.1 shows the complete set of power sources.

FIGURE 9.1 Redstone power and signal sources.

1. Redstone torch
2. Redstone block
3. Tripwire with hooks shown on either side
4. Wooden and stone buttons
5. Daylight sensor
6. Lever
7. Wooden and stone pressure plates
8. Detector rail
9. Iron and gold weighted pressure plates

Signals and *power sources* provide the same redstone energy and are somewhat interchangeable as terms, but consider signals to be intermittent, providing that energy when an event occurs, such as someone or something stepping on a pressure plate. Power sources provide a continuous flow of power, like a signal switched on permanently. Here's the most essential information on each type of signal or power source:

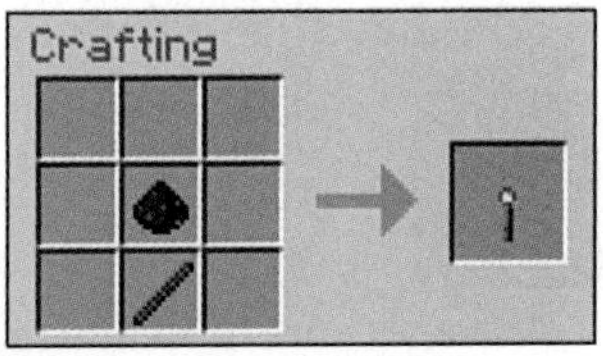

- **Redstone torch**—The torch is Minecraft's electric utility. It's clean, green energy, even if it's red. It provides a continuous source of power but also has a few handy tricks up its sleeve. Feed a power source into a torch, and you will be able to turn the torch off and on, making it a useful switching mechanism for almost every circuit. You'll see many examples of this later. Craft a torch from a stick and a chunk of redstone.

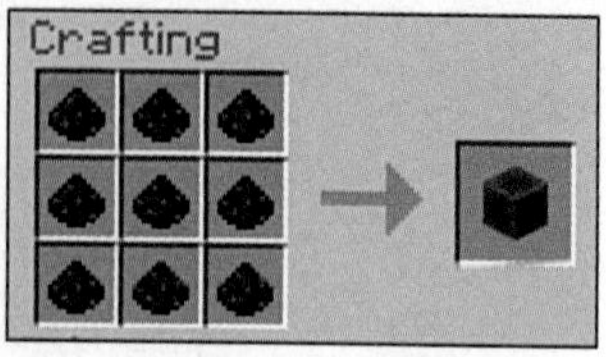

- **Redstone block**—A redstone block is crafted from nine pieces of harvested redstone. It acts as a continuous power source to any nearby wiring, modifiers, and devices. It is also the only power source that can be moved by pistons, which turns a block into a handy mechanical junction box. Redstone blocks are useful for storing large quantities of redstone ore. A stack of 64 redstone blocks can hold up to 576 pieces of ore in a single storage slot in your inventory or a chest.

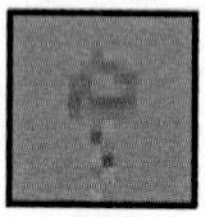

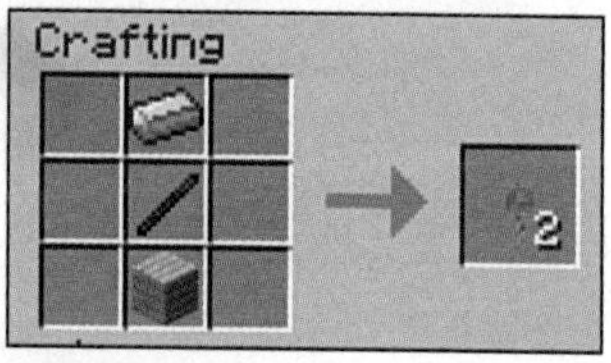

- **Tripwire hook**—Use string and two tripwire hooks to create a devious detection system, with two tripwire hooks placed up to 40 blocks apart in a straight line. Join them by placing string between. The string creates a tiny, difficult-to-see texture between the hooks, making it a favorite trap creator. It's also an efficient way to "string up" a perimeter alarm. The hooks generate power while any mob is standing on or in the same block occupied by the string. Elevate a tripwire to one block above a minecart track, and it can detect a minecart carrying a mob, including yourself, making it an easy way to separate minecarts by load and switch tracks, shunting items in one direction and players in another.

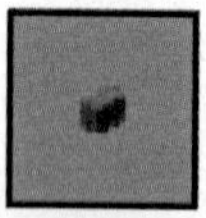

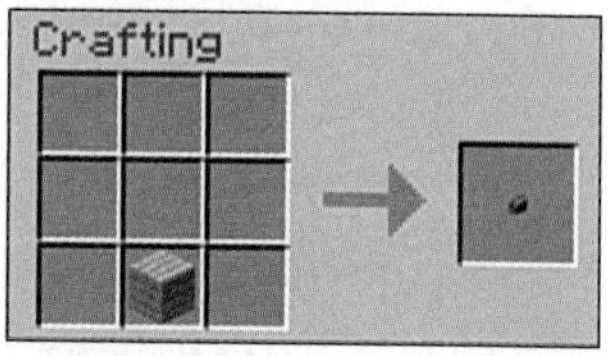

- **Button**—There are two types of buttons: stone and wooden. A stone button provides a 1-second pulse of power. A wooden button delivers a pulse for 1.5 seconds and, if you're a sharp enough shot, you can activate the wooden button by shooting it with an arrow. For an extra challenge, try doing that while galloping by on horseback. Craft a button from one wood plank block or a block of stone obtained by mining stone with a pickaxe charmed with silk touch or by smelting cobblestone back into a stone block.

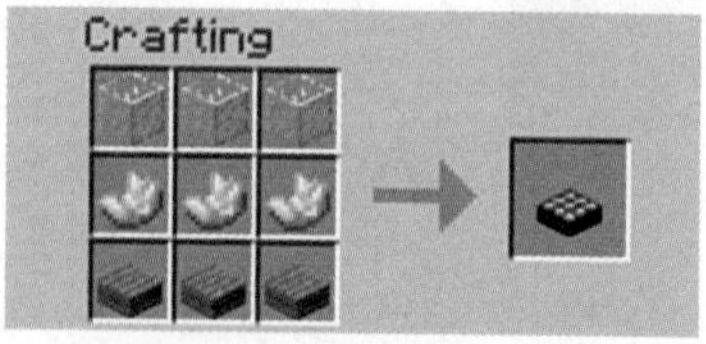

- **Daylight sensor**—These sensors act similarly to a solar panel, outputting a current directly proportional to the amount of daylight they are currently receiving. You'll need Nether quartz, wooden slabs, and glass blocks to build one. Right-clicking a daylight sensor causes it to invert and change color slightly and become a night-time sensor that sends out full current in pitch-black and none in broad daylight.

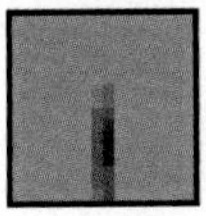

- **Lever**—A Minecraft lever acts like an on/off switch, but spruced up with its own built-in power generation. Like buttons, they're also safe from being flipped by any of the nonplayer mobs. Wire up a set of levers as described under "Redstone Wiring," later in this chapter, to create a secure keypad entry.

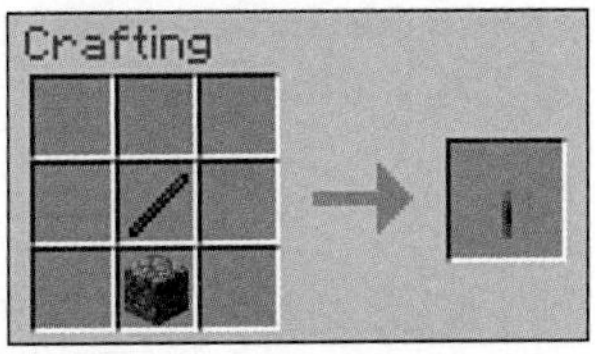

- **Pressure plate**—Like buttons, pressure plates come in wood and stone variants. Both varieties deliver continuous power while activated. Stone plates react to mobs and minecarts containing mobs; you can also activate a stone plate with a low-level fly-by in Creative mode. Dropped items, all minecarts (regardless of contents), lures on fishing rods, and arrows all trigger wooden plates.

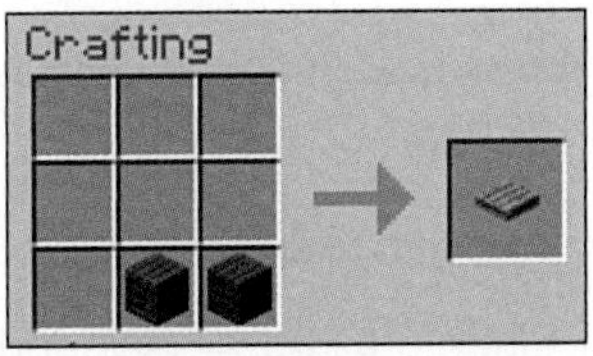

- **Detector rail**—Detector rails send off a signal as a minecart rolls over the top. You can use them to switch tracks, turn off other powered rails to prevent collisions, open doors, fill and empty hoppers, and so on. Connect a comparator to a detector rail to trigger a signal that can shunt full minecarts in one direction and empty ones in another. This is useful for shunting aside empty minecarts, ready for reuse, while sending a full one (one that you might be riding) to another destination, such as a train station, but there also are many other ways to use them.

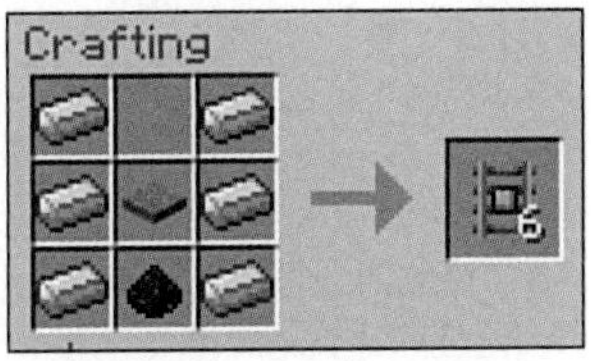

- **Weighted pressure plate**—Although similar to a standard plate, a weighted pressure plate emits a signal of strength 1 to 15, according to the number of items on the plate. There are two versions. The gold plate, made from two gold ingots, is more sensitive, stepping the signal 1 lever for every 4 items placed. The iron plate, made from two iron ingots, jumps the signal output every 42 items. The plates can count dropped items, but the items must be loose and risk despawning unless they're sucked back up into a hopper. They also can work for creating a lock where placing a particular weight of items unlocks a door, or even for creating a payment system in an adventure map. A sign placed nearby might say "Place eight gold bars on the plate to move to the next stage."

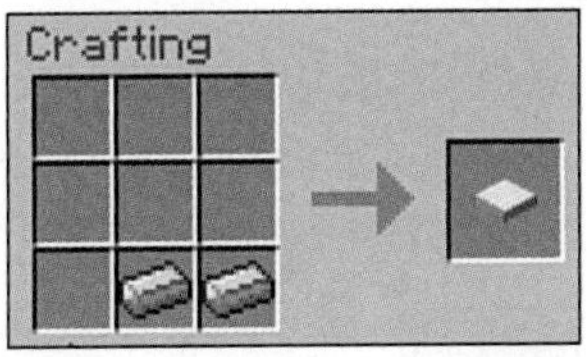

CAUTION

Don't Run Off the Rails

Pressure plates disrupt a contiguous minecart rail, so they are most reliably used at the end of a line. Detector rails and tripwire are often better alternatives.

TIP

Trapped Chests in Multiplayer Worlds

Place a tripwire hook and a standard chest on a crafting table to create a trapped chest. This sends a signal when opened and is great for Multiplayer mode. You can use the signal for almost anything, from kind intent to evil. Play a happy note from a note block or slide open the floor under the player's feet to boil him in a lake of lava. You can be as nice or as diabolical as you like.

A trapped chest has a small red square surrounding the latch that may send a warning to an alert player. Place a sign on the front to hide the texture. (You'll need to *sneak place* by holding down the **Shift** key while right-clicking.) The text is up to you, but saying "FREE TOOLS; HELP YOURSELF" or "DIAMOND STORE" can be devilishly effective. A small amount of the red texture remains visible but probably won't be seen by a marauding player intent on stealing your cache. You can also hide the texture entirely by digging a hole and sinking the chest into the ground.

All other containers (the chest, hopper, furnace, dropper, dispenser, jukebox, and brewing stand) also emit signals that vary in strength according to their contents. Tap the signal with a redstone comparator, described later in the chapter, to turn it into an output that you can use elsewhere.

Redstone Wiring

You harvest redstone from redstone ore with an iron, gold, or diamond pickaxe. When placed on the ground, the redstone transforms into a trail, also called *redstone wire*, that carries power or signals between other components.

Redstone wire has some interesting properties (see Figure 9.2):

- Laying a trail is quite easy because the wire automatically connects adjacent nodes. Just click on blocks where you'd like to place the wire, and it bends around corners, goes up and down solid block ramps, and creates three- and four-way junction points, as required. It's sticky stuff, so prevent separate circuits from connecting by keeping them separated by at least one block, or they'll join together to form a lattice. If space is tight and you must run two separate strands side by side, use a parallel run of repeaters instead.

- Water and electricity don't mix—but not as dangerously as in our physical world. Water just washes away the redstone wire and other devices, turning them back into collectable items. Be prepared to climb over or tunnel under any water blocks.
- Powered wire sparkles with a red glow that gradually diminishes until the current runs out in 15 blocks. You need repeaters or torches to boost the power for longer circuits, as described later in this chapter.
- The current runs in the space above the block on which the trail appears but provides power to the block underneath and the block directly in front of the end of the wire. Redstone powers the blocks on which the wire is drawn but conducts the power through the block above that. Think of the wire as actually occupying the space above its depicted location. That space must be contiguous, with the exception of slabs or transparent blocks such as glass, ice, leaves, and glowstone. Figure 9.3 shows a blocked current.

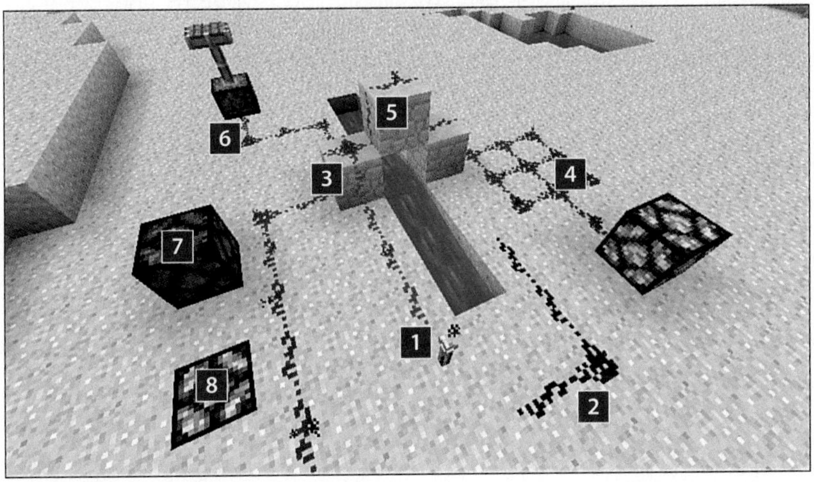

FIGURE 9.2 Redstone properties.

1. Powered wire emits a glow and sparkles.
2. Unpowered wire has a dull red color.
3. Wire transforms automatically into junctions as you place nearby nodes.
4. Connecting nearby blocks creates a lattice but continues to transmit power, without short circuits.
5. Wire can climb up and down blocks arranged in a stair-step pattern.
6. Devices can activate at the end of a wire at the same level...
7. ...but don't activate when placed next to an adjacent wire.
8. Wire powers the block below, lighting up this adjacent glowstone lamp that is sunk one block into the ground.

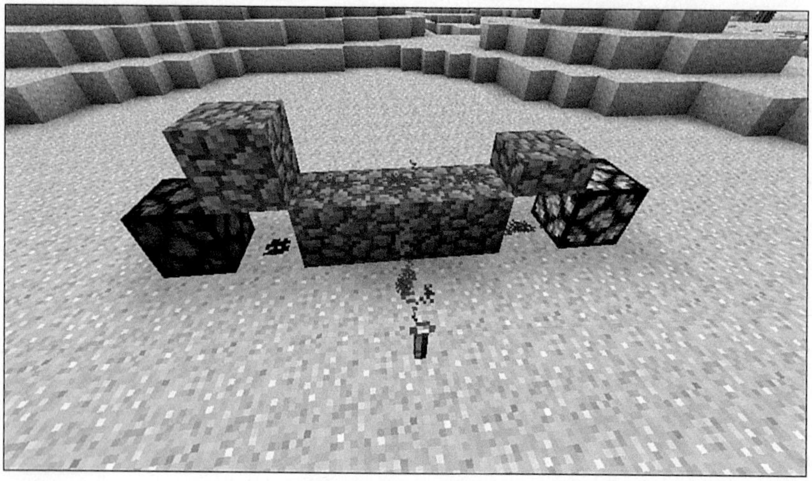

FIGURE 9.3 Blocks can break a wire's current: The block on the left prevents the current from flowing down and to the glowstone lamp, while the slab on the right (taking up just half an actual block space) allows the power to flow through it and down to the ground, lighting up the lamp. Replace the interfering block with a slab or a transparent block if keeping a similar texture is important.

Powered Blocks

Redstone power propagates from the source as *strong power*. Strong power can light up redstone wire and activate devices. Feed strong power into a normal opaque block such as dirt, cobblestone, or wood, and that block will propagate *weak power*, which can only activate devices. Basically, weak power is not strong enough to reconnect with a redstone wire and continue acting like a partial insulator. Figure 9.4 illustrates this concept.

It's also worth mentioning that a wired connection between a power source and a device isn't always necessary. Most of Minecraft's blocks—the opaque ones—can be powered directly by a source. This enables the creation of very small circuits. I included one example of this in Chapter 6, where the piston was powered by a button placed on a block. You'll see some other examples later in this chapter.

Most redstone sources are attached to a block of some kind. For example, buttons are placed on the vertical surface of a block, such as a wall, a lever to any surface, or even the ceiling. Generally speaking, the source powers the block to which it is attached (the *anchor* block), and this can then activate any devices adjacent to it. This is why a button placed on a block beside a door opens that door. It's not the button acting directly on the door through some hidden link. Rather, pushing the button powers the block to which it is attached, and that block being adjacent to the door triggers it to open.

FIGURE 9.4 Strong and weak power.

1. The cobblestone emits weak power, sufficient to activate the lamp and other devices but not enough to power the wire leading to the second lamp.
2. Running wire over a block continues the current through the space above the block.
3. The lever provides strong power to the block, firing up the wire.

NOTE

Torches Power the Block Above

There is an important exception to the rule about redstone devices powering the block to which they are attached. The redstone torch provides strong power to the block directly above it as well as to adjacent redstone wiring and devices—but not to the block to which it is attached. That said, feeding another source of power into that block, such as from a button, lever, or wire, causes the redstone torch to turn off, allowing it to act as an inverter.

Now, here's the important part. All sources except the redstone block also strongly power the space they occupy, not just the anchor. (Redstone blocks are anchored on themselves, so they only provide strong power to the space they occupy.) This provides a choice of two blocks to which you can attach components: either the anchor block or the block occupied by the power source item. Figure 9.5 shows how this works.

Keeping the two-block rule in mind gives you many more options for linking components and running circuits. In other words, more power to you!

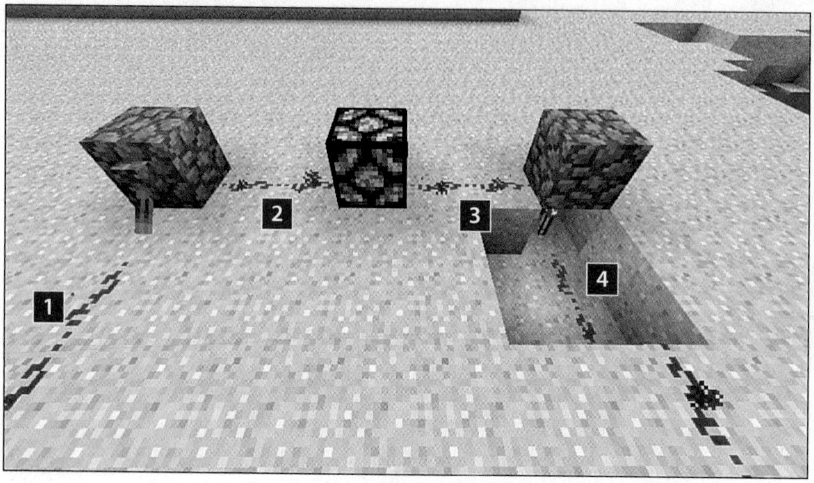

FIGURE 9.5 Sources provide strong power to two blocks each.

1. This wire is powered by the space occupied by the lever.
2. This wire gets its power from the block the lever is anchored to.
3. Redstone torches power the block above, so this wire gets its power from the cobblestone block above the torch.
4. The torch also powers the space it occupies, firing up this redstone wire.

Modifiers

Modifiers change the current in useful ways but can also be more than a little confusing. Don't worry if it doesn't all make sense right away. A little practice goes a long way. There are two types of modifiers: repeaters and comparators.

Repeaters

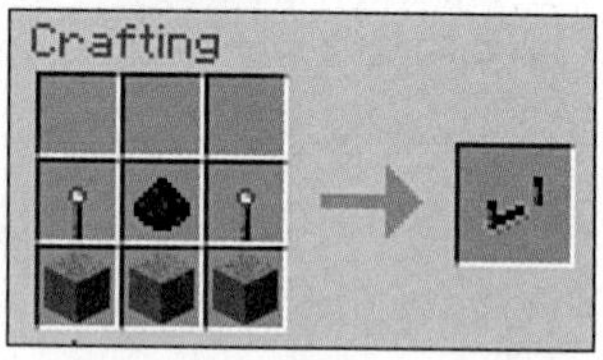

Redstone repeaters can amplify a strong or weak current and add a 0.1- to 0.4-second delay that is useful for adding timing to circuits. A repeater also acts like a diode, ensuring that current flows in only one direction.

The power-boosting function allows current to flow through solid blocks such as walls without finding a way to go over or under them. This in itself can solve some otherwise difficult design problems. Figure 9.6 shows two examples.

FIGURE 9.6 The repeater on the left picks up the weak current reaching the block and amplifies it back to strong. Without this, the block just emits a weak current that's insufficient to light the wire on the far left. The repeater on the right turns the block into a strong emitter, lighting up both redstone trails.

A repeater's current always flows in the direction of the single fixed light on the repeater. You may be able to make out a faint triangular texture on top of the repeater that shows this direction. Place the repeater facing in the direction you want the current to flow, and it will align correctly.

Right-click the repeater to add a delay to the circuit. The default is 0.1 second, increasing to 0.4 second with each right-click until the light has slid fully back to the base of its channel.

Repeaters are also useful for running current in tight spaces because they can be placed next to each other without forming the lattice effect that placed wire develops. Place them in series, as shown in Figure 9.7.

Repeaters have one other useful feature: You can T-bone one repeater's output into the side of another, and any power applied to the first locks the output of the second. This creates a latch—and, quite literally, something that can be used to provide a master lock for a door or even to create a 1-bit memory cell (see Figure 9.8).

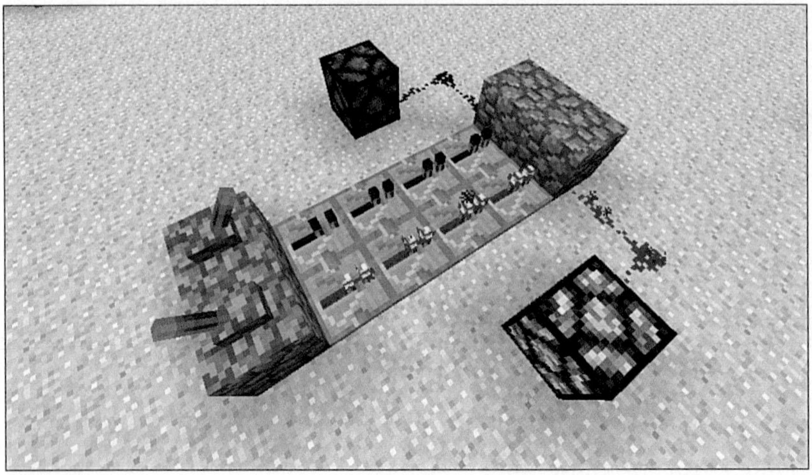

FIGURE 9.7 Two sets of repeaters keep current separate. Terminate the sets with blocks and use the sides of the blocks to run the separate strands to their destination.

FIGURE 9.8 The back repeater has latched the front repeater in a power-off state (shown by the block across the top that replaces the sliding torch), even though power reaching the repeater would normally flow through and light the lamp.

Comparators

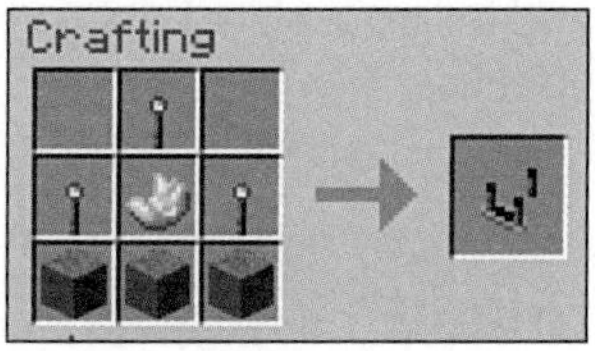

A redstone comparator increases or decreases an output signal according to the strength of the input signal. Comparators can check the contents of a chest, hopper, furnace, dropper, dispenser, jukebox, or brewing stand. They can also compare the relative storage of each and then trigger another function, such as making a railcart with a hopper move to another location for unloading (see Figure 9.9). Comparators also "read" the rotated position of an item stored in an item frame and deliver a current that ranges from a value of 1 to 8. The examples that follow show a few more useful scenarios. The comparator requires Nether quartz, which is available only in The Nether region.

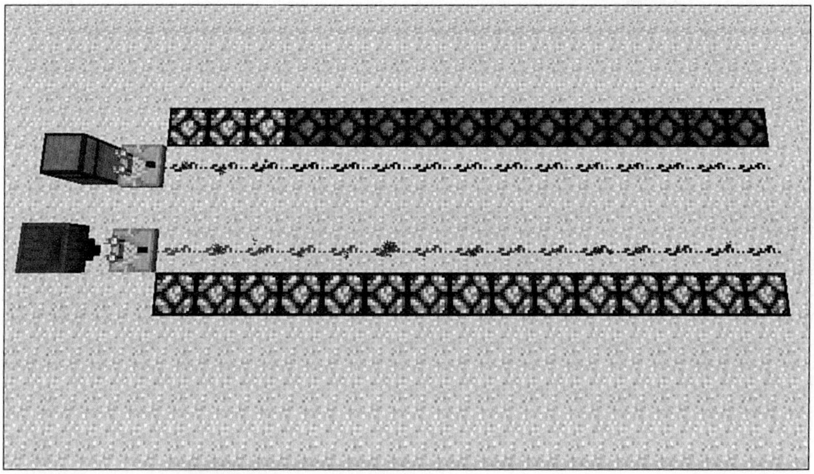

FIGURE 9.9 Comparators report inventory contents by emitting signal strength equal to the number of slots available in that item divided by the number of full slots available, converted to a percentage out of 15. The hopper and the chest shown here each have 5 full slots. Because the hopper also has only 5 slots available in total, the comparator issues a 15-strength signal, or 100%. The chest has 27 slots in all and is approximately 18% full, so the rounded emitted signal strength is 3.

Comparators always output a signal the same strength as their input signal unless they also receive a side signal, which can be delivered by any input source. In this case, they operate in two modes:

- **Compare mode**—If the side signal is greater than the input, the output is zero. In all other cases, the input equals the output.
- **Subtract mode**—If the side signal is lower than the input, the output is the input minus the side signal. In all other cases, output is zero.

As of Minecraft v1.8, redstone comparators can detect which way an item frame is rotated and deliver a signal that ranges from 1 to 8, according to the item's position. Dimmer switches, anyone?

This is a lot to take in, understandably. Some examples later in this chapter will help.

Output Devices

All of Minecraft's power sources, wiring, and modifiers are a bit useless without the circuit actually doing something. Minecraft provides a large number of devices, activators, gadgets, and more. Figure 9.10 shows the full set, described in the following list:

FIGURE 9.10 All of Minecraft's output devices.

1. Redstone lamp
2. Iron and wooden doors
3. Trapdoor (available in wood and iron variants)
4. Fence gate
5. Regular and sticky pistons
6. Powered rail
7. Dispenser
8. Hopper
9. TNT block
10. Note block

- **Redstone lamp**—The lamp, as you've seen from many of the figures in this chapter, is a handy tool for checking the output of circuits. It also happens to make a pretty good light source, although crafting one requires glowstone from The Nether. Glowstone is plentiful, but obviously you'll have to venture into The Nether to get it.

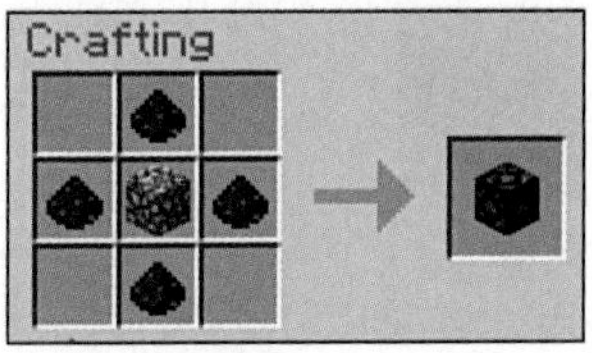

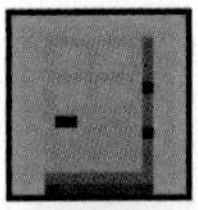

- **Doors**—Doors are the *de rigueur* entryway. Doors come in iron and wood variants and switch between a fully open or closed state instantaneously, meaning one can't hit you on the rear on the way out. Iron doors can only be opened with some sort of power input. They also keep zombies out when you're playing on Hard difficulty.

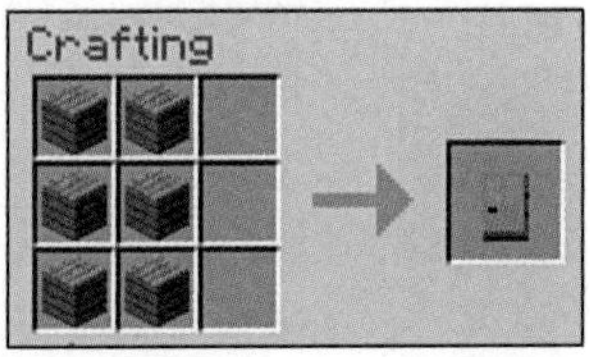

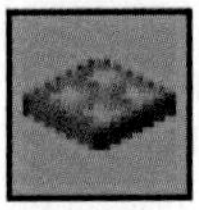

- **Trapdoors**—Trapdoors aren't going to trick anyone when used in a trap, but they're still handy. A pressure plate in front of a trapdoor will save you from fumbling for a right-mouse click. Iron trapdoors require power to open, similar to an iron door. They are crafted from iron ingots placed in the same pattern as planks for the wooden trapdoor.

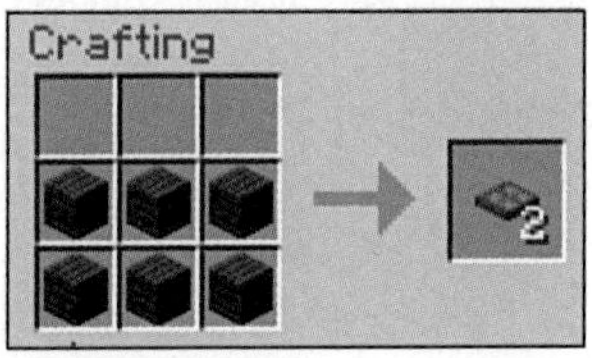

- **Pistons**—Both the regular and sticky variants are incredibly useful. You'll see some examples soon.

- **Powered rails**—Sure, you can power a minecart by jumping on board while riding a pig, but is that any way to get around? You'll be the laughing stock. Powered rails provide a more stylish way to move you and your minecarts from A to B.

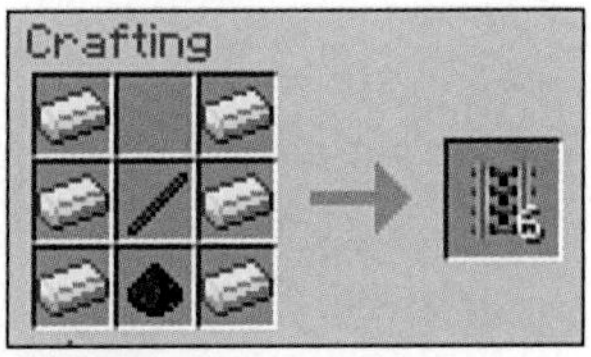

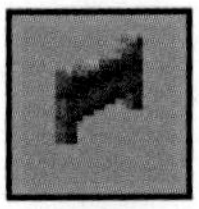

- **Fence gates**—They open, they shut, and they're good for keeping livestock in place. Place two fence gates beside each other to create a larger opening that is easier for larger livestock to navigate through. Fence gates are opened with a right-click but can also be powered with redstone, such as from a pressure plate.

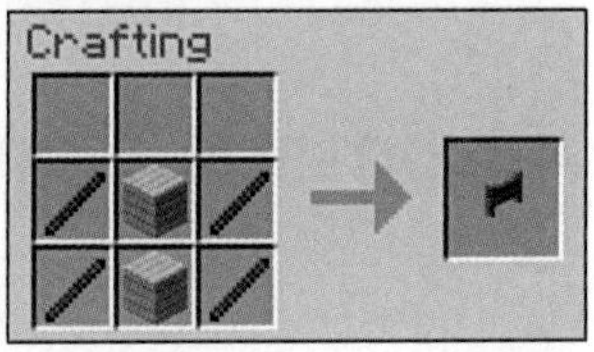

- **Dispensers**—A dispenser pumps out almost anything that's been put inside it. Typically used for firing arrows, supplying a flood of water or lava, and, well, an enormous range of other things, dispensers are an indispensable (sorry) part of any automated system. Place flint and steel inside a dispenser to make it shoot out a tongue of fire; then place a pressure plate in front and wait for mobs to wander by. (And try to not laugh evilly.)

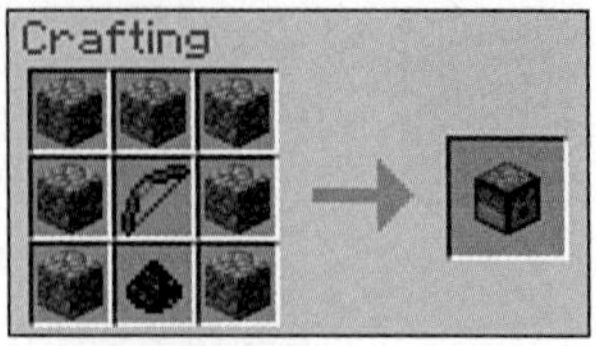

- **Hoppers**—Hoppers move items between other objects. Although hoppers don't rely on power, they'll stop transferring contents out or in when they receive a redstone signal from the side.

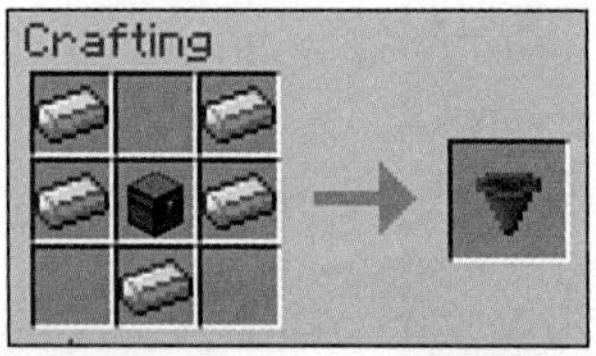

- **TNT**—TNT is the most destructive force in Minecraft, except for a creeper that's been hit by lightning, but that's incredibly rare. Set it off with a power pulse or use a minecart crafted with TNT to create a rolling disaster zone that's set off by an activator rail. Craft TNT with gunpowder collected from slain creepers (which is easier said than done) and regular sand.

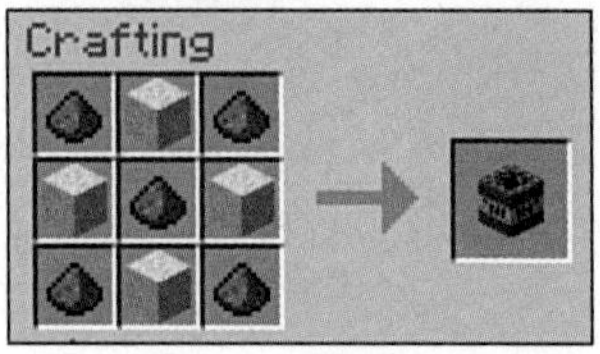

- **Note blocks**—Note blocks add a nice aesthetic to the game and let you easily create audible notifications or warnings of certain events. Right-click a note block to change the tone that plays when it receives power. You can even create your own doorbell with a string of blocks hooked up using repeaters to create delays. Try changing the instrument used by placing the note block on other types of materials and bring out your inner composer.

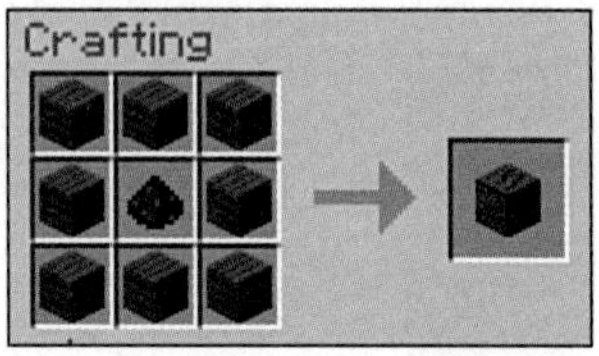

The output devices make quite a collection. You'll use them in various ways later.

You can make advanced circuits and mechanisms by combining all the components in different ways. The redstone system can do a lot more than connect a button to a light or a lever to a water dispenser.

Automatic Doors

Automatic doors can be simple and useful. You may have already experimented with them. Place a wooden or stone button on the wall next to any single door, and it will spring open. You can do the same with two doors placed side by side, but a single button placed on one side won't open them both. Wouldn't it be nice if you could link that button to both doors so they both swing open the way you'd expect?

All you need is a little redstone dust. Follow these steps and refer to Figure 9.11:

1 Position the doors. The order in which you place them is important. Place the left door first and then the right. This causes the right-hand door to flip around, becoming a mirror image of the left.
2 Place blocks to surround the doors as shown, a stack of two on each side.
3 Position the button on the top-left block. Wooden buttons provide a 1.5-second pulse of power, whereas stone buttons provide a 1-second pulse.
4 Run a trail of redstone dust from the base of one door pillar to the other in a U-shaped bend until it drives directly into the base of the other. The redstone receives its current from the space the button block occupies, transmitting the current to the opposite base block, powering that and triggering the opposite door to open.

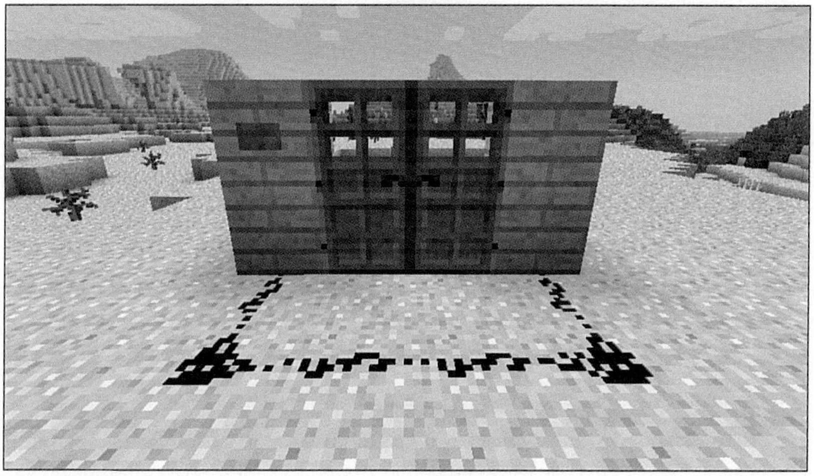

FIGURE 9.11 A simple circuit linking two doors.

The only obvious problem is one of aesthetics. You can't throw a welcome mat over it to hide the wire, but there are other ways to improve the look. One, if it suits, is to use carpet created from two blocks of wool placed side by side on the crafting table. Place that directly on top of the wiring. It will appear one block above but will create just a small step above any adjacent blocks running on either side of the redstone trail, and you can then place carpet on the adjacent blocks to completely hide the path the redstone takes. The other is to use slabs, and I'll show you how to do that here, so get ready to remove the wiring you just installed and start again.

Take a look at Figure 9.12. It's still the same concept, but the wiring now runs from the side of the button's anchor block, down a few blocks to where it can be hidden by ground cover, and back up the other side, in a mirror image.

FIGURE 9.12 It takes only a few minutes to rerun the wiring so that it can be hidden from sight. Going two blocks deep leaves room for a layer of flooring above the wire that is flush with the ground.

Follow these steps:

1. Dig out the blocks shown in Figure 9.12, although you can leave the forwardmost row in place; I removed those just to better show the circuit.
2. Add the two single side blocks on either side of the doorjambs and run redstone along the top of the blocks and down into the trench.
3. When you reach the middle, stop and place a redstone repeater to amplify the current because it needs to run a touch longer than 15 steps. Place it facing in the direction the current should run (in this example, facing toward the right) and then continue the redstone wiring out the other side and up the steps on the other side.
4. To test your setup, click the button, and both doors should spring open—the left one first, followed by the right, after a tiny tenth-of-a-second delay caused by the current running through the repeater.
5. To cover up the new wire, fill in the main trench using any material you prefer, even glass blocks if you want to see the current fire up each time you enter. Leave the two blocks at the far end empty for now. Figure 9.13 shows the blocks at the end of the trench. One is one block deep, and the other is two blocks deep.
6. Place a slab instead of a full block over the space that is two blocks deep. This gives you a surface flush with the ground while also letting the current run underneath.

FIGURE 9.13 Cover the space on the right with a slab to allow the current to run down and into the trench.

7 Build up other blocks around and on top of the wiring until you've achieved the desired result. Figure 9.14 shows an example that turns the entry into something a little grander while also hiding all the wiring.

FIGURE 9.14 A completed portico. I've used fence posts and wooden slabs to create the roof.

8 Position a couple of pressure plates behind the door for an easy exit. The plates aren't quite perfect. Each one opens just the door directly in front. For extra props, dig a trench two blocks deep under the plates and lay some redstone under both plates that connects somewhere with the other wire originating from the button. This ensures that no matter which plate is jumped on, the original double-opening circuit receives the hit and swings both doors open.

TIP

Forgot to Shut the Door on Your Way Out?

Place a wooden pressure plate inside every door leading outside, even if you don't do any other wiring. You won't need to click the door to get out, and the door will automatically close behind you every time. Dropped items also trigger wooden pressure plates. Switch to one of stone if you don't want inadvertent drops to triggers the doors.

This is just one example of connecting doors and running wiring, but there are many ways to slice this problem. The wiring could run over the top of the door. You could also make it shorter on the delivery side by placing a redstone torch two blocks under the door and powering it through an inverter—but the repeater significantly simplifies the design. And, of course, the entire thing could be flipped so that the wiring runs behind the doors.

Let's get a touch more sophisticated. Swinging doors are great, but if you have in mind something more high tech—perhaps a modern fortress decked out with everything that opens and shuts (literally)—you might consider leveling up to doors that glide open before you. They're not whisper quiet, and they don't even give that swoosh sound of the doors in every sci-fi show. However, they do look great, and you can make them from any material, including glass blocks, so they'll add a certain something to any construction.

For sliding doors you add an extra circuit to the loop. The pistons have to stay powered and therefore extended for the door to stay closed. But pressing the button delivers power rather than cutting it off, and flipping a lever will just keep the doors in one state or the other. What this circuit needs is a method of keeping the pistons powered constantly and a way of interrupting only when the button supplies its own current. This setup is known as an *inverter*, or a *NOT* gate, and is provided by a redstone torch attached to the button block.

Figure 9.15 shows the basic layout, with all components identified. The image shows the pistons powered. They'll be retracted at first, but you can place the actual door blocks either in the middle or up against the pistons, and they'll work just fine as soon as the pistons are extended for the first time.

I've shown the wiring at ground level for simplicity, but you can bury it the same way as for the wooden doors example and then build up the rest of the entry way to hide everything. Figure 9.16 shows one example, but feel free to create any look you like. Piston doors provide quite an entrance into a fortress buried into the side of a hill, where you can place natural terrain to hide the inner workings. You can also flip the workings 90 degrees and make doors open vertically or add some vertical doors and pistons on top of the horizontal ones to create a three-way iris.

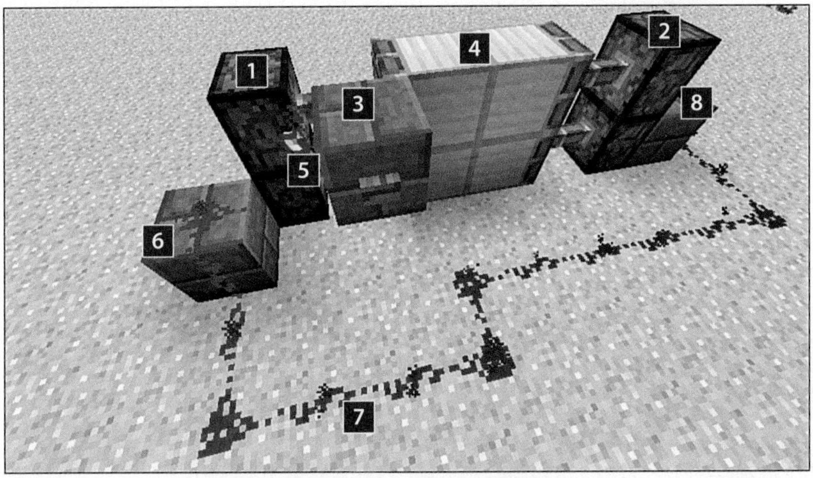

FIGURE 9.15 Place these components to create the mechanics of a sliding door.

1. A double-stack of sticky pistons
2. The second stack of sticky pistons required for the opposite slider
3. Block with button attached
4. Blocks for the door; I've used iron for that fortress look
5. Redstone torch attached to button block, forming an inverter
6. Start of redstone wiring
7. The wiring must step around the block beneath the button's own space so it isn't fired when the button is pressed.
8. Place the trail up and onto the block behind the second piston stack.

FIGURE 9.16 One approach to hiding piston door wiring.

Try the same design with an added latch circuit: Run wire from pressure plates through the latch, feeding the power into the side repeater from a lever inside. Use the pressure plates to get in and out quickly and then use the lever to lock the doors closed at night.

One final example of piston-controlled devices: Figure 9.17 shows a set of three automatic iron block storm shutters hidden within a wall cavity. (I've opened up the inner wooden wall and floor so you can see the workings.) A system like this, controlled by a lever, provides more blast resistance than glass, and you can open it up to take pot shots at mobs. Wire this up to a lever and bury the wiring under your floor.

FIGURE 9.17 Sliding windows created with sticky pistons. The repeaters keep the current feeding directly into the base block under the pistons. Without them, the wiring would revert to a lattice and stop working.

Vertical Currents

Although redstone wiring can easily climb and descend steps, you'll sometimes want to send it vertically instead. The easiest way to do this is to use an alternating series of redstone torches and ensure that the final one is in sync (not inverting) with the current at the base of the tower. See Figure 9.18 for an example.

FIGURE 9.18 Redstone torches power the block above, so using them is an easy way to create a vertically ascending current.

TIP

1×1 Vertical Ascending Alternative

You can make current (or, really, the current's signal) ascend in a 1×1 pattern by placing redstone torches on top rather than on the side of each block. This requires a temporary tower behind the planned ascent that you can remove when you're done, but it's also ideal if you can just place the ascent against a wall. Attach blocks to the tower or wall every second space. Fix redstone torches to the top of each block, and they'll pass their signal to the block above until you can draw power from a final torch placed into the side of the uppermost block.

The only way to descend a current is through a 2×2 staircase (see "The Spiral Staircase" on page 85). You may want to use this in Survival mode as well as for ascending currents because it provides an easy way to get up and down the circuit.

Advanced Circuits

The creators of Minecraft did something interesting when they designed the redstone system: They made it possible to mimic the binary logic system that is also at the heart of every integrated circuit that runs your electronics. It's nowhere near as crazily complicated as today's CPUs, and it's more like a breadboard of wires studded with vacuum tubes, but the basics are there. Let's take a look at some prototypical logic gates and how they're used to do actually useful things.

NOT Gates, aka Inverters

A NOT gate takes an input value and flips the output value. For example, if the incoming current is on, the output of the NOT gate is off. If the current is off, the output is on. Redstone torches act like this. By default, they supply a current, but if the block they are attached to is powered by another source, the torch flips off. NOT gates are also known as inverters because they invert the current.

We used an inverter to flip the current from the torch with a button in the sliding doors example. Inverters have many other uses, though. For example, two inverters in a row act as an amplifier, just like a repeater (see Figure 9.19).

FIGURE 9.19 Inverters as amplifiers: The foremost inverter pair is a more compressed version of the furthest set (two inverters in sequence).

Inverters can also turn a daylight sensor into a night-light, as shown in Figure 9.20. The daylight sensor emits a signal according to the amount of light it's receiving. Feeding this into an inverter turns the lamp on when the sensor is off and vice versa.

OR Gates, or Any Input Will Do

OR gates provide a positive output if any of the inputs is also true. This is a natural function of redstone wiring. Just connect two or more wires to a T-junction, and the single output will always be on if any input is on or off if all inputs are off. Figure 9.21 shows an OR gate with three types of input, any of which can light the lamp.

OR gates have many uses, primarily because they allow multiple inputs to feed into the one circuit. For example, a row of pressure plates or strands of tripwire around the perimeter can hook up to a single wire that runs into your house, creating a perimeter alarm system. You can also add a timed circuit to a note block to create an audible beeping alarm.

I'm sure you'll find many other uses.

FIGURE 9.20 Need a night-light? That's easy to arrange, and you can add further lamps and note blocks to create a full lighting system with an audible sound as night hits.

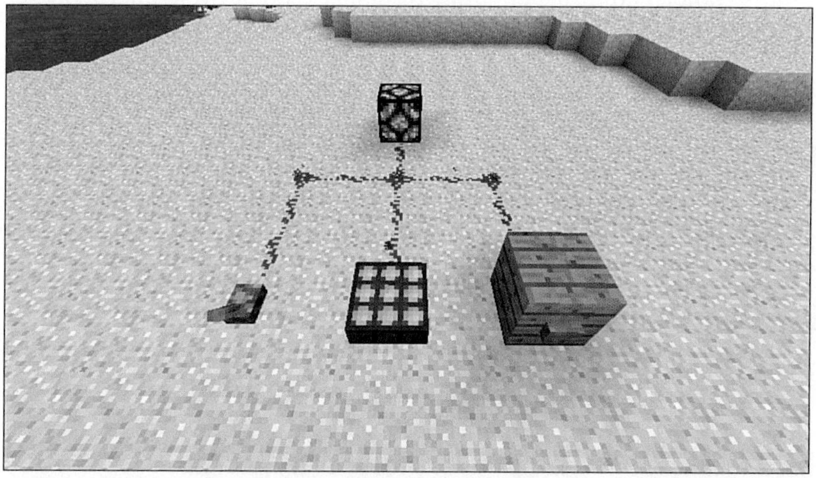

FIGURE 9.21 The OR gate is represented by the junction point of the wiring. In this case, the daylight sensor is providing the power that lights up all the wires. Use repeaters or inverters on each strand if it's important for the current to always flow in just one direction.

NOTE

If It's Not OR, It's NOR

NOR gates operate as OR gates but with the output signal inverted. Think of it as NOT+OR. In these gates, the output signal is TRUE only if both inputs are FALSE. Just place an inverter on the single-wire output from the OR gate to create a NOR.

AND Gates, Two TRUE

AND gates output current (or a value of TRUE) only if both inputs are also TRUE. In real life, this is often used in security systems where two keys must be inserted to open a vault. You can do something similar to create a secure room, and this can be especially useful in Multiplayer mode. Place a lever close to the door (although not so close that it can directly activate it) and hide a lever in another part of the structure. String them together and feed the output to the door. Now the obviously placed button won't work unless the hidden lever is also flipped on.

The AND gate is a more complex construction, using three inverters for two inputs and one output. Figure 9.22 shows the gate with both inputs on, and Figure 9.23 shows the same with one input off.

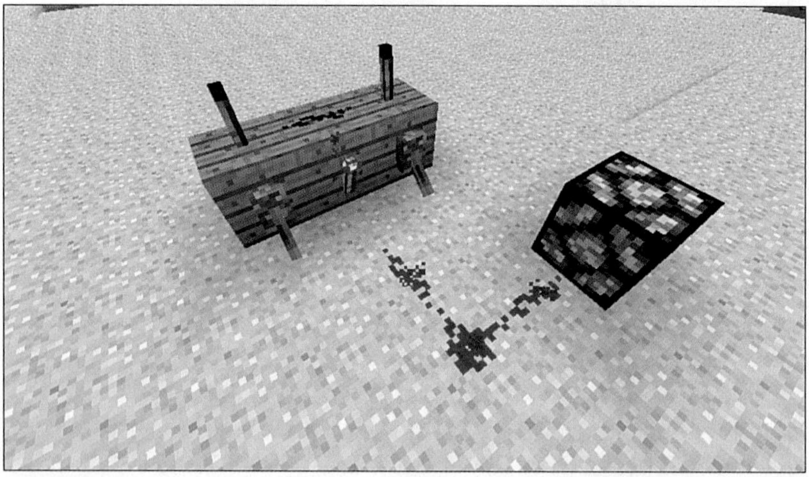

FIGURE 9.22 An AND gate with both levers switched on. This cuts both torches above the levers, ensuring that no current flows to the inverter on the side of the block. That inverter therefore sends power to the output wire lighting the lamp.

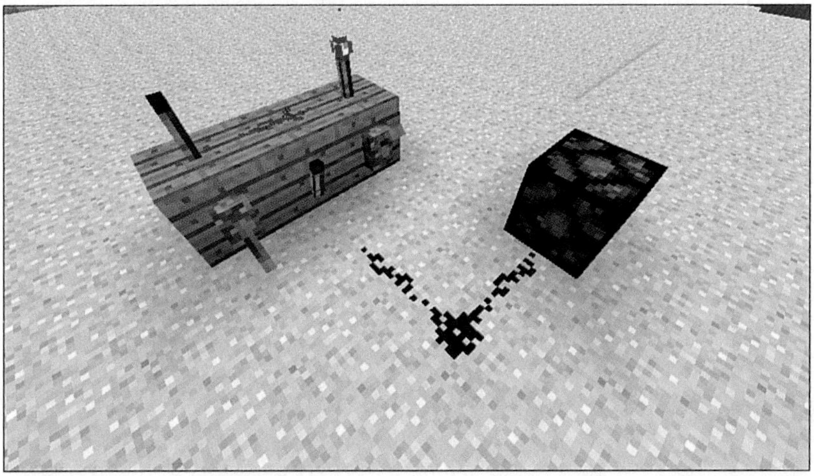

FIGURE 9.23 With one lever turned off, current flows from its torch to the output inverter, cutting its own current.

Repeater Loops

Loops set up a pulsing circuit. They're possible with just some redstone torches, but you can use redstone repeaters to make them more compact, with adjustable timing, by changing the repeater delays with a right-click.

Figure 9.24 shows a prototypical design with a single repeater adjusted back to provide a 0.4-second delay. The torch adds another 0.1 second to that, making this a 0.5-second loop. You can extend the circuit by adding more repeaters to increase the delay. Replace the lever with wire connected to any other power source or signal to hook up the repeater to other circuits.

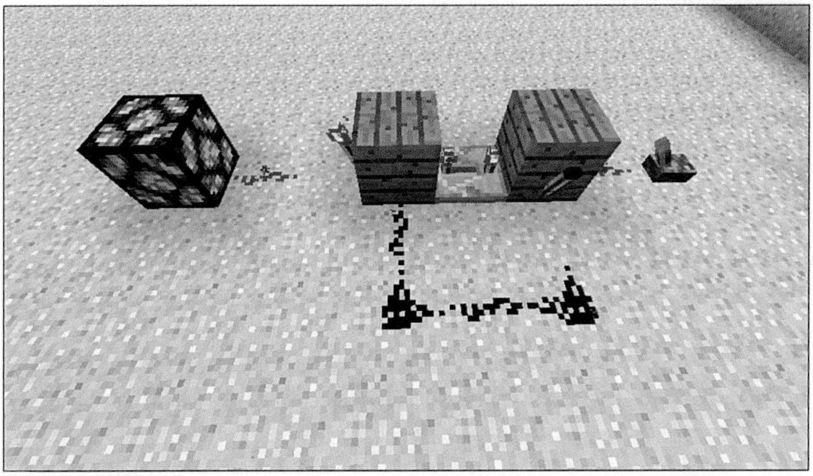

FIGURE 9.24 The repeater loop works off any type of input.

For an extra challenge, turn the repeater into a trip circuit—so that the loop runs permanently on the input of any signal until it's reset, like an alarm system. An easy way to do this is to use a redstone block sliding between two regular (not sticky) pistons. Figure 9.25 shows this approach. Note that an inverter has been added before the lamp so that its usual condition is off. The additional repeater is just there to extend the circuit.

FIGURE 9.25 A repeater circuit with a trip system. The push button on the right triggers the repeater loop by pushing the block away from the circuit, allowing the repeater loop to fire. The loop will keep running until the push button on the left pushes the redstone block back to its original position.

Rail Transport

Minecraft's rail transport system, like a lot of other things in Minecraft, can be as simple or crazily complex as you like. It is definitely part of the charm and the challenge. It can operate in a simple way, but the tendrils of redstone work their way deep into the rail system. Powered and detector rails provide key hooks that integrate rail and redstone into a homogenous whole.

In earlier versions of Minecraft, before the Horse Update (v1.6) that introduced a slew of equine-related features, rail travel was the fastest way to get from A to Z, via B to Y if you prefer a scenic route. The carts travel at an average speed of 8 meters (or blocks) per second and can climb hills, traverse valleys, and, depending on how you design the track, offer something of a rollercoaster thrill ride in between. You won't break any land-speed records, and it's not as fast as a fast horse, but it's definitely better than walking, and it remains a great system for moving items, resources, and yourself, especially from the depths of a mine.

The system is limited only by your imagination. This section introduces you to the basic components, track-laying strategies, and some more advanced hints and tricks—enough to get you more than chugging along.

Have Minecart, Will Travel

A rail without rolling stock is about as useful as a car jacked on bricks. (I'm waiting for a maglev mod—maybe TrainCraft will float one in. See Chapter 13, "Mods and Multiplayer.")

There are several versions of the standard carriage shown in Figure 9.26. It would be wonderful if these were glorious celebrations of the gilded age of the iron horse; they aren't. They're not even steampunk. But they do the job. Let's take a look in the stable:

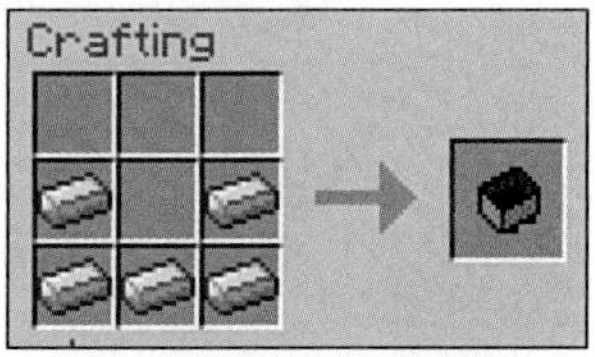

- **Minecart**—This is the barebones version of the rolling chariot. Hop aboard by right-clicking the empty cart and get taken for a ride. Use the forward key (**W**) to move in the direction you're facing. There's no way to slow down or reverse direction except to press the left **Shift** key to exit the minecart, after which it will quickly stop. Interestingly, other mobs can also ride in this type of minecart, and pigs will give it a good kick along. Self-propelling is effective but slow. Downward slopes (if you have the inclination), a powered minecart, or powered rails will speed things up.

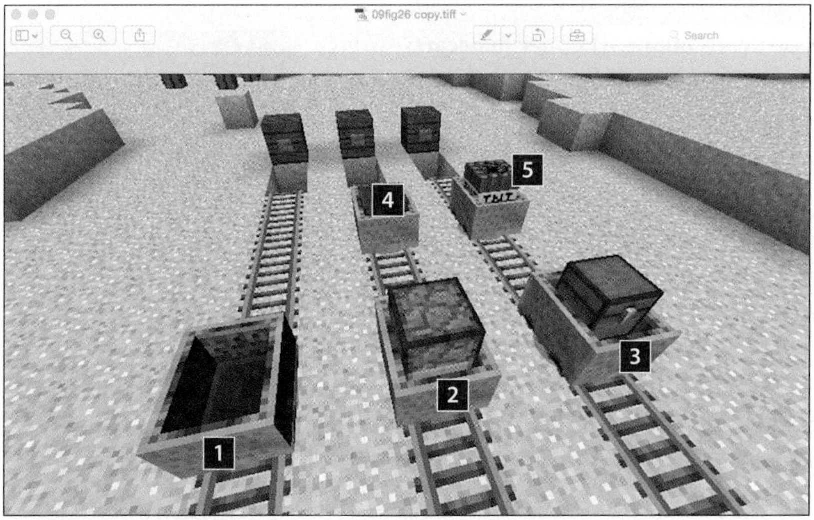

FIGURE 9.26 Minecarts.

1. Standard minecart
2. Powered minecart
3. Storage minecart
4. Hopper minecart
5. TNT minecart

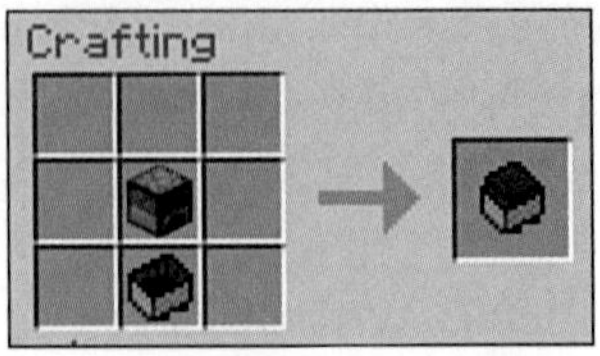

- **Minecart with furnace (powered minecart)**—Burn, baby, burn! The furnace cart is powered by coal or charcoal and can push other carts in front. It's bidirectional: Just click on one with the fuel in hand facing in the direction you want it to go. You can also change its direction at any time with another click. The engine runs for 3 minutes on each piece of fuel (enough to travel about 600 blocks), and you can fuel it for a long haul (a little more than 3 hours) by providing it with a full stack of 64 pieces of coal or charcoal. A single powered cart can push numerous other minecarts, although some glitches may occur, leaving carts jammed or stranded. It can also pull a string of carts if they have first been shunted together, such as by being backed up against a wall.

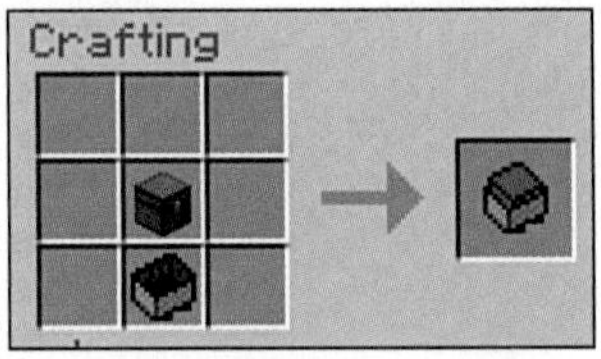

- **Minecart with chest (storage minecart)**—Add a chest to a standard minecart to gain another 15 fully stackable slots. This minecart rolls with the same momentum as an occupied minecart, regardless of the contents of the chest. Place a hopper underneath the track to automatically unload the chest and a chest under the hopper to create an automated unloading and storage system.

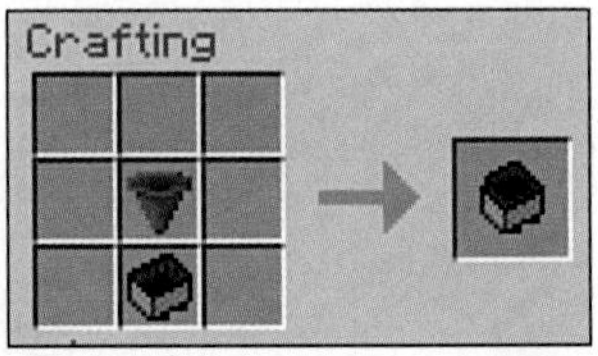

- **Minecart with hopper (hopper minecart)**—Craft a minecart with a hopper to create a hopper minecart. These minecarts automatically scoop up loose items lying on the track and can be filled up with the contents of a container such as a chest or another hopper placed in the space above the track.

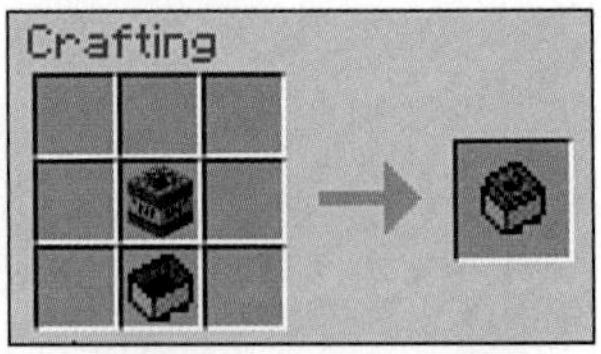

- **Minecart with TNT (a.k.a. the TNT minecart)**—Exploding minecarts? Why not? Actually, they're a little special because the TNT will destroy nearby blocks but doesn't destroy the rail tracks or their directly underlying blocks. This is a little hit and miss, though, and you may find some unintended collateral damage. TNT carts are a fun addition to Minecraft, but they aren't the most effective method for mining. Use a powered activator rail to set them off. They can also be set off through collisions with other blocks or carts, by falling more than three blocks, and by fire, lava, or other explosions.

If you plan to build a bunch of minecarts and treat them like a train, keep in mind that they don't latch together but instead can be used to push each other along. This works best with a powered cart doing the pushing. But even if you're just propelling yourself in a standard minecart, you'll find that you can push a practically unlimited string of storage carts ahead of you simply by bumping into them—shunting them along, as it were—as long as you stay on the flat. A powered minecart can push about four carts up a hill, but this doesn't always work out well in practice because the minecarts sometimes get stuck as the chain works its way around corners and over slope transitions.

As Mojang developed version 1.8 of the game—in particular the 14w11a development snapshot—it made some significant changes to minecart mechanics. For example, the standard running speed was boosted to 20 meters/second—which is fast!

A complication with the speed increase was the chance that minecarts can derail if you hit a corner too quickly. Minecarts could also "refuse" to go uphill if the minecart was traveling too rapidly.

Due to customer outrage, Mojang reverted to the old minecart physics as of snapshot 14w17a. However, this doesn't mean it won't tweak the system in the future.

NOTE

Destroying and Reusing Minecarts

You can destroy minecarts with a few hits from any tool and place them back in your inventory for reuse. You can also load them into a dispenser placed at the start of your track for easy one-click deployment.

TIP

Build Now, Rail Later

Real-life cities tend to be a mess of transportation compromises. Roads and rails fight for space with buildings, sidewalks, parks, and utilities, not to mention utility infrastructure. Take a leaf from their book: tunnel. Put your rails underground rather than demolishing your hard-built structures and pop aboveground with access points when you can. The ability to run rails on a 45-degree slope makes your life much easier than that of a city planner, and subways with underground concourses add unique ambience to a vibrant metropolis.

Rolling on Rails

Minecraft has four types of rails. Some are more resource expensive than others, but fortunately they don't need to be used all the time. Here's a quick guide:

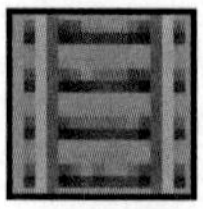

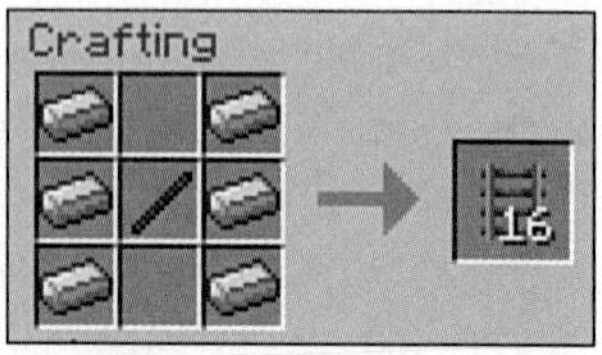

- **Normal rail**—Use six iron ingots and a stick of wood to create 16 rail track segments. Place them with a right-click, and the system takes care of bending them around corners or up and down terrain. You can use normal rail exclusively if you like, trundling along in a minecart, but your speed is somewhat limited. Only normal rails can bend into curves or a T-junction.

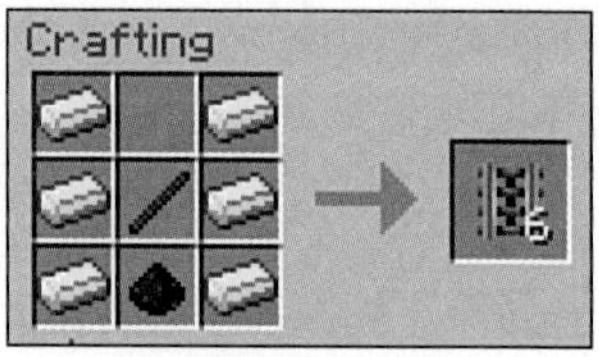

- **Powered rail**—Powered rail is expensive. For six gold ingots, a stick, and a lump of redstone, you get just six segments, so use wisely! Fortunately, you don't need a lot because a single rail can boost an occupied minecart or storage minecart for 80 blocks on level ground. (Unoccupied minecarts lose steam after just 8 blocks.) The rail is itself powered by any redstone source, but some of those sources work better than others, and I'll use them in the examples that follow. These rails light up when powered and so are easy to recognize.

When this type of rail is unpowered, it slows you down, so it's a good rail for placing at the start and end of a track for a soft landing. Just one block can stop a minecart, even one that's trundling down a slope. Powered rails provide a boost in the direction the minecart is moving, or, if stopped on a slope, the minecart will always head down the slope when the rail becomes powered.

If the minecart is stationery and at the end of a track with a block in front, the rail will instead give the minecart a kick in the direction it can travel. This is really the key to making a station where you can board a cart without trying to jump on one that's trundling past.

A single power source such as a redstone torch stuck in the ground beside the rail can provide juice to a chain of up to eight powered rail segments. Generally speaking, one powered rail is needed for every four steps up a slope, although you can work this as two rails in every eight to make it a bit easier to manage the power supply. On the flat, you should place one powered rail every 37 blocks to keep an occupied minecart zipping along at a moderate pace or two powered rails to stay at high speed.

- **Detector rail**—These rails are like a standard rail combined with a pressure plate, emitting a redstone current when a minecart rolls over the top. You can use this current or signal for anything really, including controlling hoppers, opening doors to a tunnel, setting off a note block, switching tracks at a T-junction, and so on.

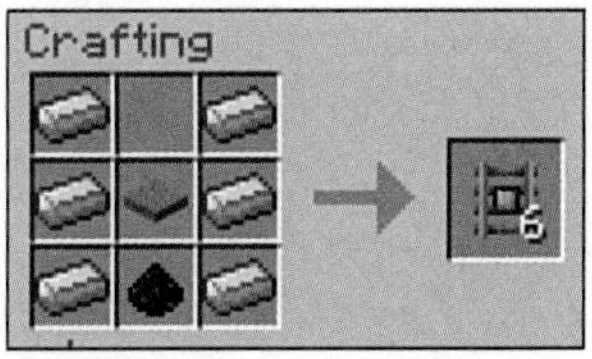

- **Activator rail**—These rails have just two purposes: to enable or disable a hopper minecart passing over the top and to set off a minecart with TNT. The size of the explosion is proportional to the speed of the TNT minecart, and the rail needs to be powered before it becomes operational. When unpowered, it acts like any other rail track.Powered activator rails also shake up minecarts, potentially causing riders to fall out.

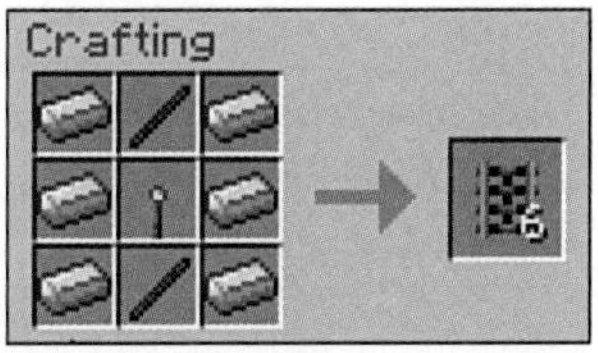

Making Tracks and Stations

It's easy to lay tracks: Just right-click where you want to place them. If you make a mistake, you can easily dig up the tracks and reuse them. This allows for some trial and error, especially when you're working out the minimum placements required for the expensive powered rails.

TIP

Zigzag to Speed Up

Whereas a cart travels on level ground at a maximum of 8 blocks per second, a slight sideways dodge boosts this to 11 blocks. Lay diagonal tracks in a continuous zigzag pattern to get this free speed boost. They'll look a little off on the ground, but the minecart will travel over them smoothly. Lay the tracks on diagonally adjoining blocks, and they'll connect with a series of corner tracks, creating the zigzag pattern for you.

TIP

Efficient Powered Rails

The cheapest way to permanently power a rail is with a lever rather than a redstone torch. You just need a piece of cobblestone and a stick to craft the lever. Then place it by the track and flick it on. If you prefer to leave your power sources hidden, place a redstone torch under one of the blocks holding a powered rail, and the rail will transmit the power to any adjoining powered rails.

As you lay tracks, you need to consider inserting powered rails. The first place to start is really at the beginning of the track. Create a small launch station, using Figure 9.27 as a guide. The station works like this:

1 The single powered track at the end acts as the launcher, gaining its power from the button attached to the wood block.

2 You place a cart at the end, hop aboard, and push the button.

3 You accelerate out of the dip and then get a speed boost from the track powered by the lever.

4 When you return, that same powered track gives your cart a speed boost sufficient to nestle it back against the block at the end of the line, ready for the next launch.

FIGURE 9.27 A simple minecart station that returns carts to their ideal starting position.

T-Junctions

A T-junction allows a train track to branch off in two directions, with the direction controlled either via detector plates or some other power source. Create this track by placing your rails into a T-section. Minecraft takes care of converting the head of the T into a working junction. Generally speaking, the most useful way to switch the tracks is to place a lever at the top of the T, as shown in Figure 9.28, but you can also run redstone to achieve the same result—perhaps all the way back to a destination switching board at the station. The power needs to terminate at the block underneath the track, making it possible to hide any wiring from view.

FIGURE 9.28 Switch the lever to choose a different track branch.

Halfway Stations

One final note before I leave you to your own track-laying devices. So far, you've seen stations at the end of a track, but what about those along the way? Creating a midpoint station provides a convenient stop 'n' go system. Midpoint stations use the same principle as the end stations, with powered rails in an unpowered state to slow you down. Create them by digging a trench one block deep and two blocks long and place the track in the trench so it forms a V shape, as shown in Figure 9.29.

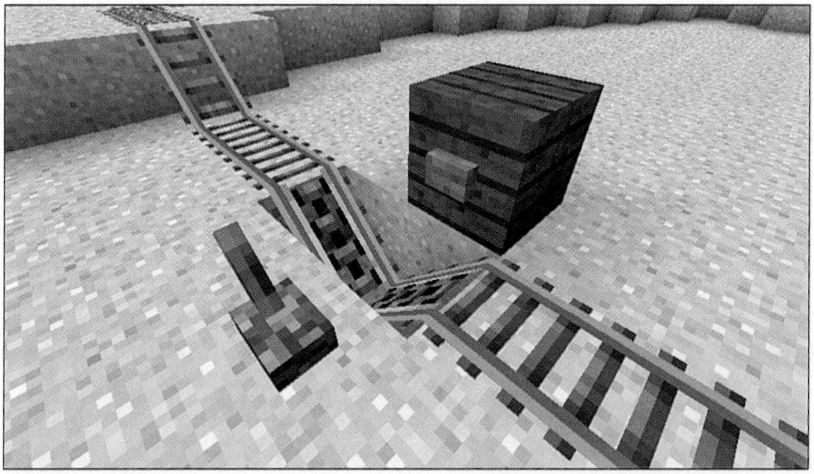

FIGURE 9.29 Switch the lever to choose a different track branch.

The minecart will stop on a downward-facing track in the direction of travel, and a quick click of the button on the side will get you moving again. The lever provides an override that permanently powers the tracks in case you decide you don't always need to stop here. If you do have to bail out as you go flying by, you can be thankful that empty minecarts stop after 8 blocks or so rather than 80! It's easy to collect again and be on your way.

CAUTION

Protecting Tracks from Mobs

In Survival mode, you are as vulnerable riding in a minecart as you are at any other time. Carts don't, unfortunately, run over hostile mobs and turn them into mincemeat. They just stop or bounce off them. Either way, it's a problem. If you are serious about using minecarts to get around, consider building them underground in well-lit, protected corridors or put up fences when they have to run aboveground.

A Word About Hoppers

Before I close this rather lengthy chapter, there's one final, brief topic: hoppers. The humble hopper is really like an automatic item-feeding system. It connects containers such as chests to other things, like a furnace or a dispenser. Essentially, it moves items between containers while also offering five inventory slots of its own. As mentioned earlier, you can also place a hopper on wheels by combining it with a minecart, and you can use a hopper to unload a minecart with a chest when placed underneath the track. (You'll need to place the hopper first and then hold down the left **Shift** key while right-clicking to sneakily place the rail on top of the hopper.)

Figure 9.30 shows a fairly extreme example to demonstrate how wildly complicated a hopper system can become—although even this layout could be extended more or less indefinitely. Once you've fed in enough raw materials, the entire thing automatically drops raw materials into the top of the furnace, fuel into the side, and the end result into the chest at ground level. It's set and forget.

Hoppers configure themselves automatically, according to their attachment point. (You need to sneakily place them onto chests and other containers that react to a right-click.) You can also connect them to each other to create a sort of endless conveyor belt that feeds items to the side and down.

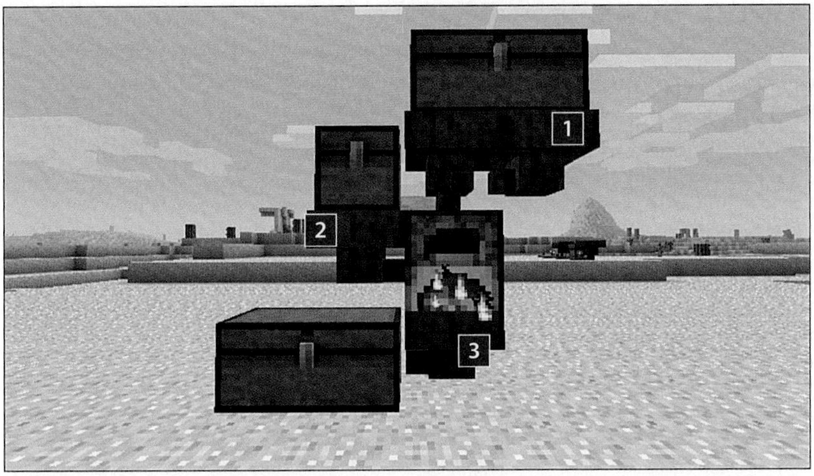

FIGURE 9.30 Switch the lever to choose a different track branch.

1. Two hoppers side by side can support a large chest—in this case feeding raw material into the top of the furnace.
2. The side hopper supplies fuel, even buckets of lava to provide an incredible amount of smelting power from a single chest.
3. The hopper under the furnace collects its output and sends it to the large chest next door.

Craft a hopper from five iron ingots and a chest. The hopper has five inventory slots of its own but acts to transfer items stored above it to anything below it at a rate of 2.5 items per second unless the transfer is stopped with a redstone signal. Place a redstone comparator next to a hopper to receive a signal when it contains items.

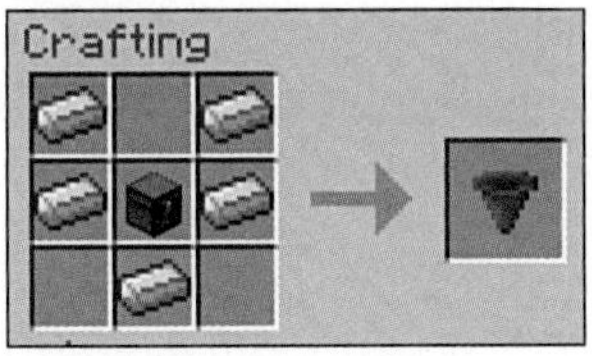

The Bottom Line

As you've seen, redstone offers many interesting possibilities. Like so much else in Minecraft, redstone is limited only by your imagination. Although redstone differs enough from electricity to give an engineer conniptions, it's a lot easier to work with, and you're not going to die from an electric shock if you cross wires. You'll just get a nice little wire lattice instead.

Redstone also plays nicely with the rail transport system, providing fast transport and an easy way to move items and other resources. Rails are quite resource intensive, so in most survival worlds, you'll probably start with something simple and efficient. But when you spend just a few hours digging out mines and exploring caverns, you will uncover more than enough iron and gold to build extensive railways. And, of course, in pure Creative mode, there really are no limits at all.

Enchanting, Anvils, and Brewing

In This Chapter

- Learn Minecraft's enchanting ways.
- Safely store your hard-earned experience levels.
- Spruce up your weapons, enhance your armor, and improve your tools.
- Hammer something out on the anvil for better repairs.
- Mix up some magic in the brewing stand.

By now, you've probably made it all the way to a diamond sword, your base is nothing short of a warlord's fortress, and you're so armored up you can take on a corps of creepers without breaking a sweat on your squared-off brow.

All's good in The Overworld. But it could always be better. This chapter walks you through a few extra skills involving a special crafting table, a very large block of iron, and a few wee drams of potion.

Enchanting Wiles

Experience points (XPs) accrue through the normal course of the game, providing small green nudges to the experience bar shown in your heads-up display (HUD). (Those colored orbs flying toward you after you bravely slay a mob or patiently smelt a batch of iron all devolve into experience points. Don't forget to run over and pick them up if they drop too far away.) There are quite a few ways to gain XP including smelting, cooking, mining, and fishing, although slaying mobs is one of the most effective. When the bar fills, it delivers an XP level—a type of currency—and promptly resets. Spend that XP wisely through enchantments, and you can power up your weapons, armor, and tools.

Enchantments improve an object's core abilities. Among other things, they can help a pickaxe mine with more efficiency, make a sword cause more damage and become unbreakable, make your armor practically (although not completely) impregnable, and build up a lot of other vital improvements that will help you in The Nether and End regions.

Enchantments also add capabilities that are a little more mystical: The respiration enchantment can dramatically increase your underwater survivability, a bow with infinity enchantment will never run out of arrows (at least not until the bow breaks), and your enchanted boots will let you leap off tall cliffs with nary a thought for a distinct lack of feathers. Enchantments also have a practical use: They can help your tools gather more resources from every mined block or even pull out whole blocks in their original form instead of just digging out dropped components.

So how do you start enchanting? It's actually pretty easy, and there are several ways to go about it:

- Use an enchantment table to apply a random enchantment to an item, at the cost of XPs.
- Pay a village priest with emeralds in return for a specific enchantment on an item you already have in your inventory. This can also work like a free repair service, where you swap a damaged item for an undamaged, enchanted equivalent.
- Combine an enchanted book with an item at an anvil. This costs some XPs but at a discounted rate compared to creating the original enchanted book. This is a bargain if you've been fortunate enough to find an enchanted book in one of the chests scattered around the world in villages and dungeons and so on. Village librarians will also trade them for other items.
- There's a small chance of gaining an enchanted item by killing a skeleton or zombie that's carrying one or by fishing.
- Combine an item with an enchanted item of the same type at an anvil. If you combine two items with different but compatible enchantments, the final item gains both enchantments. You can also use anvils to repair and rename items in a process not dissimilar to using them to enchant items.

Let's start with the simplest method: using an enchantment table (see Figure 10.1). We'll get to the bookshelves surrounding it shortly.

An enchantment table takes up one block, just like a crafting table, but creating one is a little more difficult because it requires two diamond gems, a book, and four obsidian blocks.

NOTE

Think This Is Hard?

If making an enchantment table seems challenging, I must warn you that it's a lot easier than creating the brewing stand later in this chapter! Consider this a warm-up for the lavish lava lakes you'll need to deal with in The Nether dimension.

FIGURE 10.1 An enchantment table surrounded with 15 power-boosting bookshelves.

Of all the ingredients you need here, you might find obsidian the most difficult to obtain. It lurks in some village chests, but otherwise you need to discover it in a natural setting or create it yourself with a steamy combination of water and lava. It's quite prevalent down in the depths near layer 11, but remember that you'll need a diamond pickaxe to dig it up.

Creating and Mining Obsidian

Forming obsidian requires *flowing water* to meet *still* (not flowing) *lava*. This is key: Any other variation of water and lava, flowing or not, in either order, just results in cobblestone, and that's not going to put a spell on anything.

Obsidian is practically indestructible, so it's a great construction material, but it's a little risky to mine, given its close proximity to lava and the latter's proclivity for turning your character into instant Korean barbecue.

But enchantment tables don't require very much obsidian, and I'll show you a surefire technique for getting there. Just follow these steps:

1. Fill some buckets with water. You might need only one, but take some backups just in case.
2. Locate a lava pool. If you're lucky, you've spotted these on the surface, but your surest bet is to head down to the lowest levels of your mine, where you've probably already stumbled on several. Lava is most common below layer 11, counting up from the unbroken bedrock that exists at layer 0. If you're still looking, head back down your mine and dig some additional branch lines until you do. It shouldn't take long.
3. If you find a lava pool with water that has already flowed over some part of it (Figure 10.2 shows an example), you can try to block the water source by fencing it off with cobblestone or any other handy blocks to dry up the flow and then mine the obsidian

exposed underneath. Figure 10.3 shows the result. A further border of cobblestone dropped into the lava lake along the obsidian border allows you to mine the obsidian without fear of getting swamped by the molten magma. Don't forget to use the left **Shift** key to sneak around the lava so that you don't fall in.

FIGURE 10.2 A natural lava pool and water flow. The obsidian already formed by the water creates a thin black line under the front edge of the water flow.

1. Flowing water that has already covered some of this lava pool
2. A still (not flowing) lava pool

FIGURE 10.3 Fencing or blocking off the water flow with a cobblestone barrier exposes the obsidian.

1. The flowing water has been blocked off from the still lava pool with cobblestone.

4 If there's no water nearby, stand back a little and pour water from one of your buckets so that it spills down onto a bordering block and then flows over the lava. The best way to do this is to stand at least one block up. Place a block and jump on it if a block isn't there already (or if there's no nearby ledge). This ensures that you won't be washed toward the lava or back into another danger zone.

TIP

Is the Lava the Only Source of Light?

Place some torches around before you extinguish the lava so that you're not left standing in the dark.

5 Let the water flow as far as it can, converting the lava lake to an expanse of obsidian, and then fill your bucket from the water source block to remove the water and expose it, as shown in Figure 10.4. If you can't pick up the water source block, place other blocks around to stop its flow and dry things up.

FIGURE 10.4 Water poured from a bucket has converted the entire lava pool to obsidian.

1. Obsidian

6 Take your diamond pickaxe in hand and start mining obsidian. Breaking obsidian takes a while, so be patient. There's also a good chance you'll expose more lava under the obsidian as you go. Pour some more water on top of that lava to convert any surrounding blocks to obsidian and then scoop the water back up into your bucket to use again. Mine more obsidian than just the 4 blocks you need for the enchantment table. Try to

gather at least 14 blocks in all, as you'll use the remaining 10 to create a Nether portal in Chapter 12, "Playing Through: The Nether and The End." You'll need to visit The Nether before creating a brewing stand later in this chapter.

Crafting Books

Books have several uses: for crafting the enchantment table, for boosting its powers with bookshelves, and for storing enchantments. (They can also help you play Minecraft.)

A book requires three pieces of paper and one piece of leather, although on the Pocket Edition you can leave out the leather.

Start by crafting paper from three pieces of sugarcane. Then bind the paper with leather to make a book. Go ahead and make as many as possible, as you'll need up to 45 books to create a full set of shelves to surround the enchanting table. (Don't drop everything to do this, though. You can build up to the full set later and get reasonable results with just a few to start.)

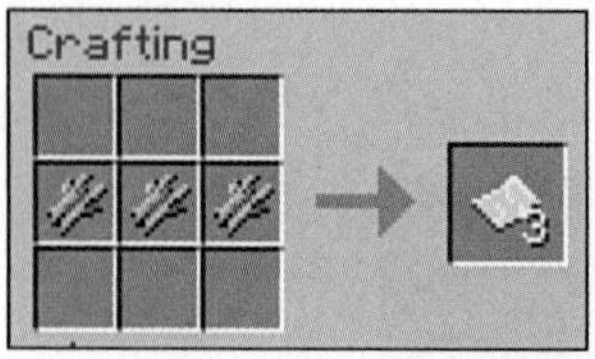

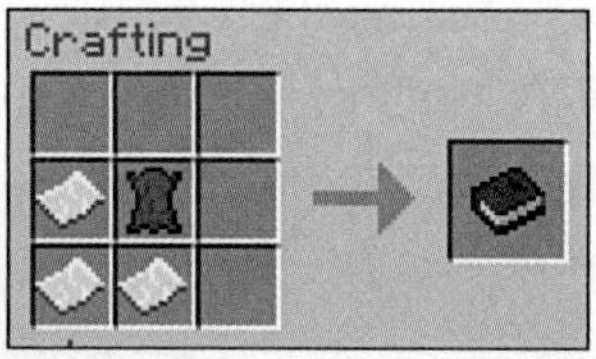

Casting Enchantments

Now that you have the raw ingredients, the whole enchantments deal becomes much easier. Follow these steps:

1 Create and place an enchantment table. Leave a perimeter of two clear spaces between the table and any walls for future bookshelves, as shown in Figure 10.1. As you approach the table, the book flips through a few pages in a rather nice animation.

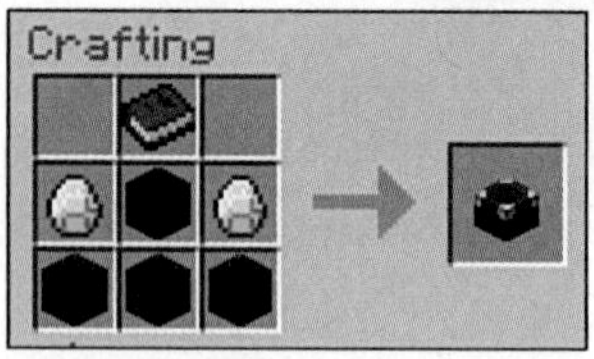

2 Right-click the table to view the enchantment interface.

3 Place the item you want to enchant (a weapon, a tool, armor, or a book) in the empty slot beneath the book. You'll see a list of three possible enchantments appear to the right, as shown in Figure 10.5. You also need to add one, two, or three pieces of lapis lazuli to the enchantment table, according to the enchantment level. (Gather lapis lazuli by mining the bright blue lapis lazuli ore.)

FIGURE 10.5 Enchanting a diamond sword.

4 The enchantments listed are unreadable and randomly generated. However, the name of one of the enchantments appears as a ToolTip when you hover your mouse over the enchantment label area. The numbering to the left of each enchantment shows the number of pieces of lapis lazuli required to cast it, while the value to the right shows the enchantment levels that will be expended. The enchantment you get is, essentially, up to a roll of the dice. You'll never know which one actually belongs to the ToolTip. An enchantment can run up 30 XPs in cost, but the higher the level, the better the chance you have of gaining a more powerful enchantment. Any enchantments for which you don't have sufficient XPs are grayed out, and an enchant table without nearby bookshelves can offer enchantments only up to level 8.

5 Select an enchantment from the list. Stay at the lower levels for now, saving your XPs for additional enchantments. You can also use the anvil to repair an item, but bear in mind that the number of times an item has been repaired attracts an XP penalty that impacts its potential enchantment level.

6 Drag the enchanted item back to your inventory. Hover your mouse over the item to see the enchantments applied.

TIP

Chancy Enchantment Tables

The formulas Minecraft uses for generating the list of enchantments aren't exactly obvious. Too many random factors are involved to provide a generic table of probabilities. A few sites online use the actual program code to generate a guide. To gain more insight, visit http://www.minecraftenchantmentcalculator.com and select the material, tool, and enchantment level. This neat utility will roll the die 10,000 times, collate the results, and give you a list of possible enchantments, along with their likelihood.

CAUTION

Repairs and Removing Enchantments

Repairing an enchanted item by combining it with another on the crafting table destroys any attached enchantments. Use the anvil for the repair if you want to retain and combine the enchantments.

Improving Enchantment Chances with Bookshelves

Bookshelves open up higher levels of enchantments. Craft them from three books and six wood plank blocks—any wood will do.

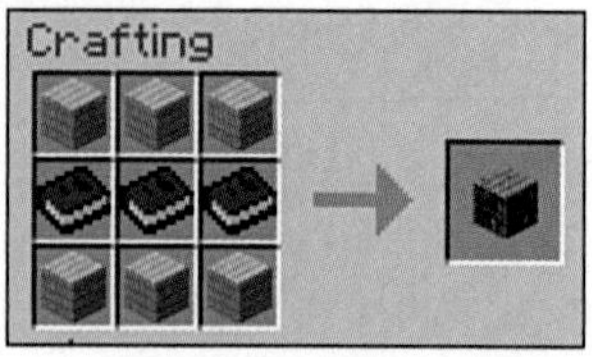

Bookshelves improve the enchantment levels in the following ways:

- Each bookshelf unit boosts the level by 1 to 2 points, with 15 bookshelves delivering the highest enchantment level possible.
- The shelves must be placed two spaces from the table, with nothing in the intervening space. Torches, snow cover, and anything else will block the boost from the shelf.
- Even with a full set of bookshelves, you'll continue to see enchantments at the lower power. There's a random distribution of levels from the lowest to the highest possible between the three enchantment slots.

- The bookshelves must be on the same level as the table or one block higher. A single layer of 15 shelves looks as shown in Figure 10.1, but you can also stack the shelves two blocks high against the walls (see Figure 10.6) to achieve the same power boost and leave the other two sides clear.
- Stacking objects such as chests and torches directly on top of the bookshelves won't block their usefulness. You can also place another bookshelf on the two-wall layout to make the shelves symmetrical, even though this won't improve the actual enchanting.

FIGURE 10.6 A slightly different bookshelf layout that still provides the maximum power boost to the table. Objects placed on top don't reduce a bookshelf's effectiveness.

TIP

Choosing and Storing Enchantments with Books

Books provide an opportunity to be more selective with the enchantments that are applied to an item. Enchant a book at the table in the usual way. The result is still random until it's complete, but it carries an identifiable enchantment as soon as you drag it back into your inventory. Combine the one you want with an item at the anvil for a small additional cost in XPs. Store any others in a chest to keep them safe.

Earning and Managing Experience

XPs are earned through different actions and then "spent" through enchanting or using the anvil. What's the quickest way to gain XPs fast, and how can you maximize your return on XPs? Read on:

- Gain XPs by killing mobs, mining, smelting, cooking, fishing, and breeding friendly mobs. (An added bonus is that if you cook the food, it becomes more nutritious.) A quick way to gain lots of XPs is therefore to breed animals to increase the population as quickly as possible and then kill any extras, pick up their dropped meat, and cook it in your furnace. Breeding chickens is easy because the seed is available anywhere there is tall grass, but cows are more useful because you can also use their leather to create books in the PC and console editions. You gain more XPs by killing hostile mobs than friendly ones.
- Try to stay long enough to collect the colored experience orbs that gradually float your way after an XP-earning event.
- Enchant gold weapons and armor. Gold benefits the most from enchanting and has a better chance of getting a higher-level enchantment than iron or diamonds.
- Pay a priest villager with emeralds to enchant items, and you won't take a hit to XPs.
- Start with low-level enchantments first, in the 1 to 10 range on the enchantment table. There's little difference in the enchantments that can be had at the cost of 1 XP to 10 XPs, so stay low and grow.
- The first 16 XP levels are the easiest. At 17 and above, it becomes gradually more difficult to climb each level, so if you want to enchant a lot of items quickly, keep your XP below 17, spend it, and then build it up again.
- All XP levels disappear on death, and while some experience orbs may drop for collection after your respawn, at best they'll only be sufficient to build you back up to level 5. If you have spare XPs (say, anything above level 17) but don't have anything to enchant, use those spare XP levels to enchant books. Store them in a chest so that they survive your death, and you can apply them to new items when you come back from the afterlife.

TIP

Adding XP Levels with a Cheat

If you're playing with cheats enabled and want to add some XPs fast, use the cheat command **/XP <*amount*>L** to quickly gain any number of XP levels. For example, **/XP 30L** adds 30 levels of experience to your character. A negative amount subtracts it instead.

Sprucing Up Your Weapons

Show your foes the thin edge of the wedge with a range of powerful weapon enhancements. You'll be amazed at how quickly you can dispatch a zombie with a sharper blade or how far you can fling a creeper with the knockback enchantment. Table 10.1 shows the full list. All the levels in Minecraft use roman numerals.

TABLE 10.1 Combat Enchantments

Enchantment	Maximum Level Attainable	Table Items	Anvil Items	Description
Sharpness, smite, and bane of arthropods	V	Sword	Axe	Increases inflicted damage. Sharpness works on all mobs, smite on the undead, and bane of arthropods on spiders, cave spiders, and silverfish. An anvil is required to gain level V on diamond weapons. Note that you can apply only one of these enchantments at a time.
Knockback	II	Sword	None	Knocks back an entity farther than a sprinting attack. Combine with sprinting for even greater efficacy.
Fire aspect	II	Sword	None	Sets the target of your attack on fire for 3 to 7 ticks, according to the level, but has no effect on mobs from The Nether.
Looting	III	Sword	None	Improves the number of items killed and the number of mobs dropped and improves the chance of zombies and Zombie Pigmen dropping additional items, such as iron or gold ingots. Grants an extra 1% probability of getting rare loot per XP level.
Power	V	Bow	None	Increases arrow damage from 50% to 150%, according to the level.
Punch	II	Bow	None	Increases the knockback that a mob experiences from a hit with an arrow.
Flame	I	Bow	None	Sets an arrow on fire, causing fire damage to any mob hit except for those from The Nether.
Infinity	I	Bow	None	Provides an infinite supply of arrows until the bow breaks, but those arrows can't be collected in Survival mode for reuse.

Enhancing Your Armor

Iron Man is a trademark, so I won't run that gauntlet, but armor enchantments do give you the Armor-All of defense, allowing blows to slide off your polished pauldrons like so much Teflon.

All of the "protection" enchantments combine to an upper limit set by the item's material. Table 10.2 shows the full list. Keep in mind that the upper limit for enchantments runs from lowest to highest as follows: iron, diamond, chain, leather, and gold.

TABLE 10.2 Defensive Enchantments

Enchantment	Maximum Level Attainable	Table Items	Anvil Items	Description
Protection, fire protection, blast protection, and projectile protection	IV	Helmet, chestplate, leggings, and boots	None	"Protection" reduces the damage passed on for that piece, up to a total for all pieces, varying according to the material. The other enchantments help more specifically against fire, explosions, and ranged weapons. These enchantments are mutually exclusive.
Feather falling	IV	Boots	None	Reduces damage experienced from falling farther than three blocks.
Respiration	III	Helmet	None	Increases the time you can breathe underwater by 15 seconds per level while also delaying suffocation damage by 1 second per level. Also improves underwater vision by reducing the opaque blue haze.
Aqua affinity	I	Helmet	None	Removes the speed penalty associated with underwater mining.
Thorns	III	Chestplate	Helmet, legging, and boots	Provides a chance that the armor will cause damage to an attacker, at the cost of the armor's durability. The effect is noncumulative, so the highest-scoring armor piece wins.
Depth strider	III	Boots	None	Allows you to move faster while underwater.

Improving Your Tools

Of all your activities in Minecraft, resource collection is one of the most important. The enchantments described in Table 10.3 provide ways to gather new types of resources, ways to improve their speed and efficiency, and ways to help them last longer.

TABLE 10.3 Tool Enchantments

Enchantment	Maximum Level Attainable	Table Items	Anvil Items	Description
Efficiency	V	Pickaxe, shovel, and axe	Shears	Increases mining speed from 0.3 times faster to almost 4 times, according to the level.
Silk touch	I	Pickaxe, shovel, and axe	Shears	Allows certain blocks to drop as themselves instead of as their usual derivatives. Applies to grass blocks, coal ore, diamond ore, cobwebs, ice, and Nether quartz ore, among others. Cannot be used at the same time as fortune.
Fortune	III	Pickaxe, shovel, and axe	None	Provides a better chance that a breakable block will drop more items and increases the rate of flint production from gravel.
Unbreaking	III	Pickaxe, shovel, and axe	All weapons, other tools, fishing rods, flint, and steel	Improves the tool's durability by reducing the chance of wear from normal use.

Enchantments are incredibly useful, but they usually last only for the durability of the item and are lost in their entirety when repaired at the crafting table. What? You'd like to repair an item without losing the enchantment and even add an additional enchantment to it? Meet the anvil.

Hammering It Out with the Anvil

The anvil has many talents. It can repair and rename items, apply enchantments from books, combine two similar enchanted items, and combine the enchantments in two enchanted books, as long as the enchantments are compatible.

An anvil does, however, require a lot of iron: 31 ingots in all.

Start by crafting 3 blocks from 27 ingots. Then combine the blocks with another 4 ingots to create the anvil.

Place the anvil somewhere handy (see Figure 10.7), and nowhere that it's likely to drop on your head. Falling anvils do cause damage and, for reasons Wile E. Coyote could well attest, are quite popular in multiplayer traps.

FIGURE 10.7 The anvil is the largest chunk of iron in the game. Fortunately, there's no damage from stubbing one's toe.

The anvil provides a single interface for all its different actions. Right-click it to open the Repair & Name window shown in Figure 10.8.

Here's how you use the anvil:

- **Repairing an item**—Place the item to be repaired in the first item slot and the raw material in the second item slot. The item can be any item with a durability value. Figure 10.8 shows an iron pickaxe being repaired, courtesy of three iron blocks, at a cost of between two and five XP levels. (You may need to place more than one of the raw material in the slot to bring the item back to full or close to full durability.) In the example shown in Figure 10.8, the pick was so worn out it required three iron ingots to be completely restored. Hover over the proposed repaired item to see its resultant durability value. (You may need to press **F3+H** from the normal view to turn this on.) Don't over-repair items; you'll receive no bonus for using additional repairs above the item's maximum durability level.

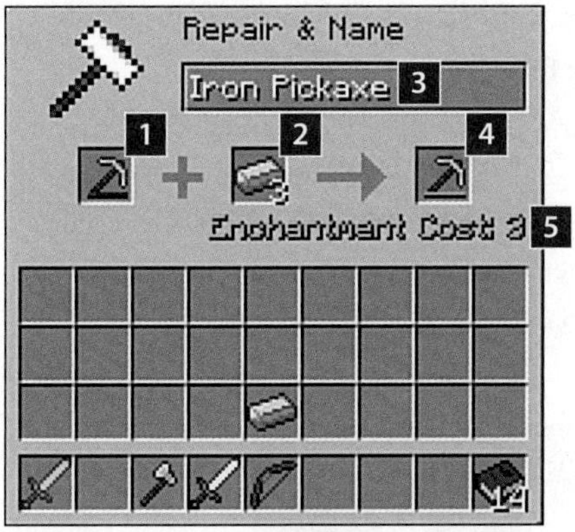

FIGURE 10.8 Repair, combine, or enchant items at the anvil—at a cost.

1. First item slot
2. Second item slot
3. Renaming box
4. Output slot
5. XP level cost to complete

- **Combining two items**—Place the items to be combined in the first and second item slots. To be successful, the items must be compatible, and the total XP cost must be less than 40. This applies to weapons, tools, and armor, as well as enchanted books.
- **Enchanting items**—Place the item to be enchanted in the first slot and the enchanted book in the second slot. The enchantment from the book transfers to the item.
- **Combining enchantments**—Place the enchanted weapons, tool, armor, or books in each slot and pick up the item with the combined enchantments from the output slot.
- **Renaming items**—Use the renaming box to name an item while carrying out any of the other anvil operations or as a singular operation on its own. Renaming costs just one XP level. A renamed sword with particular enchantments is easier to find when you're rummaging in a chest among a collection of enchanted swords whose icons are otherwise identical. You can also use the renaming facility to assign names to nametags found in dungeons and Nether fortresses. Attach them to friendly mobs to get yourself a Fido, Killer, Daisy, or whatever you like. The mob's name is visible up to seven blocks away.

Brewing Potions

Ready to brew up some trouble? Potions give you an offensive and defensive advantage that will keep limb attached to limb in The Overworld. More importantly, potions help you complete the other regions. Although potions don't require an eye of newt or toe of frog, they do, like a hell-broth, require a trip to The Nether for some core ingredients.

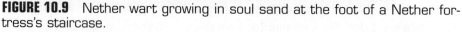

The first essential ingredient is Nether wart, the starting point for almost all the potions. It generally grows in pits dug around the bases of staircases in Nether fortresses (see Figure 10.9), although you may find it elsewhere. Those planting grounds and The Nether itself also contain the soul sand you'll need to start a Nether wart farm back home. Fortunately, soul sand is quite plentiful, growing in dull gray tracts around many of the lava lakes you'll find.

FIGURE 10.9 Nether wart growing in soul sand at the foot of a Nether fortress's staircase.

The other elusive component is the blaze rod, which is required for creating the brewing apparatus. Obtain this by defeating a blaze, which is a hostile that inhabits Nether fortresses. This, admittedly, is something of a challenge. You won't do it in 5 minutes. Chapter 12 will help you prepare for that journey, handle the hostiles, and get you home in at least one piece. If this is your first venture into The Nether, treat it as a quick snatch and grab. You don't want to spend too much time down there until you're truly prepared. You will, however, want to get a range of protection enchantments (fire protection is vital) and try to get an enchantment of feather falling for your boots. An unbreaking enchantment on tools will save you some trips back to The Overworld until you've had time to create a well-stocked Nether-base.

Head over to Chapter 12 now and come back when you have a blaze rod, Nether wart, and soul sand. You'll also need some glass blocks (smelted from sand) and a supply of water, although even a single block of water will fill an endless number of bottles. Figure 10.10 shows my own brewing chamber.

NOTE

Nether Not Yet?

Try some of the potion recipes that follow in a different world set to Creative to learn how they work and to test the results. Sprint around with a 40% speed boost (it's quite an exhilaration after the normal plod/sprint) and try some combat at Normal and Hard difficulty. Try swimming across a lava lake with the fire resistance potion. Experiment with the other potions to see their effects firsthand. Minecraft is all about exploration, and you can do this exploration before tackling some of the tougher scenarios on Survival mode.

FIGURE 10.10 My "Home Brew Club," with a brewing stand on a crafting table, a water supply, a Nether wart farm, a furnace for creating glass bottles, and a chest for storing the results.

TIP

Plant Those Nether Warts First

Nether wart grows only in soul sand, but it doesn't have irrigation or light requirements. Given the challenge in collecting Nether wart, you should use any Nether wart and soul sand you collected from your trip to build a Nether wart farm. Do this *before* you start using Nether wart for brewing. The simplicity of growing Nether wart means you can put the farm just about anywhere, including inside a small chamber reserved for your potable magic.

Brewing Up a Storm

Brewing up a batch of potions takes some initial work but always delivers rewarding results. You've already done the hard part: getting the initial ingredients together. The rest is easy. Creating potions is a useful, easily replicated exercise.

Follow these steps to get start brewing your own potions:

1 Craft a brewing stand from three cobblestone blocks and a blaze rod. Place it somewhere convenient.

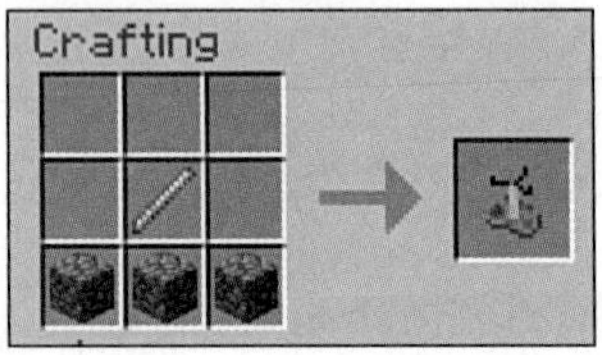

2 Create at least a few glass bottles from three glass blocks. Fill the bottles from your water supply.

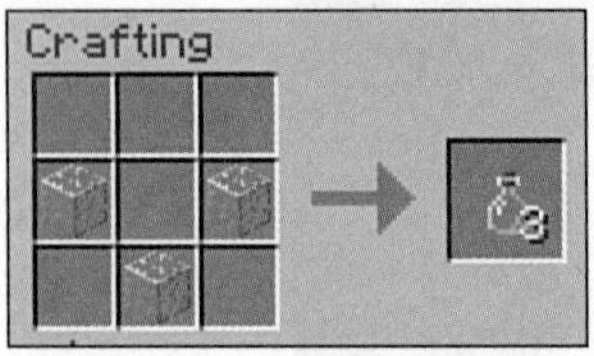

3 Right-click the base of the brewing stand to open the brewing window and then place the glass bottles in the output slots as shown in Figure 10.11. (You can place from one to three bottles, depending on how much of any potion you want to create. In this first instance, you're creating the base awkward potion. Because this potion is required for most others, it's efficient to create three of these at a time.)

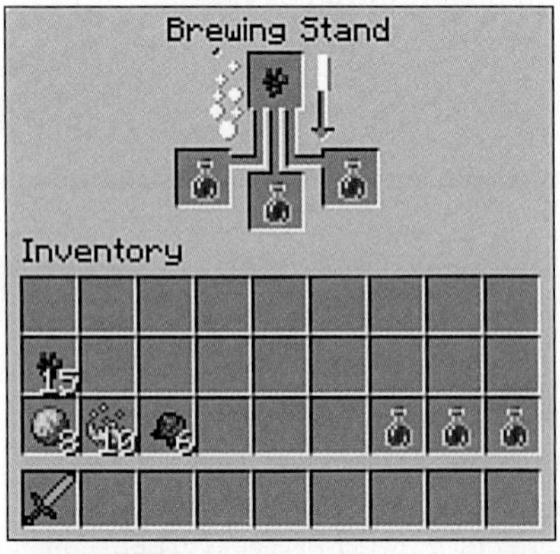

FIGURE 10.11 Drag the brewing ingredient to the top slot and the bottles (water or another potion) to the three output slots.

4 Place one Nether wart in the top of the stand. After a short while and a brief brewing animation, the three water bottles are converted into three bottles of awkward potion. There's no visual change to the bottles, but when you hover your mouse over them, you see their new name in the ToolTip.

Awkward potion is inert. It's the wallflower of potions. Turn it into something more outgoing by adding one of the secondary ingredients to create the potions listed in Table 10.4. These potions are usually referred to as *positive potions* because they have a beneficial effect on the player's character. There are also negative variants of most of these that you can throw at other mobs to cause damaging effects, with some caveats discussed in the note "When Positive Becomes Negative," later in this chapter.

TABLE 10.4 Positive-Effect Potions

Potion	Effect	Secondary Ingredient	Obtained From
Swiftness	+20% speed for 3 minutes.	Sugar	Sugar cane
Strength	+130% damage for 3 minutes.	Blaze powder	Blaze rods (with each making 2 blaze powders)
Healing	Instantly restore two hearts.	Glistering melon	Melon + eight gold nuggets (with 1 gold ingot producing 9 gold nuggets)
Regeneration	Restores 9 hearts over 45 seconds.	Ghast tear	Ghast drops
Fire resistance	Complete protection from fire and lava for 3 minutes. You can even swim across a lake of lava as long as you get to the other side in time! Also provides protection from ranged blaze attacks.	Magma cream	Magma cube drops or blaze powder + a slime ball
Night vision	See perfectly at night and underwater for 3 minutes.	Golden carrot	Carrot + 8 gold nuggets
Invisibility	Become invisible to all mobs for 3 minutes.	Potion of night vision	

Use the potions the same way you eat food: Select the potion and hold down the right mouse button to drink it. The potion of healing takes immediate effect, whereas others last for the specified duration. Open your inventory screen to see all the active potions and their remaining duration, as shown in Figure 10.12. You'll also see a bubble effect come up in the view through the main gameplay window while any potions are in effect. It's not possible to pause a potion's effects, so make the most of them while you can.

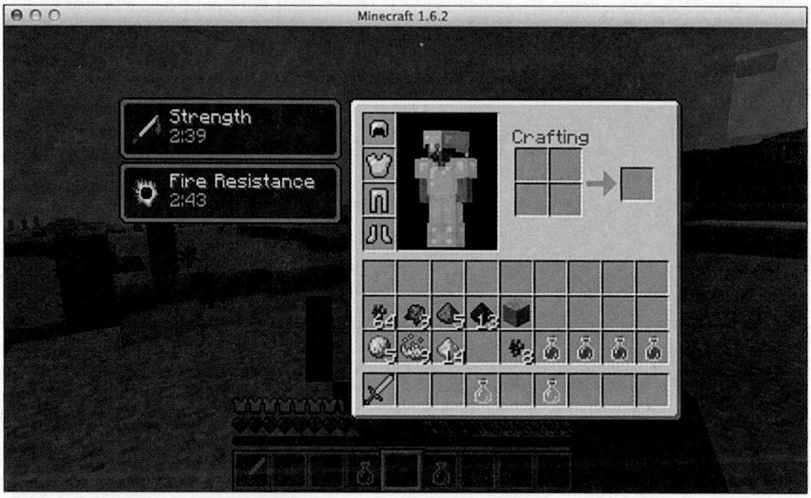

FIGURE 10.12 Active potions show their remaining duration in a box to the left of the inventory window.

Enhancing Potions

Potions provide a particular boost over a specified duration. You can add a third brewing cycle to modify their boost or their duration and then convert them into a throwable splash potion, also known as a negative potion:

- **Glowstone dust**—Doubles the effectiveness of the potion where possible, typically at the expense of duration. Applies to swiftness, healing, regeneration, and strength. Replaces the use of redstone dust, as discussed next.
- **Redstone dust**—Doubles the duration of the potion but replaces the use of glowstone dust.
- **Gunpowder**—Converts the potion into a splash potion at the cost of a 25% weaker effect. You'll see the shape of the bottle change so that it looks a little like it's grown a small hand-grenade pin on the side. Throw splash potions at mobs or down at your feet if you want to get an immediate effect from the potion without taking the time to drink it.
- **Fermented spider eye**—Add this curious crafting to transform the potion into a negative potion. Table 10.5 lists all the ones that are available, along with other negative-effect potions that can be brewed without using a positive-effect potion as the base. Craft this ingredient from a spider eye (dropped by spiders), a brown mushroom, and sugar.

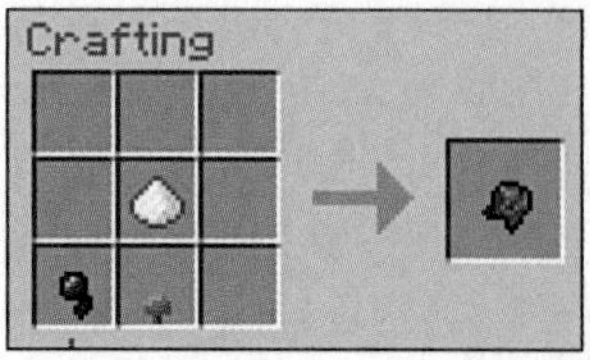

Glowstone and redstone cannot be combined through additional brewing cycles; only the last one used takes effect. However, gunpowder and fermented spider eye definitely are often used together to create a throwable version of a potion that will have negative effects when it affects the enemy. You can add them after glowstone or redstone dust to enhance the effects of any throwable positive or negative potion.

TABLE 10.5 Negative-Effect Potions

Potion	Initial Potion	Effect
Slowness	Swiftness	–15% speed for 1.5 minutes
Weakness	Strength (or brew a base potion using a water bottle and add a fermented spider eye)	Reduces melee damage by half a heart for 1.5 minutes
Harming	Healing	Causes 3 hearts of immediate damage
Invisibility	Night vision	Lets you become invisible to all mobs for 3 minutes
Poison	Awkward (add a normal spider eye through brewing)	Causes up to 18 points of damage over 45 seconds but does not cause death

NOTE

When Positive Becomes Negative

Not all negative potions have deleterious effects on mobs. Throwing a potion of harming at the undead (zombies and skeletons) helps them heal. Whoops! Throw potions of healing instead to cause them harm. This is particularly useful when you're in a tight battle with these particular mobs because you can just toss a potion of healing at your feet and improve your health while causing harm to any undead currently in close combat.

The Bottom Line

Minecraft's magical effects are potent and powerful.

Start with enchantments because their toughest barrier to entry is a natural by-product of cooking, smelting, and taking care of mobs. You'll gain XPs step by step.

Use the anvil to manage your enchantment inventory by storing enchantments in books, repairing items when needed, and combining enchantments for even more powerful results.

Potions provide your final boost, and they are the most powerful enhancements in Minecraft.

The next chapter takes a small step back from combat preparedness but is important nonetheless. Your world contains numerous villages and a host of hidden structures containing items and resources that will help your push into the game's other dimensions.

Villages and Other Structures

In This Chapter

- Meet the village people and trade your way up in the game.
- Learn about the villagers' professions and the different trades they offer.
- Explore hidden temples, dungeons, and mine shafts.
- Discover witches, warts and all.
- Craft a map.
- Clock on and off. It's easy!

In Minecraft, you are never truly alone. There are villages teeming with people, mysterious temples containing hidden treasures, and gigantic structures buried deep in the ground. A village offers the potential bonanza of finding a chest or three packed with useful items. Also, the villagers are more than happy to strike deals for certain resources and items. This chapter takes you on an exploration of the structures in The Overworld and their eccentric inhabitants.

Village Life

Villages are havens of useful resources. Finding a good-sized village early on can provide a significant advantage: chests containing useful items; rows of wheat, carrots, beetroot, and potatoes; and opportunities to trade emeralds for other items from the proboscisally endowed villagers. (Okay, that's not a real word, but you'll understand when you see the villagers.)

The only problem with villages is that they are not very common. They only appear in the desert and plains biomes, and not too often at that. They are a lot more prevalent in any world with the **Large Biomes** option turned on during initial generation, as long as **Generate Structures** is selected under **More World Options**. The villages that appear in the two biomes use construction materials native to those biomes, so you'll see a lot of wood and cobblestone in a village located in the plains (see Figure 11.1) and a lot more sandstone in a village situated in a desert.

FIGURE 11.1 Villages spawn with a varying number of buildings and inhabitants. This one is located in a plains biome.

Villages add a useful dynamic to the game. They're not essential, and you can get by just fine without them, but knowing how to make use of them will help you make the most of them.

Here are the essentials:

- Villages can appear in almost any form, from a single dwelling to a dozen buildings or more. The buildings are any of 10 different designs, from small huts to large taverns and churches.
- Your interaction with the village's inhabitants affects your popularity within that village, and attacking a few—or, even worse, killing them—can result in them sending an iron golem to attack you, although golems appear only in larger villages. Villagers won't attack you back, no matter how mean you are to them.
- Villages are a lodestone for zombies, where zombie sieges can occur, with hordes of zombies swarming the village at night. The zombies spawn anywhere in the village itself, including inside rooms, and attack any villagers present. Dead villagers can then turn into zombie villagers, increasing the havoc (see Figure 11.2).

  Cure a zombie villager by throwing a weakness potion at him, followed by a golden apple, and try to keep him segregated because the cure takes a few minutes to work. Fortunately, as night falls, you'll see most villagers scurry for cover to their favored village building. They'll also do this if it starts to rain. Iron golems fight the good fight by attacking zombies, and they get rid of them very quickly, but iron golems only spawn in villages with a population of 10 villagers and at least 21 houses.

TIP

Sleep Through the Siege

Beds don't occur naturally in villages, but if you place one and ensure that you sleep through the night, you'll spare your villagers from a zombie siege. It's a neat way to keep zombie infections to a minimum.

FIGURE 11.2 Zombies can spawn in and around a village at night in large numbers, resulting in scenes like the one shown here—a zombie siege in full swing.

- Villagers trade goods; priest villagers can enchant items; and farmer villagers plant and harvest potato, wheat, and carrot crops. These folks make a village useful to you. Look for a trade where you can obtain emeralds by harvesting wheat and then use the emeralds to pay for other types of items or services. The types of trades available are specific to each villager's profession. For example, the butchers will trade emeralds for meat. Talk to as many villagers as you can to find the best trade. Some offer rare Minecraft items such as saddles and horse armor. You can also deconstruct bookshelves in a library to obtain books, and you can happily loot any chests you find without dinging your popularity with the villagers.
- Villagers manage their population by producing children, but they won't do so until after they have had a successful trade, and even then there is a limited chance that they will mate. However, as long as two adult villagers are present, you can increase the total population capacity and, therefore, the trading opportunities by adding doors to any structure, where one side of the door is in a clear space, able to receive sunlight. The

most efficient method is to add numerous side-by-side doors to a simple box structure. (The formula built into the software results in one villager per 3.5 doors.)

- There's no particular technique for finding a village, but if you haven't found one yet in your world, despite substantial exploration, you can get a taste of the experience by searching for a game seed online. Search for something like "Minecraft village seed." It should match your version of Minecraft to ensure that the terrain generates correctly. Even though villages can be hard to find, you will find them eventually in your own world. It may just be a small clutch of houses, but there is always a chance you can stumble upon one that's much larger. If you need a quick refresher on seeds, see the section "Seeding Your World" in Chapter 1, "Getting Started." Alternatively, starting a superflat world with structures turned on will create villages that you'll have no trouble spotting from far away.

Emerald City: Your Ticket to Trade

Villages contain up to five types of villagers (see Figure 11.3), with each offering a particular set of items for trade, according to their profession and career. Emeralds are the currency in a village.

FIGURE 11.3 The village people, from left to right: blacksmith, priest, librarian (this one's a little shy), butcher, and farmer.

You can recognize a villager by his or her attire; also, the villager's career title appears at the top of the trading window. Villagers progress in their chosen profession by moving through tiers. As a villager increases his career tier, he has more buying and selling flexibility. Visit the

Minecraft wiki to read about villager career and tier specifics: http://bit.ly/1lvgzAL. In the meantime, here's a quick guide:

- **Farmers**—Dressed in brown, farmers specialize in food products and most often offer up an emerald for 18–21 sheaves of wheat. Their careers span four tiers and four jobs: fletcher, farmer, fisherman, and shepherd.
- **Librarians**—A librarian wears a white robe and offers to buy paper, books, and gold. Librarians sell, among other things, bookshelves, enchanted books, compasses, and clocks. Their careers span six tiers.
- **Priests**—You can recognize a priest by his purple robe. A priest's career spans three tiers in the "cleric" job role. Priests buy gold and sell Eyes of Ender (pricey, at 7 to 10 emeralds each), redstone, and glowstone, and they are the only source in the game for the Bottle o' Enchanting, which generates experience orbs when thrown. Priests can also enchant swords, axes, pickaxes, and armor chestplates.
- **Blacksmiths**—Blacksmiths wear brown clothes with black aprons. Their careers span four tiers in three jobs: tool smith, armorer, and weaponsmith. They buy coal, iron, gold, and diamonds and offer all the metallic items for sale, including chainmail armor, which you can't craft yourself.
- **Butchers**—Butchers have white aprons. Their careers span two or three tiers, depending on whether the butcher is, in fact, a butcher or a leatherworker. They buy raw pork chops and beef, as well as coal and gold, and they sell saddles, leather armor, cooked pork chops, and steak.

You may also spot some villager children running around, but they don't participate in trading.

Right-click on a villager to open the trading window (see Figure 11.4). Each villager starts with a single trade, either offering to sell you something for emeralds or offering to buy something from you in return for a payment of emeralds. While you can't haggle on the terms, you'll find between two and four trades on offer, and the variety will increase after the initial trades.

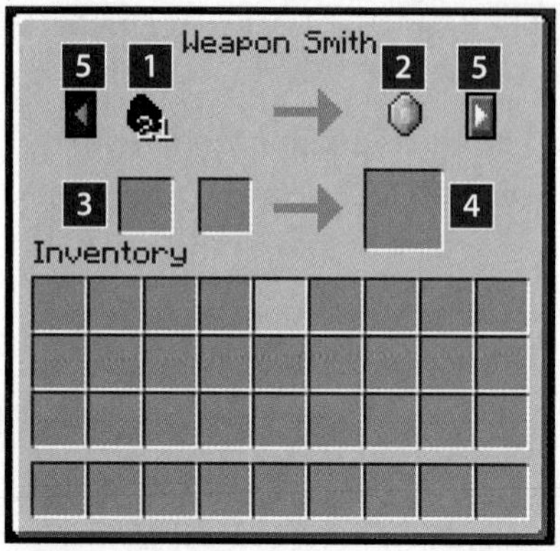

FIGURE 11.4 The goods or payment you need to supply are shown at the top left, and the goods or payment you'll receive from the villager are shown on the right, with the drop-off and pick-up slots for the trade items directly below.

1. Goods or payment required.
2. Payment or goods to be received.
3. Drop matching items for the goods or payment here.
4. Pick up the reward here.
5. Use the arrow keys to cycle through available offers.

To make a trade, just place the goods or emeralds requested in the empty slot on the left and pick up the payment or goods purchased from the empty one on the right. Trading grants experience points (XPs), so it is a useful way to get a quick bump if you are in need.

The additional slot in the middle is used for trading with priests. Place the item to be enchanted in the leftmost slot and the payment in the middle; then pick up the enchanted item from the right.

TIP

Emerald Farming

You can find emeralds in the ground, but only in the extreme hills biomes, or, if you are very lucky, in the chests hidden inside temples and dungeons, but by far the easiest way to get a decent quantity of them is to either take over the wheat farm in a village or build an even larger farm nearby. There are usually a few farmers willing to buy the wheat you collect in return for emeralds. However, take extra care at night not to get caught on the wrong side of the door if a zombie siege begins. The villagers don't mind if you move into one of their houses to stay safe or build your own nearby, and you could do them a favor by fortifying their village to help alleviate the effects of a zombie siege and keep other mobs away.

CAUTION

Not All's Well with the Well

Village wells are deep, with a lip too high for a standard jump. If you plan to spend a lot of time in a village, consider placing some blocks below the first layer of water in the well. Also, knock out one block from the wall so you can climb out if you happen to fall in. Alternatively, leave the block in place and use the well as a zombie trap. Plenty can fall in during a siege, and the shade from the roof prevents them from burning up during the day, so you can then attack them at your leisure.

Hidden Temples and Other Structures

Most villages have a chest or two tucked away, but your Minecraft world also contains other buildings that provide more valuable treasure troves. Although you will only find Nether fortresses and the End cities and ships in The Nether and The End dimensions, there are many others to explore in The Overworld.

NOTE

Less Is More: Mojang's Structures Within

Minecraft has many types of structures that are the results of specific programming code that is separate from the general terrain generation. Some of these are negative structures, adding space to the terrain in ways that expose different types of ore and often provide a geological gasp of wonder. (Caverns, ravines, and basins, I'm looking at you!) Others, such as the rivers that flow between biomes, are a clever combination of several techniques that both add and remove particular blocks, blurring what would otherwise look like jarring edges between the biomes. This note serves no other purpose except to say that this is rather clever coding, particularly the rivers. Cajoling software to create apparently natural geology is tremendously difficult. So, here's to you, Mojang, for your natural beaches, soaring overhangs, and delightful waterways.

Most of these structures contain chests with all sorts of juicy loot, but they also often contain hostile mob spawners of different types. Disable a spawner by placing a few torches nearby to raise the light level above that required for mob spawning. You can also attack a spawner with a pickaxe to break it apart. With the spawner disabled, you're free to loot in peace.

Desert Temples

Desert temples appear in the desert biome, looking like stone pyramids, each with two turrets out front (see Figure 11.5), although they are often partially buried under sand dunes. These temples are architecturally interesting, but it's the four chests hidden beneath the floor of the main chamber that make them useful.

Head toward the central chamber. In the middle is a block of blue-stained clay. The chamber with the chests sits directly beneath this, but so does this structure's biggest danger: a pressure plate connected to nine TNT blocks. Go back a few blocks and dig out a block to see the chamber. Then dig down one of the walls to get to the base (shown in Figure 11.6), break the pressure plate to make the chamber safe, and raid the chests. While you're there, you might also want to dig up the floor and retrieve the TNT blocks.

FIGURE 11.5 A desert temple in its full glory. You're likely to find them partially or even almost completely buried, so keep an eye out for any orange-colored blocks while traipsing through the deserts.

Jungle Temples

Indiana Jones faced a trap-filled jungle temple in *Raiders of the Lost Ark*. While not quite as deadly, Minecraft offer its own jungle temples, awaiting exploration. A jungle temple is a mossy vine-laden structure that occurs only in jungle biomes (see Figure 11.7). Each contains two chests, one hidden behind a set of levers and, on the lower level, another protected by two sets of tripwire connected to a couple of arrow-shooting, face-piercing dispensers. Use shears to cut the tripwire and access the first chest, then head back to the levers. These form part of a puzzle that opens a sliding block beside the stairs in the entry level. Jump down to get to the next chest. Alternatively, just smash through the wall behind the levers to get to the chest.

FIGURE 11.6 The treasure room of a desert temple. Be careful of that pressure plate! If you find such a room already blown up, it was probably caused by a mob spawning it and trampling on the plate.

FIGURE 11.7 It isn't every day that you see a temple in the middle of a jungle.

Even if the chests don't contain anything particularly valuable, the jungle temple's construction provides many useful blocks and items, including three sticky pistons, two dispensers, arrows, tripwire hooks, redstone, string, and more. Unlike Indy, you won't need to deal with any giant rolling boulders as you plunder the temple. Bring in the wrecking crew and have a ball.

Witch Huts

Witch huts, shown in Figure 11.8, spawn in swamps and aren't particularly useful on their own because they don't contain chests. However, they do sometimes host a witch, complete with prominent wart. You need to take care with these witches because they're no Glinda the Good. They'll hurl various potions your way and use other potions to counteract your own. But on death, they can drop a few useful goodies, such as glowstone dust, bottles, spider eyes, and so on, as well as an occasional potion.

Fight the witches from a distance, out of potion-tossing range, using a bow.

FIGURE 11.8 A witch and her hut.

Dungeons

Dungeons are smaller rooms buried underground that house a mob spawner and usually one or two chests. Although they can appear anywhere, they're most easily spotted when their wall intersects with the side of a large cavern or an abandoned mine shaft. Look out for the greenish moss stone shown in Figure 11.9.

The chests can hold a lot of useful loot, so disable the spawner and enjoy.

FIGURE 11.9 A dungeon connected to a cave system. Some dungeons are more useful than others. This one's chests contained enchanted books, a saddle, lots of gunpowder, and more.

Abandoned Mine Shafts

I first mentioned mine shafts in Chapter 5, "Combat School" (see page 98). They are quite liberally scattered underground and often intersect caves, which makes them easy to find (see Figure 11.10). Each is different, and these caves often sprawl across huge multilayered levels. Explore them for their chests, rails, and timber but look out for cave spiders while you do so. One small bonus: You'll find lots of cobwebs near cave spider spawners. (Deactivate a spawner by placing a torch on it or nearby to raise the light level above the spawning threshold.)

Harvest the webs with a sword or shears to obtain string or use shears enchanted with silk touch to pull in the cobwebs. Cobwebs slow down all mobs except cave spiders, so they are useful in traps. However, they won't slow you down if you're riding a minecart, so you can use them to defend tunnels by slowing down other mobs while you speed ahead.

Strongholds

Strongholds are large underground structures. They come in a variety of sizes, often with numerous rooms and chests. More importantly, they also contain a special portal needed to reach The End region. The portal is protected by a silverfish spawner and must be activated first with Eyes of Ender.

Strongholds are tough to find. They're usually buried deep, although I have seen them in an ocean biome, where the structure could be seen by looking through the water.

Finding strongholds takes a specific technique. I cover this and the portal in Chapter 12, "Playing Through: The Nether and The End."

FIGURE 11.10 Abandoned mine shafts are renowned for their cave spiders but can contain all the other Overworld's hostile mobs, along with water and lava hazards. They're a great source of rails and wood, as well as other finds from chests.

Ocean Monuments

Ocean monuments, which appear in the Deep Ocean biome, provide a fun opportunity to explore underwater and potentially gain some golden treasure. Figure 11.11 shows an example with night vision enabled to make the water more transparent.

FIGURE 11.11 The ocean monument appears in the Deep Ocean biome in Minecraft v1.8 and later.

The structure is made of a stone-like material called prismarine and is lit by sea lantern blocks. On average, water dungeons consist of at least six rooms. In my experience, the Sea Lantern blocks are pretty darned dim, so you would be well-advised to make use of glowstone blocks as much as you can to shed some light on these watery corridors.

If you have cheats enabled, you can also give yourself underwater night vision by issuing the following command, replacing ***playername*** with your Minecraft login name: **/effect *playername* 16 3600 1 true**.

The centerpiece of the ocean monument is the treasure room, typically located in the core of the structure and guarded by several Elder Guardian mobs that act as bosses. The treasure itself consists of eight gold blocks encased in dark prismarine.

The "ordinary" guardian mobs that swim around and through the water templates aren't the friendliest, that's for sure. Their main attack mode is a laser beam; they also have a thorn-like attack performed courtesy of their barbed tails. Typically, their drops include prismarine shard, prismarine crystals, and raw fish.

If you're playing in Survival mode, you'll need to be adequately equipped to explore a water dungeon. I suggest making use of enchantments and potions wherever possible, including invisibility and the depth strider enchanted boots, which confer the ability to move quickly and breathe underwater.

NOTE

Fast-Track to an Ocean Monument

The Deep Ocean biome is, well, deep. Thus, you can use your favorite search engine to discover a Minecraft world seed that enables you to reach a water dungeon quickly and easily. For instance, start a new world session (make sure to enable cheats and Creative mode first) by using the seed ID **-7185414603555797276**. After you're in the world, use the cheat **/tp 1110 60 1692** to teleport to the structure. Have fun!

Nether Fortresses

These fortresses are huge structures that feature exclusively in The Nether region and contain unique ingredients for brewing potions and finding strongholds. They're packed with chests that can hold some powerful items. But getting to The Nether and surviving there long enough to find a fortress is a journey in itself. I show you how in Chapter 12.

Mapping, or There and Back Again

You'll likely make some significant tracks as you journey across The Overworld, finding its different structures. If pressing **F3** on Windows or **fn+F3** on OS X to constantly check coordinates seems a little like cheating, you can instead use one handy tool: maps. If you're playing on a game console, you have a map in your inventory when you start a new world, and that one map with a little coercion through zooming (see below) can display the entire world. That's not so on the PC, where the world is so much larger.

Follow these steps to start mapping:

1 Create a compass. The compass on its own isn't too useful; it *always* points to your world's original spawn point. This never changes, even after you change your own spawn point by sleeping in a bed, but if you've built your base quite close to that original spawn point, it could be useful. Just keep it in a quick access slot and follow the red needle. But let's continue on our current path and use the compass instead to make a map.

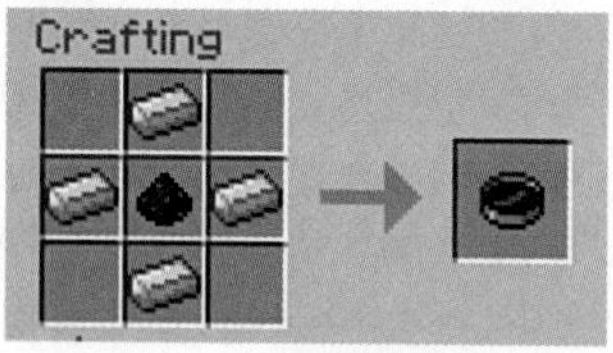

2 Place the compass in the middle of the crafting table and surround it with eight pieces of paper. (Remember: Paper is obtained from sugar cane, so it's quite easy to make.) Drag the map to a quick access slot. The map hasn't yet been used, so it shows up as empty.

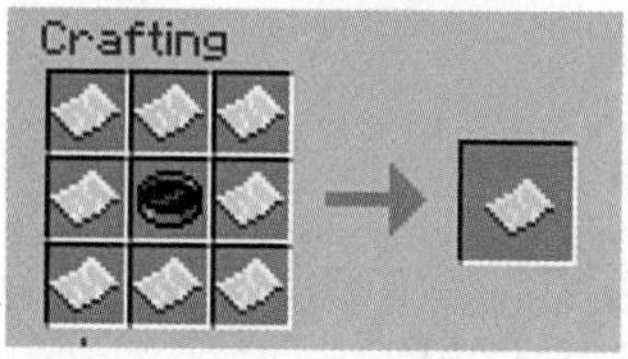

3 Select the map and right-click it to activate it. The map gradually fills in to show the landscape around you as well as structures such as villages (see Figure 11.12), although you may need to wander a little toward the edges of the map to complete the cartography because it shows only territory you've explored. Your last spawn point also shows up as a large black dot. Move your mouse up and down to bring the map to eye level or sink it down again so you can still hold it but see the territory ahead. Your approximate location at the time of activation becomes the permanent center of the map. It's approximate because maps align to an overall world grid, making it possible to create a series of maps whose edges align. Place them in a grid of item frames on a wall to create a much larger overall view of the world. Any other maps placed in frames elsewhere show up as small squares on every map covering that location, providing a way to pin locations for later reference.

FIGURE 11.12 Your location appears as a white arrow pointing in the direction you are facing. The most recent spawn point appears as a black dot, in this case just above and to the right of the arrow.

TIP

Avoid Map Confusion

Each map you create gets a unique number, and the maps are arranged sequentially from zero. You can see a map number as a ToolTip in the inventory window. This helps you keep the maps organized so you can select the correct one if you've created a few.

4 To see where you are located, look for the white arrow. Notice that it changes to a white dot if you move off the map, and this won't take long because the current map is quite small, covering an area of just 128×128 blocks, mapped as one block per pixel, or a scale of 1:1.

5 To make the map larger, zoom out by placing the map back on the crafting table and then adding another eight sheets of paper. Pick up the new map. Note that this process is not reversible. In other words, you can't zoom in a zoomed-out map. Maps can zoom out to a scale of 16:1, doubling each time.

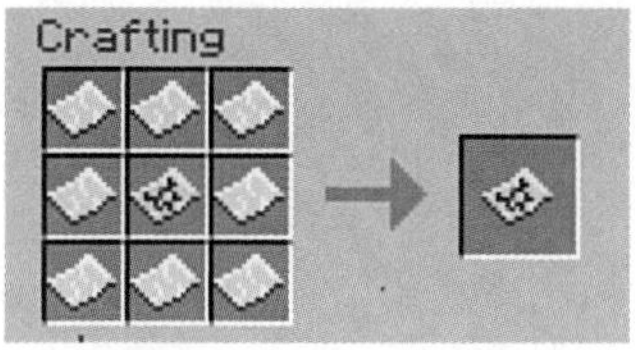

6 Place maps into a set of item frames arranged on the wall to create a seamless, much larger map.

Crafting a Clock

Clocks can help you keep track of time so that you know whether it's safe to surface while exploring structures underground or working in your mine. Craft a clock with four gold ingots and one piece of redstone.

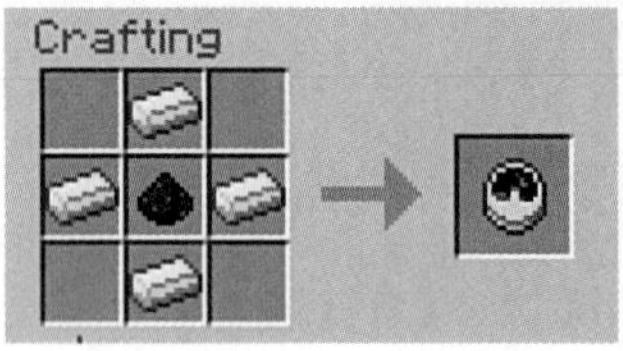

A clock works anywhere—in your inventory or in a quick access slot—and it even tells the time before you pick it up from the crafting table.

A clock works in a simple manner, rotating clockwise (appropriately enough) between night and day phases, represented by black and blue hemispheres. At midnight, you see the moon located at the 12 o'clock position. The sun rotates to the same location by noon. Figure 11.13 shows a clock mounted in an item frame with sunrise starting to approach, shown by the border between the blue hemisphere starting to push the night disk aside.

FIGURE 11.13 Time to put down tools and get back to the surface; morning has broken.

The Bottom Line

Minecraft's worlds are riddled with dungeons, abandoned mine shafts, and strongholds, as well as intricate, lengthy natural cave systems. You've probably seen some of this if you've done any flying around in Creative mode, where the landscape generates in real time in front of you, starting from the bottom up, giving you temporary x-ray vision. You'll find the largest structures below ground or under water, but temples do hold some useful bits and pieces, and trading with villages adds a whole new dynamic to the game. You can even treat the trading offers as a quest-generation system, heading out to gather the requirements for any given trade, no matter what, and without breaking the order in which they're received. Actually, as you'll see in the next chapter, the trading system can even let you skip the entire Nether region and jump straight to that epic pending battle with the Ender Dragon. Read on to learn how.

Playing Through: The Nether and The End

In This Chapter

- Get kitted up and head to The Nether.
- Find your way through a region of plummeting lava falls, endless fiery lakes, and precipitous cliffs.
- Locate The Nether fortress, defeat its mobs, and take home its horde.
- Set course for a stronghold and activate its portal.
- Travel to The End, defeat the dragon, and explore the region's islands, ships and cities.
- Build a beacon, gain additional powers, and throw a beam of light up into the sky.

Pack your bags for another field trip. You won't need your winter woolies because you'll be heading to hell and back. In this chapter, you'll explore Minecraft's other worlds: The Nether and The End. They're a little like Dante's vision of the seventh and ninth circles of hell: flaming rivers in one, an icy core in the other. Defeating the Ender dragon completes your journey through the official game structure, earning your passage back to The Overworld. You'll bring home countless treasures, valuable experience, and the priceless achievement of having won the toughest battle in Minecraft. Think of it as going from hell 9 to cloud 9.

Alternate Dimensions

The Nether (see Figure 12.1) and The End (see Figure 12.2) regions are not fun places to hang out. You need to go in with specific goals; don't dawdle too long. Both places are hazardous to your health, and any time you die, you respawn in The Overworld and lose anything you haven't been able to put away in a chest for safekeeping.

TIP

Nether Here and There

Ender Chests transport the same items between all dimensions, so they are incredibly useful for stashing valuable finds when traveling in the more dangerous regions. Die in The Nether, and you can pick up anything you've already stored in an Ender Chest back in The Overworld when you respawn. Create an Ender Chest with one Eye of Ender and eight obsidian blocks. (Of course, you need at least two Ender Chests—one at each end—to make this useful.) See "The End Game," later in the chapter, for more on creating those elusive eyes.

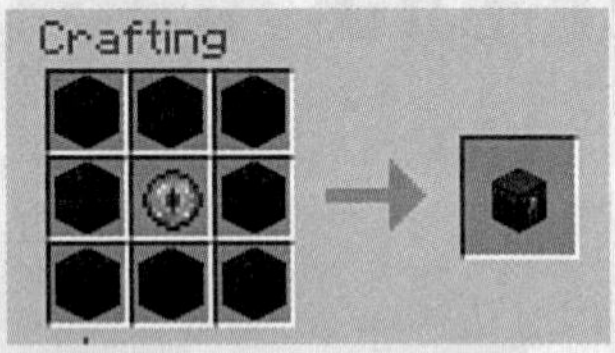

FIGURE 12.1 Seeing red? It's just The Nether: a cavernous, unforgiving place filled with more lava pools than a Krakatoan conference.

FIGURE 12.2 The End region is a dark dimension inhabited by a large dragon. It's probably high time to swap that pickaxe for something significantly sharper.

Getting through both dimensions and playing through to the end of the game takes a bit of work, but you can definitely get lucky. Although your experience will vary as much as it does in any unique Minecraft world, it will run something like this:

1 Take your time to build up your resources in The Overworld and become combat ready; you're heading into a heck of a fight, and it's going to take a lot more than just a couple of swords and some light armor to get through.

2 Build an obsidian portal to travel to The Nether.

3 Find a Nether fortress and defeat a dozen or so blaze mobs. Collecting their dropped blaze rods.

4 Return to The Overworld and craft Eyes of Ender. You'll also need to defeat about 15 Endermen in The Overworld to gain Ender Pearls for this recipe, but also see the tip "Trade Your Way to The End," which follows this list.

5 Use the Eyes of Ender to find a stronghold and activate its end portal.

6 Defeat the Ender dragon and travel through the exit portal back to The Overworld. In Minecraft's rather spare tradition, you won't see a fancy end game sequence, but you'll get to read the existential "End Poem" and see the credits roll, followed by a final score that is equal to your current experience points.

Try to be patient as you complete these six steps. This is not a first-person shooter that takes a day, some pizza, and a rack of energy drinks to finish off, although you certainly could. It also isn't an impossible challenge, and you'll see some great sights along the way.

Even better, the game isn't over once you've defeated the Ender dragon. There are new islands in The End to explore, accessed by the End gateway portal, as well as v1.9's all new End cities.

TIP

Trade Your Way to The End

Traveling to The Nether is not actually a prerequisite for completing the game. You really only need to go there to obtain the blaze rods that supply blaze powder. When you combine blaze powder with an Ender Pearl dropped by an Enderman, the result is an Eye of Ender. If you've found a village or two, look for the purple-garbed priest villager. There's about a 16% probability that he will offer to sell you an Eye of Ender for 7 to 10 emeralds a pop. Even if the initial trade isn't useful, you can use it to open additional trades until you have the one you want. This is actually a great way to get to the end of the game if you're not so much into hardcore combat. It will still take quite a bit of time, though, because you'll be extremely busy doing different tasks to complete other trades until you've amassed sufficient Eyes of Ender.

CAUTION

Chores Are Over, but Don't Make Your Bed

Sleeping in a bed in either The Nether or The End regions is definitely not a good idea. Settle in for a quick nap, and the bed explodes faster than a creeper on final fuse.

Getting to The Nether

A successful trip to The Nether is mostly about being prepared. Start by gathering the items on this survival checklist:

- **A full set of iron armor**—When it comes to armor, diamond is best, but given the scarcity of diamond blocks, and accepting the fact that you'll almost certainly die and respawn without it, just stick with iron. If you can, apply an enchantment of feather falling to your boots so you can jump down cliffs, and use any other protection enchantments you can summon up. Remember, though, that when you die, your armor doesn't come back with you, so don't go overboard. Be utilitarian rather than try to become invincible.
- **A couple of iron pickaxes and a few swords**—Make one of the swords diamond; it will help in a difficult fight.

- **An iron shovel and a full stack of gravel (64 blocks)**—You'll need this stuff for pillar jumping. The Nether has a lot of crazy-tall cliffs you'll need to get up and down.
- **Two full stacks of cobblestone**—You'll need this to create temporary shelters, bridges, and barricades.

NOTE

Forget the Water

Don't worry about bringing water with you. There's no way to place it, so you can't convert any of the numerous, enormous lava lakes to cobblestone or obsidian for easier passage.

- **A bow and a full stack of arrows**—Use these to shoot down ghasts, or use a bow with the infinity enchantment to save on arrows.
- **Snow blocks**—Turn these into snowballs to help fight blaze mobs.
- **10 obsidian blocks and a flint and steel**—Gather these in case you need to build another portal to return to The Overworld. (You'll also need 10 blocks to build the portal to get to The Nether, so aim for 20 in all.) See "Creating and Mining Obsidian" on page 225 if you need help finding obsidian.
- **Lots of torches!**—Stock yourself with as many as a full stack if you can. Torches are mostly useful for creating a trail of breadcrumbs so you can find your way back to your portal. (It's ridiculously easy to become lost down there.) Also consider bringing some jack-o'-lanterns because they are easily spotted across a longer distance.
- **A stack of wood blocks of any kind and around 20 iron ingots**—You can use these to create a crafting table and additional weapons, tools, and ladders, as needed.
- **An iron door and some iron bars**—Use these to create a temporary shelter for crafting, healing, taking a breather, and so on. Wooden doors can burn when hit by fireballs in The Nether, even though they are immune to fire in The Overworld. Don't forget to bring some iron buttons so you can open the door.
- **Food**—Aim for bread and cooked meats—at least half a stack of each. You need to keep your hunger bar full so that your health continually regenerates.
- **A chest**—An Ender Chest is fantastic, but you may not have been able to make one yet. Any other chest will do.

Arrange one of each weapon in the hotbar slots, along with the torches, shovel, gravel, cobblestone, and a couple of food stacks. You can leave the rest in the upper section of the inventory.

Ready? Let's go. The first order of business is to put up a portal.

Portal Magic

A Nether portal acts as an interdimensional transport between The Overworld and The Nether. Follow these steps:

1 Create an obsidian frame with an inner dimension that is at least three blocks high by two blocks wide (see Figure 12.3). Make the corner blocks from any material, or even leave them blank. The frame must be vertical, and it can be either free-standing or built against any type of surface.

FIGURE 12.3 Build your gateway to the underworld (I mean The Nether) with an obsidian frame.

CAUTION

Portals Are a Double-Edged Sword

Once you've built a portal in The Overworld, a second one appears in The Nether. Neither belongs to you exclusively, and they allow mobs to travel back and forth, so expect to see quite a few more Zombie Pigmen in The Overworld in the near future. (They can even spawn near them in The Overworld without coming from The Nether.)

2 Use a flint and steel to light the top of either of the two bottom blocks. The interior springs to life with a shimmering blue and purple transparent texture, as shown in Figure 12.4.

3 Okay, take a last long look at The Overworld and hope that you won't see it for a while because if you do, it probably means you've respawned. Now, jump into that frame!

4 If Minecraft needs to download terrain files, wait until you see a wavy animation that covers the whole screen and then step through the portal to enter The Nether.

FIGURE 12.4 Once lit, the frame stays that way unless it's hit by a ghast's fireball, but you only need to worry about that with the companion frame in The Nether.

Once in The Nether, you've got some work to do. Remember that your main goal is to find a Nether fortress.

The Nether has some very extreme terrain, so you may need to make use of any of the following techniques:

- Dig tunnels and stairs by mining the Netherrack with your pickaxe to move up and down cliffs. Fortunately, Netherrack breaks extremely fast, so it's easy to get around, but be prepared for lava to break through. It flows faster down there and can catch you quite unawares.
- Remember to place torches or jack-o'-lanterns as you go, always ensuring that you can see the last one placed from the next position. If you become hopelessly lost, consider building another portal to take you back to The Overworld. You may pop up quite some distance away from where you left, though, because every block traveled in The Nether is the equivalent of eight blocks traveled in The Overworld.
- Deal with mobs carefully and don't attack Zombie Pigmen because doing so will bring an entire horde of them down on you. Your biggest risk as you explore comes from ghasts and their fireballs, but the fireballs are slow, and you can knock them straight back at a ghast with a well-timed sword swing or arrow. Zigzag if you decide to retreat so they don't keep a bearing on you with the next volley. See "Nether Mobs," later in this chapter, for specific strategies.
- Use the sneak key (left **Shift**) when you're close to any cliffs and lava lakes to avoid taking a tumble.

- Crank the screen's **Brightness** slider all the way to the right in the game's **Options > Video Settings** menu and ensure that **Render Distance** is set to its furthest setting if your computer can support it. This will help you spot Nether fortresses.
- Stop to pick up a few things as you go. The bright glowstone, red and brown mushrooms, soul sand, and Nether quartz all exist in abundance and are useful crafting and brewing ingredients.
- Pause every so often to take a good look for the fortress. They're recognizable at a distance by their wide expanses of Netherbrick, long exposed walkways and bridges, rows of windows, and, often, tall walls. You're looking for any straight-geometric structure within the geological randomness of the cave system. Figure 12.5 shows the ramparts of a Netherbrick wall, signifying a fortress. Luck dictates how quickly you find one. It might take just a few minutes, in which case you can rush in, get things done, head back, and have almost all your possessions intact. Or it could take hours of hard slog. Nether fortresses generate along the north/south axis in long lines, so the easiest way to find one is to try to head east or west. A compass won't help as it will spin randomly in The Nether, but you can use the **F3** (**fn+F3** on a Mac) trick in a pinch. The x-axis is aligned east/west and the z-axis north/south, and your direction is clearly called out in the debug data. If you don't see a fortress after traveling 160 blocks or so, head about 40 blocks north or south and try again.

FIGURE 12.5 You can spot fortresses from below by looking for the walls that extend down to the lowest levels of a cave. When looking down from above, you'll see long straight walkways and rows of window spaces.

- If you enter a fortress from below, use your pickaxe to dig out the Netherbrick and ascend until you reach a corridor. If you're coming from above, just work your way down to a walkway and enter the fortress or come in through a sidewall. You may need to navigate around broken walkways or cave-ins, but fortresses are massive, so if a viable entry isn't obvious at first, just look around until you can find a way in.

Now you're almost done. There is a bit of combat ahead, and then you can head back out to The Overworld.

Surviving the Nether Fortress

Every fortress presents a similar experience: traipsing long mazes of corridors before stumbling into a moment of extreme terror! Actually, it's not that bad. You will find many long corridors. You'll also find numerous chests filled with some of the most valuable and rare items in the game. Then, once in a while, you'll probably find a small balcony containing a spawner churning out blaze mobs (see Figure 12.6), wandering wither skeletons, and magma cubes.

FIGURE 12.6 Try not to pause in this position: There's a blaze spawner in the middle and a floating blaze on the left, emitting smoke during its cool-down period.

Follow these tips to survive:

- Place torches on the ground as you pass intersections so that you can find your way back to your original entry point and then back to the portal.
- Use blocks to create temporary barricades when attacking or being pursued by mobs. This proves particularly useful in long corridors where it's impossible to dodge away from an arrow-wielding wither skeleton or when ducking out to attack the blazes springing from a spawner.

- Loot every chest you find. It's always worthwhile!
- Avoid spending too long on open walkways, where you'll be vulnerable to ghast attacks.
- Look for the bright red Nether wart growing around the base of wide stairways. It's the base of all potions, and a few potions will help you complete the final part of the game.
- When you find a blaze spawner, put up a two-block-high barricade nearby and then wait just behind the nearest corner to attack blazes as they approach from the other side. You can duck in and out, timing your attacks for when they've finished throwing their fireballs. If all goes south, retreat back to the barricade and rebuild your health.
- Remember, you're here mainly for the blaze rods. Collect them from each killed blaze until you have 10 or so and then head back to the portal and the bright, sunny, verdant Overworld.
- Place your spoils of victory in a chest near the fortress entry point now and then, just in case you die. You can come back and pick them up later or grab them on the way out after you've hit your quota.

That's all there is to it, really. It's not so difficult on Normal difficulty, and it becomes quite easy once you've done it a few times.

Nether Mobs

You'll meet an interesting mix of mobs while exploring The Nether. If you're properly equipped, they won't present too much of a problem:

- **Zombie Pigmen**—I first introduced these in Chapter 5 ("Zombie Pigmen," page 99). Avoid fighting them because, as with zombies, you'll get rushed by a mob, and they tend to not give up for quite a while. Their drops aren't really worth the risk, and you'll find a lot more swag in a fortress.
- **Ghasts**—With a fittingly ghastly moan, these huge floating mobs attack you from a long distance (see Figure 12.7). They're quite slow moving but spit out dangerous fireballs that can cause as much damage by an indirect hit—setting the Netherrack around you on fire—as they do directly. Take care of them with two to three fully charged arrows and dodge the fireballs by moving just a few blocks out of the line of fire. If you're brave enough, you can also fish them in with a fishing rod and hack at them with a sword. Ghasts drop magma cream and ghast tears, both useful for brewing, but you'll need to find one over land or pull it in with a fishing rod so the drops don't burn up in lava.

FIGURE 12.7 Ghasts typically float through The Nether's sulphurous air, but they can also sink into a lava lake and take potshots at you, sniper-style.

- **Blazes**—You might find blazes floating down the corridors of a fortress, but they're usually near a spawner. They have a distinctive attack pattern, spinning up for a few seconds while emitting a fire effect and then firing off three quick fireballs at you. They then cool off for a while. Attack them while they're chilling down or early on, when they're spinning up. Swords work well if one separates from the pack; otherwise, use arrows and then make a dash past the entryway to the spawner to pick up the blaze rod drops.
- **Magma cubes**—These burning cubes split like slime mobs in The Overworld. They're slower but far more dangerous and harder to kill. Attack the large cubes and middle-sized cubes from a distance with arrows and then finish off the small ones with your sword. You pick up a lot of experience points and the handy magma cream.
- **Wither skeleton**—These tall versions of the regular skeleton stalk the hallways of fortresses. They usually use swords but occasionally can pick up a bow, and getting hit by one causes the wither effect, a type of soul-destroying poison that darkens your health bar for 10 seconds while causing additional damage. They're best attacked with an arrow from a distance. You can also turn the odds in your favor by creating a bolthole that's just two blocks high. The wither skeleton is a little taller than the regular skeleton and can't follow you through. The wither skeleton will occasionally drop a wither skull. After you have three of these, you can, if you care to dice with death, create a wither boss. See "Introducing the Wither Boss" next for more information.

NOTE

Introducing the Wither Boss

The Wither Boss is a player-created hostile mob, and it's incredibly tough to defeat. It can destroy every block in Minecraft except bedrock and end portal frames, and it attacks all other mobs by flinging out black and blue skulls. It also drops a Nether star on defeat, and you'll need one of those to create a beacon (discussed later in the chapter). The Wither Boss is created by placing soul sand from The Nether dimension in a T shape, much like with the iron golem, and then placing three wither skulls along the top row of the T. There's no need to create a Wither Boss to get through the game, but if you want to have some fun, spawn one by typing the command **/summon WitherBoss**. Visit http://minecraft.gamepedia.com/Wither to learn more.

- **Endermites**—This little critter sometimes spawns when an Enderman teleports or when you teleport by throwing an Ender Pearl. They are easily defeated with a couple of swift thrusts of even an iron sword.

With some blaze rods in hand, you have what you need for the final journey. The End, as they say, is nigh.

DANTE'S DIMENSIONS

It's probably all just coincidence, but there are some interesting parallels between Minecraft's other dimensions and Dante's own. Dante treated the levels of hell as concentric spheres, each becoming smaller, like the layers of an onion (with plenty of associated weeping, as well as a lot of gnashing). The seventh level, the one that most closely corresponds with The Nether, is eight layers beneath the earth. In Minecraft, The Nether has a scale 1/8 that of The Overworld, so traveling 100 blocks in The Nether and then taking a portal back to the surface would have taken you 800 blocks in The Overworld. This is exactly how it would work if The Nether were a smaller sphere beneath The Overworld, and, of course, *nether* does mean *lower*, or *under*.

Dante's ninth and final circle is a small frozen region protected by a winged Satan. Minecraft's The End region is a similarly barren, tiny region protected by a winged dragon. While Dante's Satan was trapped in the ice, and Dante and Virgil didn't have to defeat him, they nevertheless found their way back to the surface of the earth by climbing down through a hole in the center. In Minecraft, you'll jump through a portal in the middle of The End to find your way back to the sunny side.

The End Game

Are you ready to start the final phase? Just as you prepared for The Nether, you'll need to gather a few items for The End. There are two parts to the conclusion: finding a stronghold and finding The End portal and then defeating the Ender dragon. You don't need to get everything on this list, but it will give you an idea of the level of preparation:

- **Eyes of Ender**—You'll need about 15 of these, and you can get them either by trading with priest villagers or by crafting. You may need up to 12 to activate The End portal, and you'll need the rest to find the stronghold. If crafting the eyes, spend some time defeating 15 Endermen to collect 15 Ender Pearls. Endermen are easiest to find at night. Place the blaze rods you collected from The Nether on the crafting grid (saving at least one for a brewing stand if you plan to concoct some potions) and collect the blaze powder. Combine that with the Ender Pearls to create the Eyes of Ender.

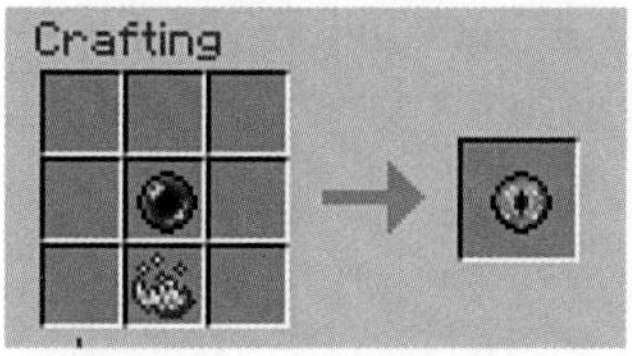

- **Weapons**—Bring a diamond sword (hopefully with a sharpness enchantment) and a couple of bows with infinity enchantments or at least two stacks of arrows. Also bring some string in case you need to build additional bows.
- **Armor**—Diamond armor is ideal, including boots with a feather fall enchantment because you'll probably suffer a couple of long drops while fighting the dragon. Bring a helmet and a pumpkin and consider using the latter so that you don't antagonize the numerous Endermen into a fight.
- **Potions**—Brew up potions of regeneration and healing. Strength potions can help, but only when you can attack the dragon with a sword. You'll mostly use a bow and arrows. See Chapter 10, "Enchanting, Anvils, and Brewing," if you aren't familiar with enchanting and brewing.
- **Food**—Pack about half as much as recommended for The Nether expedition.
- **Tools**—Bring a couple of stacks of dirt or gravel and of course an iron shovel because there will be some pillar jumping involved. Also bring two iron pickaxes because you'll need to dig down to the stronghold, and they'll help you in The End region.
- **Ladders**—Using ladders is an alternative to pillar jumping. Just plan for whichever you prefer.
- **Obsidian**—Bring about 12 blocks, just in case you need to build a bridge that the Ender dragon can't destroy.

- **Bed**—You can't use it in The End region, but you may need it while finding the stronghold. Once you have a bed, you can set it up in the portal room to create a new spawn point.
- **The kitchen sink**—Bring anything else you can think of to set up a small shelter in the stronghold to act as your base, such as wood and iron blocks for tools, additional diamonds, a crafting table, a furnace, a brewing stand, and so on. At least be prepared to make a small shelter in case you need to spend a night on your way to the stronghold.

Finding a Stronghold

Each Overworld generates with three strongholds located between 640 and 1,152 blocks from the world's original spawn point. You might be lucky and find the stronghold in just a few minutes; your search shouldn't take any longer than 20 minutes. The strongholds are spaced at equidistant angles from the spawn, 120 degrees apart, with no part rising above the general terrain. They are, however, cut by natural terrain features such as ravines and valleys, so while in most cases they're buried deep underground, there's a chance that you could stumble across an exposed section. You may even find just a stronghold's portal room sitting on its own in water.

Follow these steps to find your first stronghold:

1. Climb to a high spot, ideally with some clear space around it, and then throw an Eye of Ender. It will float into the air and zoom off in the direction of the nearest stronghold.
2. If the eye floats to the ground a short distance away (which it does in four out of five cases), pick it up to use it again, and you're already on your way to the stronghold. In some cases, the eye just explodes instead. Don't worry; just head in the same direction.
3. Keep traveling for quite some way so you don't use too many eyes; then throw another. The eyes float high when the stronghold is distant and float quickly to the ground when you're close or over the top of the stronghold. In the PC edition, the eye homes in on The End portal room, whereas in the console edition it takes you to the center of the dungeon; you need to explore the dungeon from there to find the portal room.
4. When you think you have zeroed in on the dungeon's location, start digging. Use normal mining techniques to create a staircase and turn regularly so that you stay in the same general area. You'll know you're there when you start to dig up stone or mossy bricks. Keep going until you break through into the portal room or a corridor, but don't dig straight down, or you could fall into a lava pool (see Figure 12.8). If you need to work your way down into the room, open the roof a little and sneak-place blocks against the wall to create steps.

FIGURE 12.8 Eureka! Breaking through into The End portal room.

The portal room contains a silverfish spawner. These mobs are best defeated in one blow, using a diamond sword with at least a sharpness level 1 enchantment. Taking more than one blow alerts others, and you could end up with a swarm, but they're not impossible to handle without an enchanted sword. Just try to dispatch them as quickly as possible. Silverfish can also appear when breaking a Monster Egg block, a type of block that looks just like ordinary stone, cobblestone, or brick. You'll only stumble across these in strongholds and, very rarely, an extreme hills biome.

Once you've cleared the room, there are just a few more preparatory steps:

1. Destroy the spawner with a pickaxe.
2. Block up the entrance you used to enter the portal chamber, assuming that you didn't saunter in through the iron door in the anteroom.
3. Place a bed and sleep in it to reset your spawn. If you die in The End (which is very likely), you'll come straight back here, which will save you the overland trek.
4. Place a torch in the anteroom to prevent other mobs from spawning.
5. Check the chest that's in the anteroom to see if there's anything useful there, and then dump almost everything else you're carrying in the chest. You only want to take with you the armor you're wearing (including the pumpkin that you should place on your head), one of each weapon, about two dozen food items, a pickaxe, some potions, and a shovel.
6. If you want to just take a look at The End region first, store everything you have in the chest except for a dozen or so dirt blocks or obsidian, a pickaxe, and a cheap bow and half a dozen arrows. This approach can help if you spawn in an awkward position and need to first build a bridge from obsidian to the main island. If you get swept into the void by the Ender dragon, you'll be able to come back and complete the job, bringing

a complete set of tools once you're sure you can get across. Any dropped items are not recoverable after respawning, although items placed in a chest in The End will survive. When you're ready to return, just die in some convenient way, pick up the main set of supplies stashed in the stronghold, and head back through the portal.

CAUTION

Don't Destroy the Portal!

Be extra careful not to destroy any End portal blocks. There's no way to repair them, and you'll then have to find one of the other two dungeons to continue your journey.

Now the final magic moment: activating the portal. Climb the steps and place Eyes of Ender in any of the empty slots on top of the stones surrounding the portal. You'll see it spring into deep black life, as shown in Figure 12.9.

FIGURE 12.9 The End portal, ready for action.

The portal is now ready for action...are you? That dragon has no idea what's coming. Go ahead and jump in. Then press **Esc** to pause and read on.

Defeating the Ender Dragon

The End region generates as a fairly small island comprised of end stone, floating in an endless void, dotted with obsidian towers and numerous Endermen. Your spawn point is probably located on this island, but it can also be underground (in which case you can use your pickaxe to dig out a staircase to the surface) or on an even smaller platform floating a small distance away from the mainland. If that's the case, you'll need to build a platform across, using your dirt blocks or obsidian, and keep your bow handy so that you can shoot the Ender dragon if it attacks so it doesn't push you into the void.

The Ender dragon is no quick kill. With 200 hit points and the ability to knock out up to half your health in a single blow, its wings are not easily clipped, and while it will spew acid at you if you spend too long standing still, it's also no Smaug. There's also nowhere to hide. When you get near the towers, even burrowing into the ground won't save you because the dragon can fly through the ground and any structures to reach you.

Defeat the dragon following these steps. It's actually not difficult but can take a few attempts. Always keep your hunger bar topped up so your health can continually regenerate.

The dragon draws healing power from the Ender crystals located atop eight obsidian towers of varying height, arranged in a broad circle around the portal back to The Overworld (see Figure 12.10). You won't defeat the dragon without knocking out every one of those crystals, and the portal won't activate until you've knocked him out. Follow these steps:

FIGURE 12.10 You'll probably first spot the Ender dragon in the distance. Look for the line of shimmering power as it passes by an Ender crystal.

1 Put the pumpkin on your head so you don't annoy any Endermen. They'll needlessly sap your health, so it's worth having a reduced field of view, as shown in Figure 12.11. Crank up the brightness in your video settings if you're having trouble seeing your surroundings.

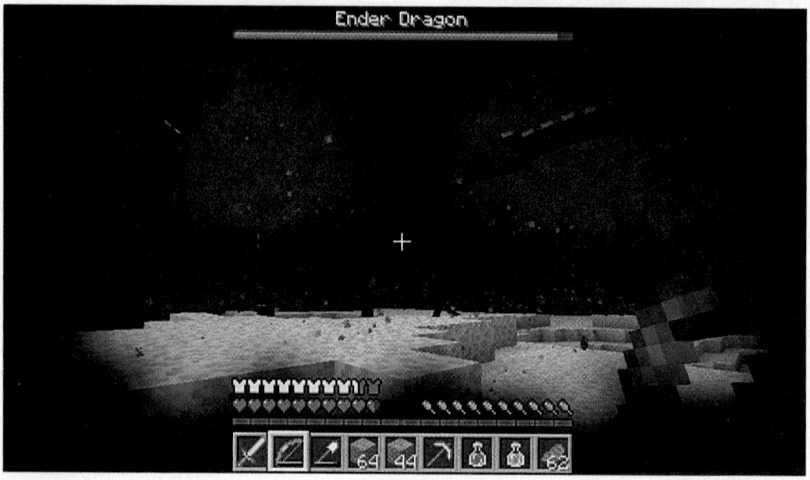

FIGURE 12.11 Wearing the pumpkin requires a bit more scanning to get the full picture, but it doesn't take too long to get used to it.

2 Head toward the nearest pillar. You'll be able to shoot out the Ender crystal on top with a single arrow shot if the pillar is low enough and not protected by an iron cage; otherwise, you need to pillar jump to climb to the top. When you see the dragon's health bar appear, you know it is close by. Take a look around and try to fire an arrow into its head (its most sensitive part) if it's on an attack run heading straight for you. Otherwise, continue pillar jumping a few more seconds and then look again. Keep in mind that the dragon will attack you by firing acid balls, and you can also get knocked off by the dragon's wing when it's just flying by. That's when armored boots with a feather falling enchantment are very handy. It may also destroy some of your ladder. If that happens, just climb back up as fast as you can, fill in the gaps, and continue to the top.

3 Break any cage surrounding the crystal, then try to hit the crystal with an arrow. This is best done from a position of cover, such as on the ladder while a block or two from the top. It's best to stay as far away as possible from your target because the resulting explosion can cause substantial damage. (That explosion can also knock out other nearby crystals, so it may benefit you.) Also, if you have diamond armor with a high-level protection enchantment, just whack the crystal with impunity.

4 Take a good look around from the top of the tower and shoot out any other crystals that are within range.

5 Head back to the ground and use your shovel to dig out the dirt blocks you placed.

6 Repeat steps 2–5 until you've taken out every crystal. You should be able to spot any you've missed by looking for the white beams that show up as the dragon draws power.

Now it's Ender dragon time. Follow these steps to deal it a deathly blow:

1 Position yourself near the final portal in the middle of the circle of towers. The dragon will alight there now and then turn to face you, spewing out acid. Just keep your distance and fire arrow after fully charged arrow into its head.

2 Keep your bow fully charged, with the arrow ready to fly with a critical hit. You can also take off the pumpkin helmet at this point to improve your vision because you really only need to look up at the dragon, so you're unlikely to antagonize any Endermen.

3 Take your time waiting for the dragon to start its attack run. It flaps around in the distance for a while. Don't waste arrows firing at the dragon until it turns to face you from its perch, but be ready to step sideways to dodge any acid balls it will throw your way when it's flying around. Figure 12.12 shows the moment you should unleash the arrow. Aim your crosshairs directly at the dragon's head to cause maximum damage. (My aim is a little off in that screenshot. Let me just say that it can be quite difficult to fight an Ender dragon *and* take screenshots at the same time!)

FIGURE 12.12 The Ender dragon, on the final stage of its attack run.

4 Still aiming directly for the Ender dragon's head to cause maximum damage, shoot an arrow. After you hit the dragon, you'll see it flash red and quickly change direction. With correct timing, you can repeatedly hit the dragon without taking any damage.

5 Repeat your attack until you've knocked the dragon's health down to zero. Then stand by for a striking purple-strobed explosion of splendid proportion (see Figure 12.13).

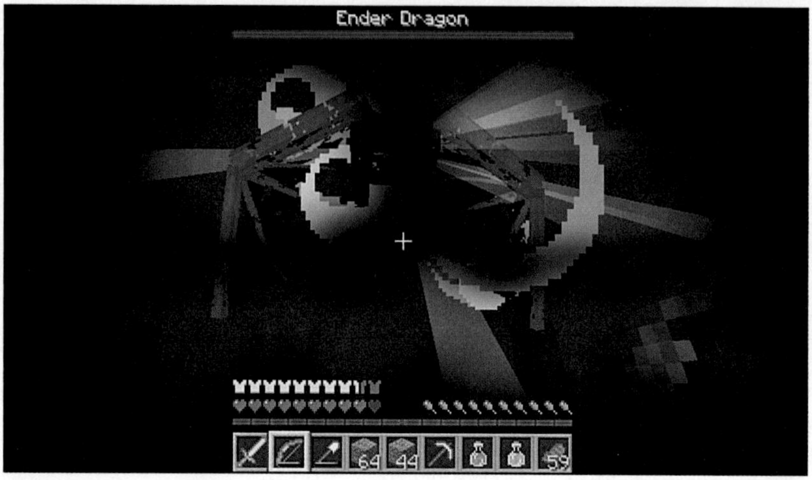

FIGURE 12.13 The final moments of the Ender dragon.

Congratulations! Notch yourself up as a dragon slayer because you've just defeated the toughest mob in Minecraft! Enjoy the spectacle; it's probably been a long time coming and is over far too fast.

Watch for a portal to appear directly beneath the dragon's last position as soon as the fireworks finish (see Figure 12.14). It will have a dragon egg perched atop—a shrine, if you like, to the dragon's defeat, or a celebration of your victory. Maybe both.

FIGURE 12.14 Grab that dragon egg for your trophy cabinet back home.

You'll also see the End gateway portal (see Figure 12.15), a way to get to the other islands in The End region. The portal entry is one block in size, so the only way in is by throwing an Ender Pearl at it. There are a few islands scattered around.

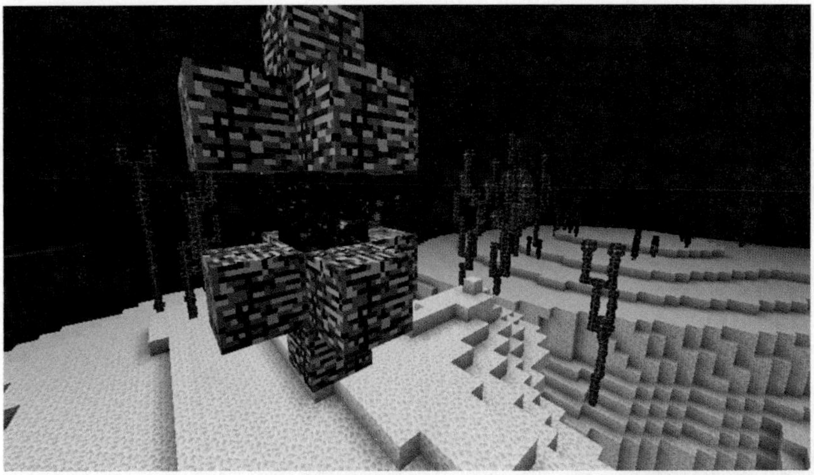

FIGURE 12.15 Use the gateway portal to jump instantly to other islands.

Throw in the Ender Pearl from different sides of the portal to visit each one, and then enjoy exploring their End cities (see Figure 12.16) and ships (see Figure 12.17), and collecting the chorus fruit from the regions odd-shaped trees. Just beware the purple-colored Shulkers, a projectile-firing mob that exists only on these islands. Getting hit by one will cause you damage and also make you levitate for a short while, making you an easier target. Fortunately, their homing projectiles travel fairly slowly.

FIGURE 12.16 End cities contain a range of treasures, although you might have to travel some way to find them.

FIGURE 12.17 Although not easy to reach, the ships in The End stash a few goodies in their hold, including a brewing stand. You'll also find something else you can't get anywhere else: a dragon's head at the prow.

Before you take the fast route home by jumping into the portal, stop to pick up the numerous experience orbs dropped by the dragon. You'll collect up to 70 XP levels. You can also keep the pumpkin helmet on and start wailing on Endermen to gather experience, but you'll need to do so without the pumpkin for them to drop Ender Pearls. That's a somewhat dangerous exercise, so it's best to make a safe exit and then return when you've restocked your weapons, armor, and supplies. You can always return through any stronghold portal later.

TIP

Wanna Grab That Egg?

Getting the dragon egg is a little tricky, and the egg itself doesn't serve any purpose except as a trophy piece to put in an item frame back home. But why not? Build a small platform up to the egg and hit it with any tool to knock it to the ground. (Actually, it teleports, but not too far.) There's only one way to crack this egg, and that's by digging two blocks under it, placing a torch on the lowest block, and then knocking out the one directly under the egg. Jump in to pick up the dropped egg and scramble out of there.

And that, as they say, is that. When you're ready, jump feet first into the portal to view the End Poem (it's worth a read) and game credits—or press **Esc** to skip (see Figure 12.18). You'll return to your last spawn point in The Overworld.

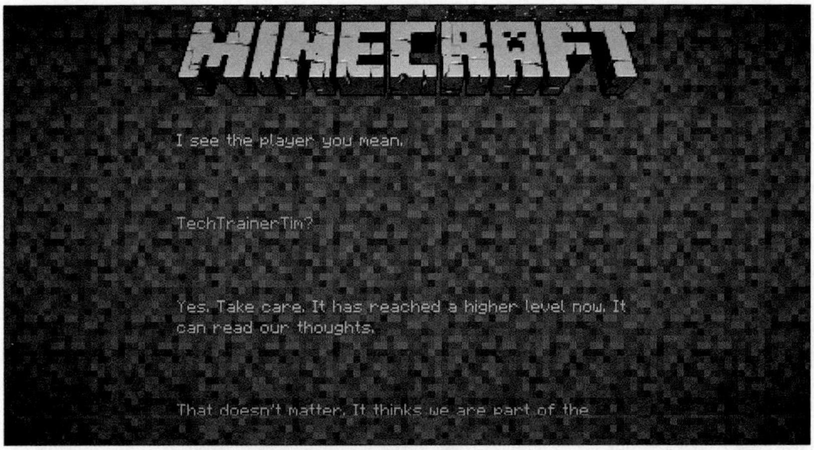

FIGURE 12.18 A sneak peek of the End Poem.

Beckoning a Beacon

The Wither Boss is the toughest mob to defeat, and the Nether star it drops also happens to lead to the most difficult item one can build in Minecraft: the beacon.

A beacon throws into the sky a light beam that is visible from the furthest render distance set in the video options. This makes it a useful marker, as it is often visible from far away. However, more importantly, the beacon casts an aura in a square shape that bestows those within range with special powers; this is called an *effect*. The way this works is quite interesting and perhaps just a little complicated. Here are the key characteristics:

- The beacon block must form the apex of a pyramid created from mineral blocks that are one to four layers deep. The block material doesn't matter. You can use blocks of iron, gold, diamond, and emerald, in any combination. Remember that a single block is formed from nine pieces of the base material.
- The beacon's capabilities depend on the height of the pyramid on which it is placed, as shown in Table 12.1. Beacons of one to three layers provide one of five primary powers. A beacon of four layers adds a secondary power of regeneration, but you can choose instead to boost the primary effect. Figure 12.19 shows beacons atop all four pyramids.
- Multiple beacons can share the same base pyramid blocks, as long as there is a regular square pyramid shape under each beacon. Even the materials can be mixed (see Figure 12.20).

- Change the color of a beam by placing stained glass above the beacon so that it intersects the beam (see Figure 12.21). Use multiple stained glass blocks to create any color in the visible spectrum. Using different colors is a useful way to identify different locations from afar.

FIGURE 12.19 Nether beacon pyramids, from one layer to four. Materials can be placed in any order and even mixed up in the one layer.

FIGURE 12.20 Beacons can share the same pyramid blocks as those adjacent, with each beacon projecting a different effect.

FIGURE 12.21 Changing beacons with stained glass blocks. Combine different colors to create the same color combinations you get from dyeing leather.

TABLE 10.1 Combat Enchantments

Pyramid Height	Blocks Required	Bottom Layer Size	Effective Area of Powers	Available Effects
1	9	3×3	20×20	Speed I (move 20% faster) Haste I (break blocks 20% faster)
2	34	5×5	30×30	Above plus: Resistance I (reduce incoming damage by 20%) Jump Boost I (jump higher by half a block)
3	83	7×7	40×40	Above plus: Strength I (increase damage dealt by 130%)
4	164	9×9	50×50	Above plus: Regeneration I (gain back 1 point of health every 2.5 seconds) Or boost any power above to level II strength, typically doubling its effectiveness

Given that pyramids work the same no matter from which mineral they are made, it makes sense to focus on using iron as the base material as it's far more plentiful than the rest. Also note that pyramids do not need to be aboveground. You could start with a single-layer pyramid and then dig into the ground to add additional layers in the future, boosting its effective area.

Top the pyramid with a beacon crafted from obsidian, glass, and a Nether star and then right-click the star to open the special Nether beacon interface, shown in Figure 12.22.

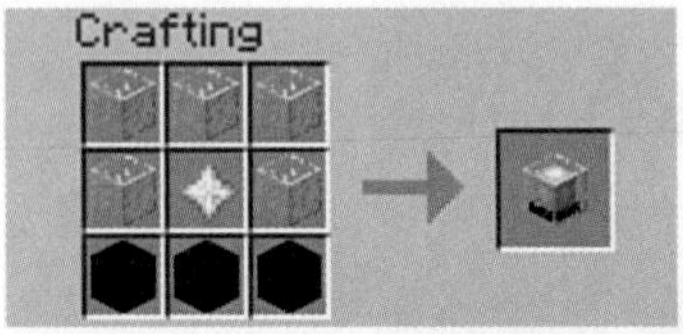

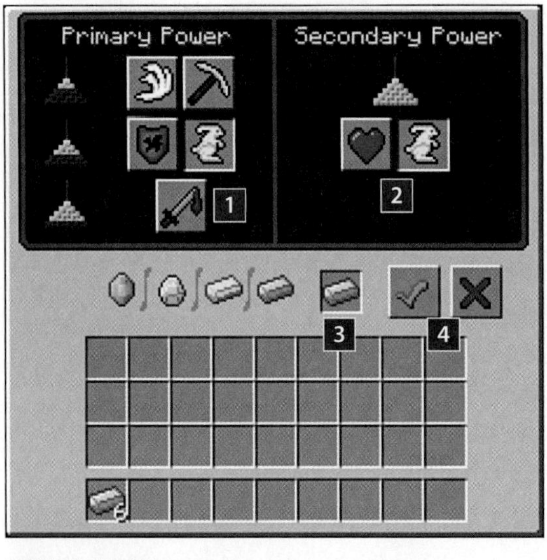

FIGURE 12.22 Configuring a beacon.

1. Select a primary effect. Only those that meet the level requirements for your pyramid are active, although all are shown.
2. If you've built a four-layer pyramid, also choose a secondary power of regeneration or boost the primary effect.
3. Place a piece of emerald, diamond, gold, or iron ore in the slot to confirm—and in the future change—the beacon's configuration. You can use any of the materials.
4. Click the checkmark to proceed or the X to cancel.

Although beacons provide only quite localized effects, you can always pick them up by mining them with any tool or your bare hands, and take them with you to a new location.

The Bottom Line

With The End game complete, you may be wondering what to do next. The End region has plenty to offer. Establish a base in the End city and build a railway network through the gateway portals. (You can avoid throwing away Ender Pearls by traveling in a minecart, a boat, or even when riding a pig). Defeat the dragon again (it respawns indefinitely) and collect its breath in bottles for potions. Back in the Overworld, you also have a stronghold to explore, and at some point you may want to get home, but in any case, I have some good news. The end of Minecraft is actually just the beginning. Build, explore, survive, and thrive. You will learn how to dramatically expand the experience in Chapter 13, "Mods and Multiplayer." Customize your experience, modify Minecraft to the hilt, and join a multitude of servers with worlds, options, trading systems, combat scenarios, and a whole host of extraordinary things to do. The possibilities are as endless as The Overworld itself.

Mods and Multiplayer

In This Chapter

- Go skin deep: Switch up your threads, adopt a guise, and give Steve the slip.
- Adopt a mod and give yourself superhero capabilities, add more creatures, or get an invaluable radar system.
- Sharing is caring: Create a multiplayer game on your LAN.
- Beam yourself and others around the world with command blocks.
- Expand your Minecraft universe with multiplayer gaming.
- Set up your own server and host a permanent world that you, your family, and your friends can all enjoy.

Taking Minecraft to the next level is a rewarding experience. As you customize it, join servers, share worlds, and add mods, you'll change the way the game plays, adding, in some cases quite literally, dimensions to the standard game.

Customizing Your Experience

You can customize Minecraft in three main ways:

- Change the main character's skin so that it looks like someone, or something, else. You can choose from hundreds of thousands of skins, including variations on the in-game mobs, superheroes (although this won't give you any additional powers), and characters from other games and movies; it's an endless list. Or you can design your own.
- Change the in-game textures and sounds, fonts, and menus with a resource pack. Resource packs dramatically improve the world's look with higher-resolution textures that smooth out the rough bitmaps (although not the actual blocks) of the default world or give it an ambience more befitting your own aesthetics—for example, stepping into a medieval, modern, cartoon, sci-fi, or dungeon look and feel. Thousands are available.
- Include a mod to add in-game functionality, new tools, items, mobs, and more.

These changes can add a lot of excitement to a single-player game, but they're also required at times to get the most from particular multiplayer worlds.

I'll walk you through each.

Changing the Skin You're In

I haven't mentioned this before, and you may know it already, but your character in Minecraft actually has a name. Sort of. The original developer, Markus "Notch" Persson, was asked one time for the character's name, and he jokingly dubbed him *Steve*. The moniker seems to have stuck, a little like Herobrine, the character that doesn't actually exist in the game but has become the stuff of legend through mods, Internet memes, and so on.

NOTE

Who Is Herobrine?

Herobrine is supposed to be a somewhat spooky character who haunts the game, building strange structures and tunnels and doing all manner of dastardly things to the player. He looks the same as Steve but with eyes lacking pupils, and he has become a favorite discussion point for Minecraft-playing kids. Mojang, the maker of Minecraft, has stoked the fires several times in version release notes by including among the usual list of bullet points about things that have changed, a not entirely innocent nod to the meme that they have "removed Herobrine." Add that to the hoax videos, the actual mods that do add a Herobrine character, and talk among kids, and Herobrine has become as real as the Slender Man, that other Internet spook.

It's all in good fun, of course, especially at Halloween when Herobrine comes knocking at your door.

So, anyway, back to Steve. Want to spruce him up? Maybe change his look entirely? Make him a her? It's nice to be distinctive, especially in a multiplayer world. You can, and it's quite easy to do. The console editions come with skin packs, but on the PC you have a choice of just two skins starting out: the male Steve and female Alex.

However, there are multitudes of further skins online, and you can create your own from scratch or use one of those preexisting as a starting point.

The first thing you need is a skin file. Figure 13.1 shows the default Steve and Alex skins splayed out. Each section corresponds to a particular facet of the character, the top half dealing with the head and the lower half, from left to right, the legs, torso, and arms. Each section wraps around the 3D model file generated by the game with two full layers available. For instance, you could add a watch to your avatar's left or right wrist, or you can put on a jacket or a cape over the first-layer skin graphic. Moreover, you can individually customize the avatar's left and right legs and feet.

FIGURE 13.1 Both Steve and Alex's skin files, splayed out so that they show every surface.

You can change the skin's display settings within Minecraft. Access them from the main screen by clicking **Options** and then **Skin Customization**. As you can see in Figure 13.2, you can toggle layered skin effects such as the cape, the jacket, and the hat.

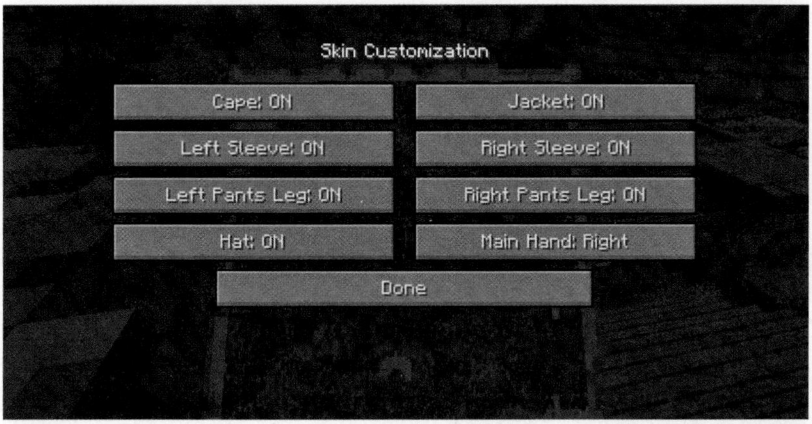

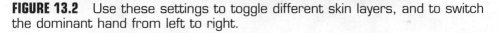

FIGURE 13.2 Use these settings to toggle different skin layers, and to switch the dominant hand from left to right.

Fortunately, you don't need to know too much about the specifics of the mapping because there are a number of excellent skin editors available online as well as on iOS and Android devices, and there are abundant preexisting community-created skin files available for easy customization.

You can access many of these through a web-based editor and then load the new skin directly into your account on Mojang's minecraft.net server. Having it on Mojang's server ensures that when you log into a multiplayer server, everyone else can also see your customized skin, but you will need to exit Minecraft and reload to also load the new skin. Use F5 to switch to an external view to admire your new attire.

Minecraft Skin Editors

There's been something of an explosion recently in the number of skin editors available online, as downloadable applications for PC, and on mobile devices. Some of the iOS and Android apps work extremely well. Most cost a few dollars, and it takes just a few taps to upload the skin so you can view it on the PC edition of Minecraft.

However, you'll find a better collection of editors online. I'll show you the best three I've found so far.

Miners Need Cool Shoes

This site http://www.needcoolshoes.com, like many others, surrounds much of the screen with TMA (too many ads), but it's worth it. The 3D editing is intuitive, it makes it easy to load in community-created skins and edit them and then send them to your Mojang account, and it supports Minecraft's v1.8 multiple layers. See Figure 13.3.

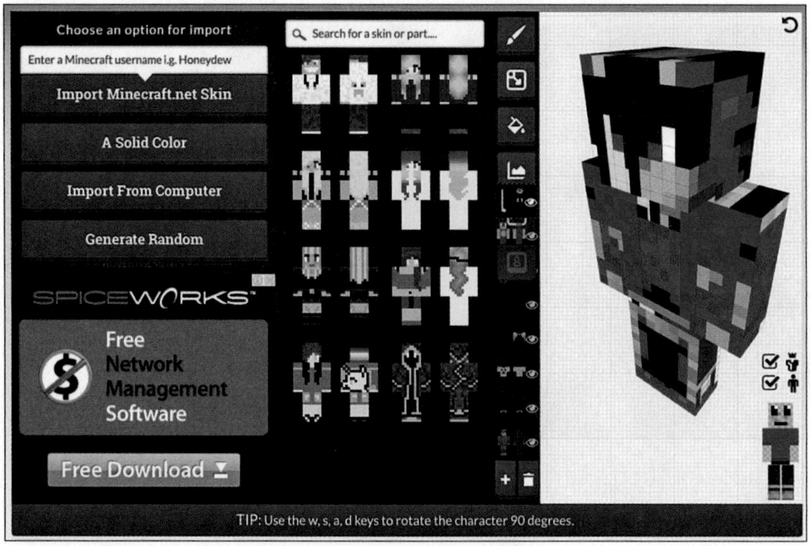

FIGURE 13.3 Miners (always) need cool skins.

The Skindex

The Skindex, at http://www.minecraftskins.com, is one of the easier-to-use free-form skin editors. It shows a skin wrapped around a 3D model (see Figure 13.4), so you can easily rotate and adjust the skin one pixel at a time. It also has extensive community integration. Visit the site, select a skin, and then click **Editor** to adjust.

Novaskin

Novaskin, at http://minecraft.novaskin.me, provides a comprehensive editing system, although with an at-times daunting interface. However, the integrated search system makes it easy to find existing skins and edit them with precision. Novaskin has a huge community with an easy search interface to find the one you want. See Figure 13.5.

FIGURE 13.4 Men in Black—or any color you like. The Skindex's editor is one of the easiest to use, with pixel-level adjustments on a 3D rotating model.

FIGURE 13.5 One of the many Sonic the Hedgehog skins loaded into the Novaskin editor.

NOTE

Slim Skins

Minecraft uses two skin wireframes for players: one with 4-pixel-wide arms for Steve and one for 3-pixel-wide-arms for Alex. When you load your skin into your Mojang account, you should also indicate whether it is based on Steve or Alex to ensure that it displays correctly. You'll see the option to do so on the upload screen.

Loading Your New Skin

These (and other) editors create new skin files that you can save to your PC. You may also be able to load them directly to your Minecraft account, but if you'd prefer to do that later or can't do so directly, follow these steps to load a saved file:

1. Log in to your account at http://minecraft.net.
2. Click the **Profile** link at the top of the screen.
3. Select Steve or Alex as the skin model.
4. Click the **Choose File** button and select the skin file you previously saved.
5. Click **Upload**.
6. Relaunch Minecraft to download the new skin. Press **F5** to toggle between the different view modes.

Resource Packs: Change Your World

Resource packs replace the default textures, sounds, menus, icons, and even the clouds, sun, and moon, although some are more complete than others. Figure 13.6 shows one example. The packs come in all shapes and sizes. Some are ambitious, whereas others are quite simple in scope. All, however, are easy to install. Just select the correct Minecraft version. While you should find that v1.7 packs work just fine, for the most part, with v1.8 and v1.9, you may want to use the exact corresponding version to be sure.

Installing a resource pack is easy:

1. Download the pack. Try one of these three:
   - **Planet Minecraft**—http://www.planetminecraft.com
   - **Minecraft Texture Packs**—http://www.minecrafttexturepacks.com
   - **MinecraftDL**—http://www.minecraftdl.com
2. Open the **Options** menu and click **Resource Packs**.
3. Select **Open resource pack folder** to open the directory where the game accesses resource packs.
4. Move the downloaded resource pack file to that folder. You can see the interface in Figure 13.7.

FIGURE 13.6 The Dokucraft: The Saga Continues resource pack, like many of the other good ones, changes the default textures and also the styling of all the interface elements and menus.

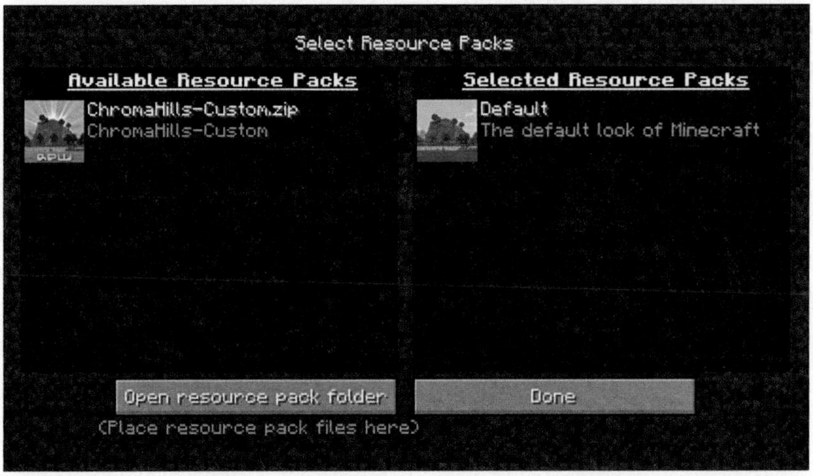

FIGURE 13.7 Resource packs on the left are available but not yet active. Those on the right, including the default, are already loaded.

TIP

Are You Packing? Try This

Among the many thousands of resource packs, there are a few that you should definitely try to get a proper taste of to see just how fabulous they can be. The ones below are carefully constructed, go beyond being just derivative, and provide a complete overhaul that's gleefully lacking glaring errors. Just remember that you'll get best results by finding the version of the resource pack that is an exact match for your current version of Minecraft, so search for them on the sites above and then select the most appropriate link.

- **Dokucraft: The Saga Continues**—A swords and sorcery pack with animated textures that enliven the game.
- **Faithful 32**—Faithful because it replicates Minecraft's default textures but in a higher-resolution format. I highly recommended this if you just want to improve the standard look.
- **Ovo's Rustic**—Beautifully designed to look like the Wild West. Once you install it, you'll love the new pickaxe.

The default Minecraft textures use a grid of 16×16 pixels. Consider this the size of the pattern placed on each side of a standard block such as cobblestone. Custom resource packs allow this to increase from 16 to 32, to 64, to as high as 128×128 pixels per texture. However, the higher the resolution, the more of a hit it will take on your computer. Typically any system can handle a texture of 32×32, and this tends to be where most of the resource packs fall, but switching to 128×128 may well make Minecraft unplayable due to the additional demands those textures place on your computer. If that happens, just restart Minecraft, open the **Options** menu before starting a game, and switch back to a lower-resolution resource pack.

5. Switch back to Minecraft, and you should see the pack's information appear in the list. If it doesn't, chances are it's not compatible, so just delete it.
6. Click to select the resource pack. You may not see anything happen for a few seconds or more, as Minecraft extracts the contents of the pack and then reloads its resources. Once it has, you'll typically see some subtle or major changes to the window, including the styling of buttons and usually a change in fonts, although this depends on the contents of the pack.
7. Press **Esc** to return to the game. (There's no need to go back through all the menus.)
8. Voilà! You've just installed your first resource pack.

Now, a caveat. There's a lot of confusing information in some of the downloads. You'll see references to MCPatcher and Optifine, complex file paths, and more. You can feel free to ignore these. They're old news, left over from earlier versions of Minecraft.

CAUTION

Beware the Pop-Ups

Downloading resource packs—and mods, for the matter—can be a tricky business. Most creators try to make some funds from their efforts, which is no problem at all (they've often put thousands of hours into them), but it does lead to one of those first-world problems: pop-ups. You can quickly become lost in a sea of spring-loaded pages, interspersed misleading download buttons, strange captcha entries, and, at times, downright duplicity. Unfortunately, there's no real way around this. Websites such as AdFly and MediaFire offer a way for the creators to make a bit of a return for their efforts, at the expense of forcing adviews on everyone downloading that pack. Pop-up blockers provide varied results, sometimes working and other times preventing the download from taking place. Just take care out there, never enter your credit card details, and watch out for misleading links.

Mind My Mods

Mods are the marvel of Minecraft because they can change almost every aspect of the game. Want the ability to fire arrows that explode on impact like a block of TNT? Why, certainly. Want radar that shows every nearby mob overlaid on a map? No problem. Explored your way through every biome there is and, gosh, just want a bit more variety? There's a mod for that, too, and it can generate worlds of fantastic variety.

So what, exactly, is a mod?

In a word, programming. Mods change the way Minecraft works by replacing parts of Minecraft's own program code with their own routines and by adding additional functionality that goes beyond the original program's design. And herein lies the danger. Mods are the equivalent of the Wild West, living within the ordered confines of Minecraft's civilized releases. They are not officially supported by Mojang, and every time a new version, or even a small update to Minecraft comes out, there's a very real risk that the new code will be sufficiently different from the previous version to turn perfectly working mods into piles of binary mush. In turn, installing a mod designed to work with a previous version of Minecraft into a new version may break Minecraft itself, forcing a complete reinstallation of the core game files.

Things become even hairier when mods try to coexist. One may change a routine on which another relies, breaking it, and so on. It's a fragile existence. I've even heard of one user, and perhaps there are many more, who continues to use Minecraft v1.4 because they don't want to lose compatibility with the 90+ mods they have installed.

CAUTION

Mods Change Worlds

Mods can add new items, block types, and all sorts of additional data to a world's saved game file. This can have a permanent effect on any world that you open in a modded version of Minecraft. If you just want to test a mod, do so by creating a new world when you have the mod loaded rather than a world to which you may want to return. Alternatively, create a backup of that world or your entire saved game folder. See "Installing Forge Mods," later in this chapter, for details on locating this folder. Copy the folder to any convenient location outside the Minecraft directory. Restore it later by copying it back over the original folder.

The good news? Modding Minecraft is no longer the minefield it used to be. There is a solution coming. Mojang has committed to releasing an official programming interface which will ensure that mods have a way to work with Minecraft without actually trampling all over the program's code. But there is no release date as yet. However, there is a similar alternative that you can use right now. It's called *Forge*.

Forge acts as a layer between Minecraft and mods. Mods designed to work with Forge talk to it instead of trying to insert themselves into Minecraft. Forge then handles the Minecraft side of the discussion. Forge is, in its way, just another mod, but it ensures that all the others using it "play nice." It also simplifies the installation of mods. You'll see how this works later in this chapter.

TIP

Worry-Free Modding

Prebuilt mod packs can prevent you from spending a lot of time worrying about compatibilities by downloading versions of Minecraft with various mods already tested and packed into a single-click installation. Check out Technic Launcher (http://technicpack.net), Feed the Beast (http://feed-the-beast.com/launcher), and ATLauncher (http://atlauncher.com/downloads) to experience Minecraft in what is often a very different form from the vanilla game.

Before we get to the step by step, I have good news and I have bad news for you concerning Forge. The good news is, as I stated, the Forge system makes installing and managing mods a headache-free process. The bad news is that Forge and, therefore, compatible mods also lag a little behind the release versions of Minecraft, so with v1.9 out, you may find that you can still only play v1.8 when using Forge.

> **TIP**
>
> **More About Forge**
>
> Programming a mod for Forge is beyond the scope of this book, but if you want to learn more about it, I highly recommend picking up a copy of *Sams Teach Yourself Minecraft Mod Development*, by Jimmy Koene, published by Sams Publishing. In addition, I've covered the subject of Forge and mod installation using different and sometimes quite simple techniques in my book, *The Advanced Minecraft Strategy Guide*.

Now, then, let's get to the good stuff.

Installing Forge Mods

Forge makes mods easy. Don't leave home without it. Follow these steps to install:

1. Download the Forge installer from http://files.minecraftforge.net. Look for the recommended file for your version of Minecraft under the Promotions list at the top of the page. (In this case, *promotions* simply means that it's a promoted file and has nothing to do with advertising.) Then click **(installer)** under the Downloads column.
2. You'll pass briefly through an ad network. Wait five seconds and then click **SKIP** in the top-right corner of the web page to download the file.
3. Open the downloaded file to install. Usually everything is correctly set by default, but ensure that **Install client** is selected (see Figure 13.8). You'll see a file path to your Minecraft application folder. I've never seen the installer get it wrong, but you can adjust it if you see a problem. Then click **OK**.
4. Within a second or two, you'll see a window confirming that Forge was successfully installed.

FIGURE 13.8 The Minecraft Forge installer.

The installer obviously installs its own files, but it does so in a clever way, by creating a new profile in the Minecraft Launcher. Select the Forge profile or your standard profile to quickly switch between the modded and un-modded versions of Minecraft.

To test the installation, open your Minecraft Launcher and click the **Profile** drop-down menu. You'll see a new profile called *Forge*. Select this and click **Play**. If your Forge installation was successful, you'll see some additional information on the title screen in the lower-left corner, as shown in Figure 13.9.

FIGURE 13.9 Forging ahead: Look for the additional text in the title screen to confirm an active Forge.

Forge on its own doesn't add any visible functionality to Minecraft. For that you need to install an actual mod. Notice the Mods button on the main game screen; you'll use that to retrieve a list of any currently installed mods.

Forge makes adding and removing mods as easy as drag and drop, although you'll first need to get to the actual mods folder. Follow these steps:

1 Click **Options** from Minecraft's title screen.

2 Select **Resource Packs.**

3 Click on **Open resource pack folder** and use your standard file system controls to go up one folder or directory level to the main Minecraft folder. Within that you'll see the **mods** folder. Forge adds this folder on installation, so you won't see it if you haven't yet installed.

4 Copy or move any forge-compatible mods into this folder.

5 Restart Minecraft to load the mod and start testing it.

NOTE

No Need to Decompress

Mods are usually found inside a .jar file or a .zip. Either works just fine; there's no need to decompress the zip first.

Here's a small list of mods you can try to get started. Remember to always download the version that corresponds to your Minecraft version; Forge doesn't remove that particular requirement, and you may need to wait a while for these mods to be updated to the latest release, but you can always adjust the Forge profile in the launcher to use an earlier version of Minecraft that is compatible.

TooManyItems

http://goo.gl/vyE3JG

TooManyItems (which everyone calls *TMI*) is one of the most popular and useful mods, providing an incredible enhancement to the inventory window (see Figure 13.10).

TMI adds a host of controls to the window for quickly setting up stacks of inventory items, enchanting items up to any level, brewing potions, and controlling other aspects of the game, such as the time, weather, and difficulty level. It also supports saving and reloading stored inventory configurations.

Although a mod such as TMI makes it ridiculously easy to get through the game in Survival mode, the ability to quickly load a particular configuration of items or blocks makes it quite useful for construction projects in Creative mode.

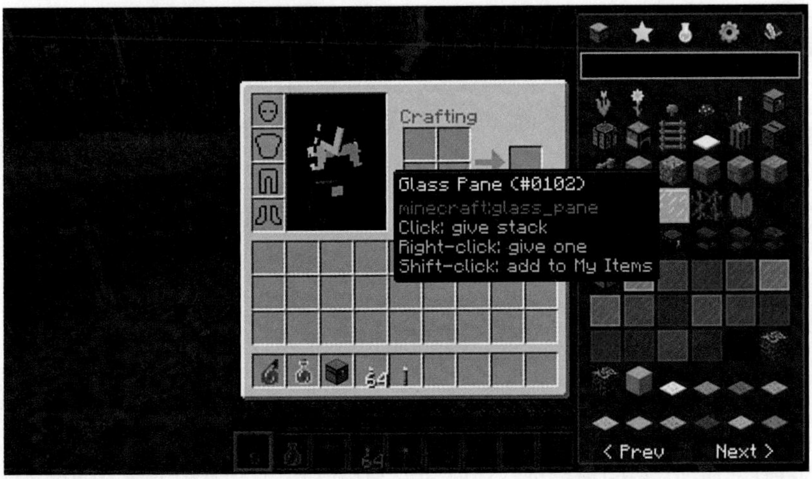

FIGURE 13.10 TooManyItems greatly expands the inventory screen.

NOTE

Not Enough Items

Another mod that is quite similar to TMI adds the useful ability to view the crafting recipe for any item in the game as well as for new items added by other mods, as long as they've been programmed to work with TMI. It isn't quite as complete as TMI in some other respects but is definitely worth a look. You'll need to install Code Chicken Core as well as the mod. You can find the latest versions of both at http://mod-minecraft.net/not-enough-items-mod/. Install them both at the same time by loading them into the mods directory and remove TMI for now, if it's already installed. Open your inventory in Minecraft, hover over any craftable item, and press **R** to see its recipe or **U** to see recipes in which the item is used.

Ruins

http://www.atomicstryker.net/ruins.php

Ruins is one of a substantial number of mods from AtomicStryker that add some epic functionality to Minecraft. This mod, in particular, will dot your worlds with a large number of different structures and dungeons. Some embed mob spawners, chests with loads of loot, traps, and more, while others, such as that shown in Figure 13.11, will give you a great place to call home.

Once you've wandered the barren lands of The Overworld to your heart's content, install this mod and pepper the landscape with an exciting range of new structures to explore.

FIGURE 13.11 Need a quick castle? Find one and so much more in the Ruins mod.

Progressive Automation

http://goo.gl/BisO9I

This mod adds a suite of useful machines to Minecraft. These can chop and plant trees, plant and harvest crops, breed and kill mobs, gather eggs, shear sheep, and much more. Each machine follows an upgrade path to make it more powerful.

Progressive Automation (see Figure 13.12) strikes a nice balance between not changing the core of Minecraft too much and yet also providing a way to start getting into aspects of machinery that take away some of the more repetitive tasks while playing on Survival. You'll find full documentation at https://goo.gl/WrMdd7.

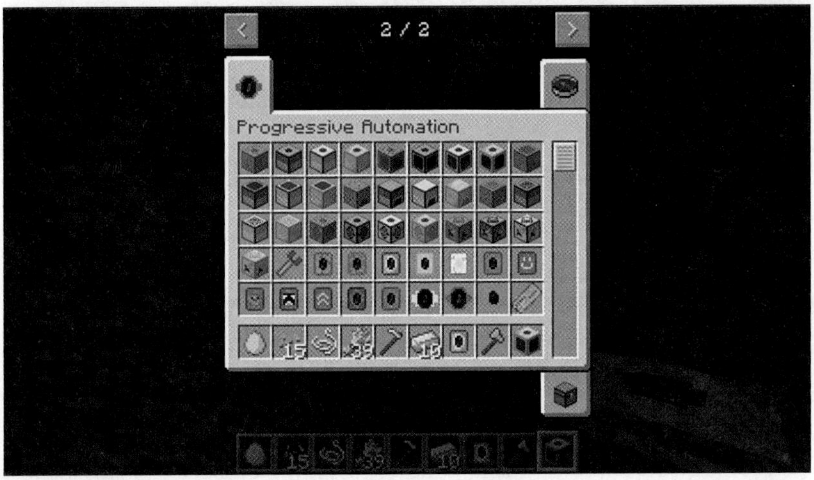

FIGURE 13.12 This may look like a lot to add to vanilla Minecraft, but the machines are actually quite easy to implement.

VoxelMap

http://goo.gl/P5XE9m

This is another community favorite. It adds a very handy and highly configurable map to the top-right corner of the screen (see Figure 13.13). It makes it easy to add multiple waypoints for navigation; move quickly between them; highlight biomes; and show nearby passive and hostile mobs. Note that you'll also need to install LiteLoader. You'll find the link for that on the VoxelMap home page.

FIGURE 13.13 VoxelMap has several useful display modes but, more importantly, also provides a fast way to set waypoints so you can find your way home—or wherever.

TIP

More Mods

There's no single go-to list of mods, but there are two good sources. Planet Minecraft provides a very comprehensive offering (http://goo.gl/1folnq). For best results, look for mods that include [FORGE] in their title and remember to match the displayed version to your own Minecraft version. Also visit MCF ModList (http://modlist.mcf.li) for a curated and easily searchable list of mods by version. You may find it a little easier to navigate than Planet Minecraft.

The mods listed in this section provide just the tiniest glimpse into what is quite an amazing amount of custom development. Mods exist that can change the tiniest detail or alter the entire experience. Just remember to tread carefully when downloading or going through a custom installation and be sure to install the mods one at a time, launching Minecraft in between to ensure that a mod hasn't broken the main game. If it has, just delete the mod and move on to the next one.

Multiplayer Madness

Playing Minecraft by yourself is all well and good ("sniff"), and there's plenty to keep one occupied. But playing as part of a group can be a lot more fun and, if creative builds are your goal, hugely more productive.

Minecraft provides several ways to party up:

- **LAN**—Share your world on your local network, and anyone on the same wired or wireless connection can join in.
- **Join a multiplayer server**—Jump into any server to join other players. Some servers support hundreds of players at the same time, engaged in acts both creative and combative. More on these below.
- **Host a multiplayer server**—Start up your own server, punch a hole through your firewall, and share your Minecraft world with the rest of the actual world.
- **Join realms**—See the "Minecraft Realms" note in the following pages.

A few prerequisites apply to joining any multiplayer game, no matter the connection method. First, each player needs his or her own account (or Minecraft license), even on a local-area network (LAN). Second, the Minecraft client has to match the server's version. This means a v1.9 client can't talk to a 1.8 server. However, remember that you can play Minecraft by using an earlier version from the Minecraft launcher. Open the **Version** drop-down list, select the target Minecraft version, and then click **Play** to continue.

Finally, some servers ban players for using mods, and on a LAN game, all the mods that change blocks or add new items must match between the client and server. Once resource packs support mods, this will probably be a much simpler requirement: Just install the recommended resource pack, and you'll be ready to go. For now, though, ensure that the contents of your mods directory match across all PCs if you're playing on a LAN.

Sharing and Joining on a LAN

To set up a LAN server, open any Minecraft world:

1. Press **Esc** to open the Options window.
2. Select **Open to LAN**.
3. Join a LAN server by clicking **Multiplayer** on the title screen and look for an available server. For instance, I have a local Minecraft server named *LAN World*, as shown in Figure 13.14. You'll also see the account name of the user hosting the session, as well as the name given to that world.
4. Double-click its name to join the server.

That's all there is to it. In a few moments, you'll appear at the world's spawn point.

FIGURE 13.14 Joining a LAN server.

TIP

Teleporting Other Players

Bring other players to your location quickly and easily with the teleport command. It's a sort of "beam me up, Scotty" for Minecraft. Make sure you start a multiplayer game with cheats on and then type **/tp *playername***, replacing ***playername*** with the name of the player you want to teleport. Press **Enter**, and you'll zap that player directly to your location. See http://www.minecraftwiki.net/wiki/Commands for a complete list of commands.

COMMAND BLOCKS

Minecraft has a special block designed specifically for Multiplayer mode, although you can also place it in a Singleplayer world. It's called the command block, and it can't be crafted; you won't even find it in the inventory in Creative mode. However, if your world has cheats enabled, or if you're running a server, you can give it to yourself or to another player. Type **/give *playername* *137*** to make a command block appear in that player's or your inventory (see Figure 13.15). When it is placed, a right-click on the block opens a command window. From here, you can type in and store any of the available commands to cause that action to occur to the player. Just set a lever, pressure plate, or button on or near the block to send a redstone pulse that triggers the command. For example, setting **/tp @p 0,0,0** will teleport the player to location coordinates x=0,y=0,z=0. Substitute the 0s for more specific coordinates, put a pressure plate next to the command block, and you can create an instant transport system between different bases, hubs, mines, and so on in your world.

FIGURE 13.15 You can use the command block (shown faintly in the background) to trigger actions on players in Minecraft multiplayer sessions.

Joining a Multiplayer Server

Just as mods expand Minecraft's functionality in any number of useful and imaginative ways, multiplayer servers create whole new worlds that can take the experience even further. These servers allow you to communicate with other players either cooperatively or combatively, depending on the server's rules. Some are plain vanilla, meaning there's not a lot of difference between them and a standard Minecraft world besides it being multiplayer, but many others are carefully constructed, elaborate masterpieces with special code that provides a heavily customized experience for players. The Shotbow Network shown in Figure 13.16 is one such example.

FIGURE 13.16 Shotbow's game lobby, showing just a few of the game types as well as other players.

NOTE

Minecraft Realms

Minecraft Realms is a subscription service that provides an easy way for families or groups of friends to host small cooperative servers of up to 20 players. Although it's simple enough to set up a LAN game if you're all on the same network, Realms works across the broader Internet, so players can get together from all over the world. The Pocket Edition also supports Realms, with the goal of supporting up to 10 players per server, and the service will no doubt make its way eventually to the console editions. Realms servers also include a range of prebuilt worlds with fun components to them, as well as mini-games that can be played at any time so that you temporarily swap out your world for one set in a battle arena, on a parkour map, or someplace else.

The first thing you should do is locate an actual server. There are literally thousands to choose from, and sites such as planetminecraft.com and minecraftservers.org do a great job of keeping complete databases running. Some servers are open to one and all, while others require registration. Most are free to some extent, although paid subscriptions may provide access to use otherwise full servers and give you other benefits.

Join a multiplayer server by following these steps:

1 Click on **Multiplayer** in the title screen.

2 Select **Add server**.

3 Type in a server name. (It can be anything you like that will help you identify that server in the future.)

4 Type in the server address and click **Done**.

5 Select the server from the list (see the earlier Figure 13.14) and click **Join Server** or just double-click the server's name.

Most servers drop you into a game lobby where you can see the different game types and read the server's rules. These usually include information on permitted mods, so make sure you read the signs or any books dropped into your inventory, as this can help you avoid getting banned.

The following are some servers to start with:

- **TeamExtreme (http://play.teamextrememc.com)**—This group claims to have the biggest Minecraft public server in the world. It is pretty heavy-handed with rules, but the world is incredibly detailed, and you can meet a lot of Minecraft-savvy players here.
- **Shotbow (http://us.shotbow.net)**—The Shotbow network hosts a huge range of game types, each with its own particular rules. It tends to have some hardcore players, so make sure that your skills are up to speed before you visit.
- **The Hive (http://eu.hivemc.com)**—The Hive is full of games that are great for kids and anyone else who wants to have a bit of fun. There's an arcade with paintball, hide-and-seek, survivor maps, and a Herobrine game.
- **Supercraft Brothers (http://mineca.de)**—Supercraft Brothers is something of a riot, offering fast-paced player-versus-player (PvP) gaming. There is quite a range of servers and game play styles, so make sure you also visit http://minecade.com/SuperCraftBrothers.
- **Phanatic (http://play.phanaticmc.com)**—This busy server offers Creative mode, a host of mini-games, and a *Hunger Games* mode, based on the premise from the popular film.
- **BeastsMC (http://c.beastsmc.com)**—Don't let the name perturb you; this is an excellent server for creative builds. The same host also offers survival and hardcore multiplayer.

You'll find a huge range of impressive servers out there, some with incredibly extensive worlds and gigantic creative builds. Look through the server lists to find one that suits you. There is, truly, something for everyone.

NOTE

Changes for Multiplayer Server Operators

Mojang made big news in June 2014 when it published a substantial change to the game's End User License Agreement (EULA). The new wording expressly forbids Minecraft multiplayer server operators from charging players real money for features that are already a part of the Minecraft code base.

For instance, historically you'll find servers that offer various incentives for players that are based in real money transactions. Some of the perks improve the user's capabilities in the multiplayer world, while some for-pay features are little more than vanities (custom titles and so forth).

This EULA change sparked a lot of controversy in the Minecraft community, both for and against. Above all else, we must remember that, at the end of the proverbial day, Mojang owns the Minecraft code and therefore has a right to define the software's acceptable use policy.

Hosting a Multiplayer Server

Hosting your own server is a rewarding way to create a consistent, stable world that you and others can connect to from anywhere. It does require a little technical knowledge—especially if you want to be able to access the server externally—but nothing insurmountable.

The basic steps are fairly simple, and you can use a *white list* to ensure that only you and your trusted family or friends can join. For now, though, I'll show you how to set up the server on the local network. You can actually do this even if you have just one PC.

Follow these steps, and you'll be up and running in no time:

1. Download the server software from http://minecraft.net/download. Choose the .exe file if you're running Windows or the .jar file for any other platform.
2. Create a new folder and move the downloaded software to it.
3. Double-click or open the downloaded file to launch the server. You'll see a window similar to that shown in Figure 13.17.

The server does a few things on the first run, generating a new world and also creating a number of configuration files. The world generates into a folder called, appropriately enough, *world*, in the same directory as the server software. Its format is the same as those that the Minecraft client creates, so if you'd like to share a world you've already created, shut down the server and copy that world from the *saves* directory of your Minecraft application into the server directory and then rename the folder *world*. Restart the server to share it.

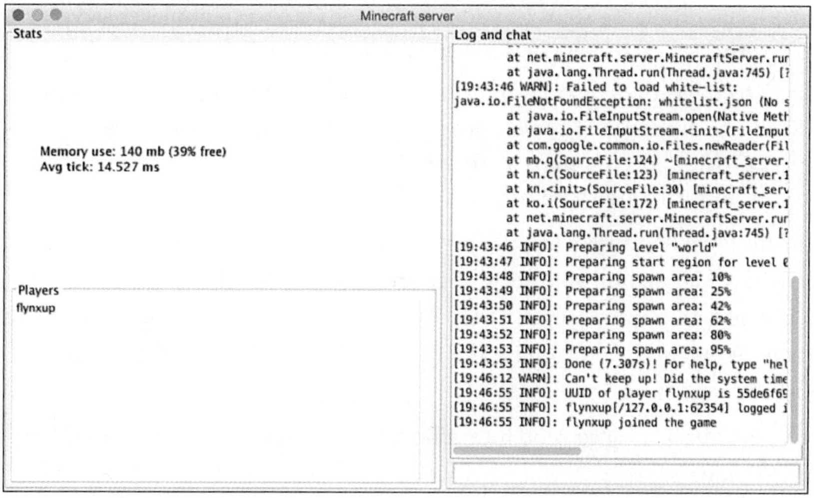

FIGURE 13.17 The Minecraft server provides a clean interface for managing players and should run well in the background on all but very low-specification computers.

TIP

Host with the Most

If hosting with your own hardware doesn't appeal to you for security or other reasons, but you still have an urge to share a world for collaborative creation or otherwise, consider using a paid hosting provider. Numerous providers online specialize in Minecraft hosting and will provide you with all you need, including configuration and customization tools. Mcprohosting.com starts for as little as $2.50 per month for five players.

Once you have a server running on your local network, you need its IP address to connect. The IP address is the address on your local network, and it usually looks like 192.168.0.*x* or 10.0.0.*x*, where *x* is the final IP number assigned to your computer.

Discovering the IP address depends on the server's operating system. On Windows, you'll find it under the network card or Wi-Fi connection in the Network and Sharing Center in the Control Panel. Select the active connection and click **Details** to see the IP address. On OS X, open **System Preferences** under the Apple menu, click **Network**, and then click the active connection. You will see the IP address under the Status line in the right panel of the window. If you're using Linux, I'm just going to go right ahead and assume that you already know the address or know how to discover it.

Connect to the server using the same steps as you use to connect to a multiplayer server, using the IP address as the server address in the Add Server window.

Opening the server up to the broader world requires a few more steps, and it is not without risks because you'll have to expose your server through the firewall to the untethered wilds of the Internet. I can't provide specific steps as this is all about router configuration, and routers are all different, but here are some pointers that should help:

- Assign a permanent local IP address to your server. You want to ensure, for example, that if your server is addressed on your local network as 192.168.0.4, it stays that way. Typically, IP addresses are dynamically assigned within the local network, but if your router supports IP reservation, you can use the MAC address of the server to assign a permanent local address.
- Use the router's port forwarding to send all traffic the router receives on port 25565 to the server's local IP address.
- In almost all cases, your Internet provider assigns you a dynamic IP address—an address that can change without notice. Static IP addresses cost extra, sometimes hundreds of dollars, so I recommend using a dynamic DNS service instead. I prefer dyndns.org, but there are many available. A dynamic IP address ensures that you or others can reach the server from anywhere with a standard address, such as http://mcserver.mydyndns.org. You then type that address rather than an IP address into Minecraft's Add Server page. In many cases, it's possible to configure the router to talk to one of the more common dynamic DNS providers, but if not, then you will be able to download a small piece of software from the provider that will keep the domain name version of the address up to date and running smoothly, even if your Internet provider changes your external numerical IP address.

Finally, you should take some steps to protect the Minecraft server application to prevent just anyone from logging in:

1. In the small chat bar just below the main window log in the server's display, t **/whitelist on**. This ensures that only people specifically approved to access the server can log in. Anyone else who tries will simply be disconnected.
2. Add the account name (the Mojang or Minecraft account used to log in to the game) for everyone you want to grant access to the server. Do this by typing **/whitelist add *playername***, replacing ***playername*** with the actual name. The white list is a file contained in the server's directory. If you need to add a lot of names, you can do so just be typing them into the file itself, using a plain text editor, with each name on a single line.
3. Add yourself as an operator so that you can control the server from any Minecraft client by typing **/op *yourname***. Again, replace the latter part with your actual account name. If there is a potential downside to multiplayer Minecraft, it is that the screen can get pretty busy with chat and status messages. Figure 13.18 shows what I'm talking about.

4 Create a startup script that will automatically restart the Minecraft server if the power goes down or the server hardware resets.

FIGURE 13.18 In a multiplayer session, type **/help** to see the commands that are available to you, based on your privilege level.

That's the essence of a Minecraft server. You can do a lot more besides, including setting up a texture pack that will automatically download to anyone who joins, adding Bukkit mods (see http://wiki.bukkit.org), and more, but I'll leave you to discover these on your own. You can find a wealth of material online, and also in my advanced guide, *The Advanced Strategy Guide to Minecraft*.

Hosting a customized Minecraft server is, perhaps, the ultimate expression of not just playing but also optimizing the Minecraft gaming experience and sharing it with others.

Spectator Mode

Minecraft includes a neat enhancement to Multiplayer mode called Spectator mode. This game mode, which can be enabled by issuing the command **/gamemode 3** or **/gamemode spectator** allows the player to fly around the world without interacting with it in any way.

While you're in Spectator mode, you can fly through blocks and entities, but you cannot impact them. Spectator mode is a "fly-only" mode, which means you won't be walking anywhere in the world while you're in that mode. Use your mouse's scroll wheel to change your speed; you can fly much faster here than in Creative mode.

As you'd expect, your avatar can't take any damage while in Spectator mode. Also, you can keep your existing inventory but cannot access it.

Finally, you can "possess" mobs by left-clicking on them. Performing this action allows you to take on their view of the multiplayer world, although at this writing, the mobs freeze in position. This may, of course, change in a future update.

The Bottom Line

Minecraft is one of the most open games on the market. From skins to mods to hosting a server, it's a malleable ball of clay, waiting to be shaped by your hands.

Fortunately, you don't need to start from scratch. Many dedicated developers, artists, and designers have traveled this road before. Thousands of mods, tens of thousands of servers, and hundreds of thousands of skins are already out there.

The ultimate player is not the one who simply finishes the game but the one who takes it ever further—from fantastic constructions to amazing redstone contraptions, from ludicrously complicated automated farms to tricks (the TNT cannon comes to mind) that go far beyond any of the game's original intentions. Minecraft is fertile ground, an endless expanse of possibility both within gameplay and also deep within its code. Multiple mods can spawn something like programmatic chaos, but when well orchestrated can result in an experience that sings.

Enjoy, and if you ever think you've gone as far as you can go, take another look. There's a new experience just around the corner. I hope to see you there.

INDEX

Symbols

A

B

C

D

E

G

H

I

J

K

L

M

N

P

Q

R

S

T

U

V

W